HARLEM

BETWEEN HEAVEN AND HELL

Monique M. Taylor

HARLEM

BETWEEN HEAVEN AND HELL

University of Minnesota Press
Minneapolis • London

All photographs in this book were taken by the author.

The University of Minnesota Press gratefully acknowledges permission to reprint poetry by Langston Hughes in this book. These poems, or excerpts from poems, are from *The Collected Poems of Langston Hughes,* by Langston Hughes, copyright 1994 by The Estate of Langston Hughes. Reprinted by permission of Alfred A. Knopf, a division of Random House, Inc.

Published by the University of Minnesota Press
111 Third Avenue South, Suite 290
Minneapolis, MN 55401-2520
http://www.upress.umn.edu

Printed in the United States of America on acid-free paper

Library of Congress Cataloging-in-Publication Data

Taylor, Monique M.
Harlem between heaven and hell / Monique M. Taylor.
p. cm.
Includes bibliographical references and index.
ISBN 0-8166-4051-3 (acid-free paper) — ISBN 0-8166-4052-1 (pbk: acid-free paper)
1. Harlem (New York, N.Y.)—Social life and customs. 2. Harlem (New York, N.Y.)—Social conditions. 3. Harlem (New York, N.Y.)—Race relations. 4. African Americans—New York (State)—New York—Social conditions. 5. African Americans—New York (State)—New York—Economic conditions. 6. African Americans—Race identity—New York (State)—New York. 7. Middle class—New York (State)—New York. 8. New York (N.Y.)—Social life and customs. 9. New York (N.Y.)—Social conditions. 10. New York (N.Y.)—Race relations. I. Title.
F128.68.H3 T39 2002
305.8'009747'1—dc21

2002007142

The University of Minnesota is an equal-opportunity educator and employer.

12 11 10 09 08 07 06 05 04 03 02 10 9 8 7 6 5 4 3 2 1

Here's to Harlem!
They say Heaven is Paradise.
If Harlem ain't Heaven,
Then a mouse ain't mice!

—Langston Hughes, "A Toast to Harlem"

So we stand here
On the edge of hell
In Harlem
And look out on the world
And wonder
What we're gonna do
In the face of
What we remember.

—Langston Hughes, "Puzzled"

Contents

Introduction: Welcome to Harlem, USA ix

1. Harlem between Heaven and Hell 1

2. Insiders and Outsiders 29

3. The Dilemma of Racial Difference 57

4. Class Conflict and Harlem's Black Gentry 85

5. Racial Bonds and the Communion of Fellowship 129

6. Home Ownership and Political Participation 159

Conclusion: The End of the Line? 171

Acknowledgments 179

Notes 181

Bibliography 187

Index 201

APOLLO
APOLLO

introduction

Welcome to Harlem, USA

Starbucks has arrived in Harlem. The upscale coffee emporium shares a corner with the 125th Street subway station, which takes in and disgorges an endless stream of travelers. At this corner, one emerges to vendors hawking incense, black-nationalist pamphlets, books and tapes, and black-themed Mother's Day cards. Outside this key entrance to the famous black community, a sea of black, brown, and tan faces is a reminder of how far a quick subway ride transports one from downtown Manhattan. The 125th Street subway station is a portal to a black world still markedly defined by its difference.

But to enter Starbucks in Harlem is to come face to face with a jarring realization: This Starbucks exhibits the corporate sameness of its other, now ubiquitous outlets. The chain-store uniformity is all around, from its tables and chairs, its background wall art, napkins, and green server aprons, right down to the lingo that distinguishes its coffee all over. Enter Harlem's Starbucks and you could be anywhere.

Starbucks is not the only striking new arrival uptown in Harlem. Old Navy, a Disney Store, The Body Shop, and Blockbuster Video also have set up shop along 125th Street—the community's commercial thoroughfare. This formerly decrepit commercial strip is humming with its own version of the market bustle that accompanies the rest of New York City's 1990s renaissance. For a change, it seems, the once segregated and oft neglected Harlem has joined in to take part in sweeping changes occurring across America's urban and suburban commercial landscapes.

These changes are the commercial manifestation of gentrification that has been taking place in Harlem's history-laden streets for three decades. This gentrification has been mostly residential and has bolstered a black middle class in Harlem. Black newcomers have been attracted by Harlem's mythic stature as the cradle of black culture in the twentieth century. I was drawn to the story because its protagonists—the black middle class—are so often overlooked by news media and academics focused on the racial aspects of poverty and the black underclass. Moreover, it did not escape my notice that in other places during the 1980s, when gentrification was chiefly featured as a trend driven by white yuppies, here was a group of black actors, themselves engaging in yuppie behavior, but with an implicit political dimension. Given that many structural changes since the 1960s ushered in a new dynamic in race relations by opening fresh opportunities and increasing the ranks of the black middle class, it seemed timely to explore the lifestyles and trends of the black yuppie. And Harlem, as the cultural heart of black America, seemed an unusually rich location to explore changes of the sort ushered in by the civil rights movement of the 1960s.

This book is primarily a study of race, class, and culture and not a strict gentrification study, nor does it seek to be. During the course of my research, I found it necessary to familiarize myself with the literature on gentrification as a way of improving my understanding of what was producing some of the social roles and political tensions and their cultural ties to a racial meaning in contemporary Harlem.

The primary objective of this book is to explore the forms that middle-class black identity and group solidarity take by looking at a set of black gentrifiers who have experienced interracial contact in other, more integrated settings. While one sign of progress in black–white relations is measured in the integration of schools, colleges and universities, neighborhoods and communities, and workplaces, statistics alone fall short of illuminating the subtle complexities these changes hold for the formation of racial identity.

It has been argued that decreasing segregation and greater equal opportunity have increased the gap between the haves and have-nots in the black world. The black middle class described in classic works by E. Franklin Frazier, W. E. B. Du Bois, Horace Cayton, and St. Clair Drake lived in a world inhabited by blacks of lower socioeconomic status because of a castelike system of racial stratification. Thus, black neighborhoods and communities, shaped by de jure segregation, were, of necessity, home to a range of classes. Group identity and consciousness were shaped by a physical proximity born of circumstance. With the loosening of segregation, middle-class migration away from traditionally black neighborhoods broke up this class diversity.

Black gentrification in Harlem—in effect, a reversal of this exodus—would seem to defy this trend.

A construction I call the "rhetoric of return" is used to analyze the causes and consequences of middle-class blacks moving to Harlem. This rhetoric of return, I maintain, helps to clarify some of the real, imagined, exaggerated, and manipulated concepts invoked by black gentry to explain themselves as rightfully belonging in Harlem. The rhetoric of return is also used by others—redevelopment officials in Harlem, other long-term brownstone owners, the media—to discuss why and how this group functions in Harlem today.

The stories that the middle-class black newcomers to Harlem tell make use of its spaces and other residents to present and explain themselves as actors returning to the ghetto and rescuing it. Other than events I have directly witnessed or drawn from my own field notes, these stories are their own depictions, replete with self-interest and class anxiety, and not an "objective" Harlem reality. However, the stories yield valuable insights into the importance of race identity for a group of blacks who supposedly have greater chances for assimilation.

A second objective of the book is to examine the nature of intragroup identity for the newest members of the black middle class. Against a backdrop of increased opportunity and upward mobility, the book explores the voluntary choice to settle in a black community as a window into how self- and group-identification is defined for middle-class blacks in terms of class, race, and a mix of class and race. And where race and class intersect, I will examine how the establishment of a middle-class black identity is accompanied by tensions in both their black and white worlds.

By examining a group of black "yuppies" and their return to a historically black community widely known today for its poverty, the book explores the contradictory and complicated nature of group boundaries, class mobility, and racial integration in modern America. The most recent class cleavages in the black community challenge our understanding about how race functions in shaping identity and interests for individual blacks and their relationships to the wider black community.

A final objective of the book is to examine the role of history, symbolism, and culture in shaping community preservation within the black community today. As they engage in an ongoing struggle to apply the symbolism of a once segregated black community to their lives in the post–civil rights era, Harlemites represent an important link connecting Harlem's present and past. The result is an examination of the meaning and significance of race and class identity in contemporary America told through Harlem's experience.

In the seventeenth-floor office of the Harlem Urban Development Corporation, a wall of windows offers sweeping views of Harlem. From this height, agency chief Charles Landell directs my attention from easels that hold architectural plans to panoramic views outside of sites where condominiums and townhouses will soon sprout. A young black woman from an advertising agency interrupts to show off her artwork for a poster promoting HUDC-sponsored brownstone condominiums. The poster is a palette of muted pastels: a young professional couple stands in the middle of a clean, sunlit, tree-lined street, flanked by grandiose brownstones. The father holds a small child in his arms. Another youngster clings to the leg of his smiling mother. Even the family dog is in the picture, rounding out the complete image of the "yuppie" family HUDC hopes to attract.

The noteworthy feature of the poster is that the family is black. In fact, Landell, the artist, and I discuss how dark, or light, the skin tone of the family should be. Landell explains that HUDC is very aware of the role that black professionals might play in the redevelopment of Harlem. His strategy, he tells me, is to actively recruit this group by promoting the idea that life in Harlem does not have to be incompatible with middle-class family life.

This moment, in 1992, would presage the steady transformation of residential Harlem during the rest of the decade—changes capped by the influx of corporate name-brand chains. By 2000, banners hung up and down Malcolm X Boulevard/Lenox Avenue by the city's Department of Housing Preservation and Development proclaim: "BREAKING NEW GROUND." Across the street from Starbucks, look skyward and your gaze is met by another banner, equally optimistic in tone: "Empowerment Zone—THE FUTURE'S LOOKING UP."

Throughout Harlem, new housing appears here and there in what appears to be a more random pattern than the 125th Street makeover. Along the mostly residential, numbered side streets are conspicuous pockets of change. Curbside garbage dumpsters brim with the dusty, tangled mess of guts that signal a house in the midst of renovation. Four and five levels up, brownstone windows sport signs advertising those in the business of rehabilitation. "HOME AGAIN IN HARLEM: newly renovated and affordable," announces a poster that contains address, telephone number, and Web site information.

Recently completed renovations dot the side streets they share with scaffold-encased buildings undergoing remodeling, empty lots, and dilapidated older structures. The remodeled homes are easily identified by their gleaming wooden doors, shiny brass house numbers, security bars, and signs that announce: "PRIVATE PROPERTY: NO SITTING ON STOOP." Old warehouse and commercial spaces advertise phone numbers under promises of loft conversions soon to come.

To be sure, these changes potentially promise greater racial and economic integration in the historically black and economically marginal community. They signal a welcome shift from a long and deep segregation, an isolation that continues to mark many impoverished urban pockets across America. But a number of troubling questions accompany the emerging Harlem. For whom are the shopping and commercial changes meant? Who will live behind the facades of the posh housing renovations? Would too many newcomers, especially a large number of upper-income whites, threaten the racial and historic importance of the community?

Here and elsewhere in America, redevelopment that attracts national chain stores also brings groans and criticism aimed at "disneyfication" and homogenization of our public and private lives. Where the downtown renovation is a makeover that threatens with its corporate blandness, communities, villages, and towns fret over the potential loss of identity as they see familiar "mom-and-pop" stores losing out in a Darwinian struggle of capital and commerce. So, too, in Harlem do these changes arrive amid fear and apprehension.

Not only does the new development raise the potential for clashes along racial and economic lines, it opens up questions about the role of local power and participation in neighborhood development. In the long run, what remains to be seen is whether any of this development presages demographic shifts of the sort that would spell the demise of historic black Harlem. But this story does not begin with the arrival of Starbucks and other chain retailers in Harlem.

All of the transformation one sees in Harlem during the spring of 2000, both in commercial and residential realms, has been decades in the making. For much of the twentieth century, Harlem's fortunes have risen, fallen, and risen again with shifts in U.S. racial politics. The buffeting effects of a rising and declining urban industrialism and the onset of deindustrialization also have contributed to the roller-coasterlike ups and downs in the community's economic life.

Its wildly varying fortunes are readily evident to even casual visitors. A walk west on 125th Street leads away from Starbucks and into the heart of Harlem. This stretch takes you past a large image of Dr. Martin Luther King, his stern visage staring out from a brightly colored mural. Depicted with a raised finger stabbing at the air, Dr. King most certainly commands attention: "REMEMBER I HAD A DREAM AND IT'S UP TO YOU TO FINISH IT." The black lettering stands out against the dancing swirls of the mural's yellow, blue, red, green, and orange.

Midway along the east–west boulevard sits the famed Apollo Theater, and just across, the forlorn Mart 125—a two-level covered market that at one time was to solve the problem of too many sidewalk vendors clogging the boulevard with unlicensed street commerce. Once hailed for providing opportunities for local merchants, small entrepreneurs, and start-up businesses, the Mart now sits nearly empty, most of its tenants evicted and embroiled in a legal controversy with the city government over the duration of its leases.

On a spring day, the mall is like a ghost town, its offerings sparse. A staccato rap from a blaring radio competes with plaintive wails of Bob Marley that echo through the emptiness. Many of the closed stalls have on their darkened windows an *Amsterdam News* article detailing the controversy raised by the Mart's closure. Old photocopied signs of protest are partially torn. Messages that invite attendance at community meetings and supply addresses for letters to state officials are nearly plastered over with other announcements.

"STAND UP FOR MUMIA," urges a wall poster plastered in a three-by-three matrix. Whoever worked this stretch with Mumia posters was diligent. Lampposts, brick walls, empty doorways, and bus shelters—all become platforms advertising a protest gathering in support of the death-row inmate. A walk that is less than ten minutes from the Starbucks at the 125th Street subway station brings you right to the enormous and shiny new glass and concrete Harlem versions of Disney and Old Navy.

Around the corner on Adam Clayton Powell Jr. Boulevard, community activists inhabit a storefront office. On its doors and windows are photocopied flyers that reveal a telling blend of confrontation and acceptance aimed at the arrival of the stores. A hip young woman with funky glasses and a coif of messy dreadlocks runs the office, a joint venture of two community organizing groups. She presses flyers and pamphlets into my hands as she explains their mission. At issue is not whether the chain stores should be here, but rather how they can contribute to community improvement by providing jobs, training, and benefits for Harlem's neediest residents.

Today, one can walk for blocks in Harlem through stretches that bespeak the community's fall from better days. At the corner of 138th Street, a faded and rusty sign on the Casino Renaissance is as weathered and forlorn as other buildings that share the surrounding block. Streets like 138th, once celebrated for architectural grandeur, are now also defined by decrepit buildings.

This morning, an elderly man who is shabbily dressed pauses, leaning one hand against the building's faded red brick. Beneath the rusty sign and its long-spent neon, he urinates into a darkened door well, ignoring a posted ordinance: NO PUBLIC URINATION. All around him, other abandoned buildings are sprayed with jagged flourishes of graffiti; their stairwells hold rubbish—fast-food containers, empty bottles and cans, tires, mattresses, old shoes missing their mates. Demolition and arson have lent the streets a gap-toothed look.

Yet some of Harlem's streets remain guarded by well-preserved brownstones that have kept their grandeur. Neighborhoods such as Sugar Hill and Hamilton Heights, officially designated as a historic district, sport clean, quiet tree-lined streets that exude a middle-class respectability and hint at a rich history. The historic black community, which covers 3,829 acres, is surrounded on three sides by the East, Harlem, and Hudson rivers; its official boundaries run south to north from Ninety-sixth Street to 178th Street of upper Manhattan.

But Harlem spills beyond geography. It stretches beyond the confines of its physical space to gather in a far-flung African diaspora. The distinctiveness of African, Caribbean, and southern and midwestern U.S. blackness abounds in the sights, sounds, colors, and flavors of the traditions and day-to-day life in the community. Many of the streets in Harlem are identified by pairs of green street signs suggestive of the black claim. Lenox Avenue stretches uptown into Harlem, where it becomes Malcolm X Boulevard. Here, 125th Street is Martin Luther King Jr. Boulevard; Seventh Avenue is Adam Clayton Powell Jr. Boulevard; Eighth Avenue is Frederick Douglass Boulevard. Important figures in black history—Jackie Robinson, Paul Lawrence Dunbar, Sojourner Truth, Mahalia Jackson—identify schools and housing complexes. Marcus Garvey Park sits on Fifth Avenue between 120th and 124th Streets.

The New York Public Library Schomburg Center for Research in Black Culture, the Apollo Theater, and the Abyssinian Baptist Church are among Harlem's famous institutions. Among some of New York City's better-known landmark buildings, these spaces celebrate a black cultural heritage. In a blacktop lot at the 135th Street YMCA (where many Harlem luminaries first stayed upon arriving uptown) young boys play basketball in a fenced-in space. Bold black letters on the stone wall behind them declare: HARLEM PLAYS THE BEST BALL IN THE COUNTRY.

Just across the street from the YMCA and the Schomburg Center, a little more than ten blocks from Harlem's new Starbucks, sits Pan Pan, a local coffee shop. After hours of walking the boulevards and side streets, taking measure of the old and new in the community, I slip into the cozy familiarity for a cup of coffee and a grilled cheese sandwich, and to read the *Amsterdam*

News. It is well into the afternoon, and the three sections of low counter and swivel-style stools are alive with customers and conversation. I slide into an available space, listening as waitresses shout out orders for grits, eggs over easy, and other greasy-spoon delights.

As they sit over their cups of coffee, the men and women in Pan Pan ask after each others' health, catch up on children, grandchildren, and family matters—pictures are passed around. At my section of counter, a small group mulls over suspected racist conspiracies. Today's topics range from Adam Clayton Powell to Martin Luther King Jr. to J. Edgar Hoover. The group works through the complications of extending sympathies over the recent announcement that the New York mayor, whose racial politics leave much to be desired, has cancer. "Too bad indeed, uhmmm, hmmm," one of the men concludes, as heads nod in agreement. The men seem uncomfortable.

But their "race talk" continues. Somehow a royal plot against Britain's Princess Diana (who was, these talkers state matter-of-factly, involved in an interracial relationship) is worked into the ranging conversation, and with a smoothness born of a well-practiced art, they turn back to America, New York, and the storied streets of Harlem. Pan Pan is as typical of "old" Harlem as Starbucks is reflective of an emergent Harlem. Businesses such as the Disney Store and Blockbuster stand out next to fried-chicken vendors, check-cashing outlets, social service agencies, and bargain-priced shoe, clothing, human hair, and jewelry stores.

I first stepped into this story in the late 1980s. A newspaper headline and photos grabbed my attention. As the real-estate section of the *New York Times* told it, middle-class blacks were moving to Harlem in hopes of spurring a "second renaissance." The story's headline and photo captions were intriguing. The reporter relied on dramatic historic imagery and community lore. And by playing up Harlem's storied past, a portrait emerged of a black middle-class group that was as success-minded and upwardly mobile as it was duty-filled and politically committed to the black community.

It did not hurt that some of the renovations these newcomers had completed made for eye-catching real-estate photo spreads. In these photos one could see how the investment of time and money had restored the interiors and exteriors of elegant turn-of-the-century homes. Beaming owners posed on gleaming wood floors rescued from years and layers of linoleum and paint. Polished marble stairs led to grand entrances beneath ornate turrets and retouched archways. Close-ups showed a range of intricate details, restored.

I started doing fieldwork in Harlem in 1987, intending to interview Harlem's newest residents—an increasing number of black professionals, some married, others single, some families with children, others childless. The story I had read in the *New York Times,* along with others on the same theme, helped me locate many of these individuals. Not only were they eager to talk about Harlem and their lives, they were instrumental in helping me establish further contacts within their own formal and informal communities, neighborhood, and professional networks. What these initial contacts also opened up for me was a far more complex story about what was going on in Harlem. As I worked my way through borrowed Rolodex entries and met more people at community events—the reinauguration of Little League in Harlem, a photo exhibit at the Schomburg Center, for example—I also met middle-class Harlemites who had lived in the community for many years.

These people cast my glance back to the middle to late 1960s and early 1970s as they shared memories and told of their own participation in struggles against urban renewal that had foreshadowed by two decades the current gentrification in Harlem. Little by little, I learned that this latest influx of black middle-class actors into Harlem was a story of race, class, and community change that needed to be placed in a broader context.

During the first half of the twentieth century, studies by sociologists and anthropologists explored the culture, psychology, political attitudes, and economic standing of the black middle class, as well as its relations with poor and working-class blacks (Cayton and Drake, Frazier, Du Bois and Oliver Cox). Now that we are beyond the legal parameters of rigid segregation, studies of race *and* class must take on a world moved beyond caste *and* class constraints. Historic and structural shifts brought on by the dismantling of American apartheid provide a different context for the lifestyles, values, and attitudes of the black middle class. Public interactions and exchanges between blacks and whites have followed educational integration, equal opportunity in the workplace, and antidiscriminatory housing laws. Still, a more subtle type of racism has emerged—one that challenges optimistic conclusions about integration and increasing racial equality.[1]

With its growing numbers and visible success, the black middle class has, as Mary Pattillo-McCoy effectively argues, been ignored due to a policy and academic focus on black poverty. Elijah Anderson argues in a similar vein that the success and higher visibility of blacks in the workplace lead fewer Americans to see the need for affirmative action. Pattillo-McCoy's book *Black Picket Fences* urges greater focus on middle-class black life in the post–civil rights era: "the growth of the black middle class has been hailed as one of the major triumphs of the civil rights movement, but if we have so little information on this group and what their lives are like, how can we be so sure that triumphant progress is the full story?"[2]

Despite a significant amount of "black flight" during the waning years of racially restrictive barriers in America's housing markets, the Harlem community had never been entirely abandoned by the black middle class. Nor was the 1980s the first time Harlem had acted to solidify racial pride and identity through the use of historic preservation as a defense against "outsider" development.

Throughout five years of conducting interviews and participating in community events, I expanded my study to include both long-term and newer black middle-class residents. I also interviewed members of the business, redevelopment, and real-estate community in Harlem, the community's cultural and religious leaders, and neighborhood and political activists.

My interviews placed me in a variety of settings. During the summer, I lived in an apartment in Harlem with an aunt and uncle, who were not part of the study. I visited numerous community institutions—always with a neighborhood map, plenty of subway tokens, a tape recorder, extra batteries, and a notebook. I spent time at churches and restaurants, uptown and downtown offices, beauty salons, galleries and museums, the Mart 125, and the Apollo Theater, among other places. At private homes, I listened at kitchen and dining room tables, in lushly landscaped rose gardens, on front stoops, and in formal parlors and informal television rooms.

Typically my interviews ranged from thirty minutes to an hour. Sometimes I was able to spend hours with a subject. These interview sessions ran late into the night or were conducted while touring the neighborhood on foot or by car. Interview subjects were asked to talk about specific details of their work lives as well as their residential experiences in Harlem. These questions addressed length of residence, reasons for moving to Harlem, the nature and level of activity and involvement in the community, and interactions with neighbors and other residents. I also pushed subjects to comment on race, racism, and race relations in contemporary America and in their lives. This moved interviews beyond simply talking about life in Harlem to touch on personal experiences of race and integration in other neighborhoods, work, school, and social settings, which helped me place their contemporary accounts in a broader structural and historical context.

Not only did these individuals contribute to my understanding of events in contemporary Harlem, they also helped me work back through time, to the defining moment for Harlem's significance to black America—the Harlem Renaissance of the 1920s and 1930s. From the community's poets and historians, I was directed to the important studies, biographies, films, and recordings that had chronicled Harlem's life since the early 1920s.

In addition to the tape-recorded interviews, I filled boxes and notebooks with copies and originals of materials as varied as old news clippings, development reports, theater programs, menus, newsletters, photos, and flyers. Assorted scraps and documents of the community's past poured forth from closets and storage spaces, desk drawers, office file drawers and cardboard folders, scrapbooks and photo albums. Again and again, my contacts allowed me to look back through time and space in order to situate current events in Harlem in a broader course of political, social, and historical narrative.

While this work has its origins in an academic dissertation, it is now told in a manner that should be accessible to academic and general audiences alike. In the absence of what ought to be serious and ongoing discussions about the cultural, political, and social realities that shape race relations in America, we too often ignore the inner workings of daily experiences of race. Such insights are a necessary part of exploring the complicated architecture of our nation's ignominious racial past and present.

The material that makes up the chapters in this book is drawn from a variety of sources: historical accounts along with the literature and poetry of the Harlem Renaissance, documents from Harlem community agencies concerning redevelopment, interviews with new and long-term Harlemites conducted in homes and workplaces inside and outside of Harlem, newspaper and magazine accounts of gentrification in Harlem, as well as observational and descriptive material drawn from my own fieldwork in Harlem from 1987 to 1992. For readers unfamiliar with ethnographic practice, I have sought to maintain the anonymity of interview subjects by giving them pseudonyms and changing their job titles and distinguishing details about their homes. In the same spirit, I have changed the names of some institutions that I visited in Harlem. Other more famous or historical locations retain their names.

In chapter 1, I examine the historical and symbolic importance of Harlem. Why does so much symbolic meaning—hope, haven, home, promise, pride, and community—reside in Harlem, according to both opponents of and participants in gentrification? In part, the answer derives from the fact that Harlem, as a site of black America's cultural past, represents history and tradition in the African American community.

Because Harlem is a powerful cultural symbol with a complex racial meaning, its oppositional and marginal characteristics stand out as available symbols in a *racially* charged struggle. In a new era of American race relations, modified since the civil rights era, important but thorny questions arise about the ways in which race functions as part of the current transition in Harlem.

To understand the range of responses that have arisen today concerning Harlem as symbolic space in transition, it is important to establish the source of this community's meaning as well as the complexity and contradictions within Harlem's symbolic meaning. In earlier times, a more simplistic dichotomy of race was enough to maintain Harlem's larger oppositional meaning against the white world, without revealing internal contradictions.

But with America's shift beyond de jure segregation and the rigid boundaries that accompanied it, the black community now finds itself confronting the many, sometimes contrasting meanings attached to its symbols and culture. That there is a multivocality—or range of multiple meanings—attached to Harlem as a symbol is apparent in the variety of conflicting responses to 1960s and 1970s redevelopment that presaged gentrification in Harlem.

Chapter 2 begins by looking at the Harlem State Office Building controversy of the early 1970s. This episode laid the groundwork for how the community, in particular middle-class residents who played a central role in resistance to urban renewal plans hatched by the city, would respond to more recent renovation and renewal. The chapter examines the role of homeowners, real-estate brokers, and redevelopment officials in influencing the shape of urban renewal and later gentrification. The chapter combines interviews, newsletters from that time, accounts of meetings and protests, and redevelopment agency documents to identify the roots of a carefully defined strategy that would place a premium on attracting black middle-class homeowners to Harlem as part of economic revitalization. My interviews with key players show a clear desire to attract middle-class *and* black residents but reveal sharply split opinions over whether whites who might follow would be compatible with historic and cultural preservation.

Chapter 3 examines the black gentrifiers in the 1980s and 1990s. Many seem to be drawn to the community in order to connect with what they see as a needed respite from integration and the largely white worlds in which they work and previously lived. Firsthand accounts of their participation in the gentrification of Harlem offer a look at the ways in which memories and images, drawn from representations of Harlem's past, are based on a nostalgic view of Harlem that is heroic and vital, if at times mythical.

In extensive interviews, I identify a racially tinged set of push and pull factors that account for migration to Harlem. The people I interviewed relate stories of exclusion, hostility, and more subtle forms of marginalization in integrated settings, predominantly white neighborhoods and workplaces where these gentrifiers have achieved some measure of professional success. What makes their stories significant is that their decision to move to a largely black and troubled community comes at a moment when America is increasingly opening its doors to minorities as a result of civil rights reforms aimed at dismantling discrimination in jobs, housing, and other areas.

In chapters 4, 5, and 6, I continue my analysis of middle-class black gentrifiers and their lives in Harlem. Chapter 4 looks at the reality that greets them when they arrive in Harlem. In this chapter they confront the conflicts and class tensions that surround them as property owners who stand out in a community in transition. In interviews, we hear how they define themselves in the sometimes uncomfortable role of gentrifiers and how they describe their conduct as home owners. Just as dilemmas of difference in chapter 3 focused on race, the dilemmas illuminated in chapter 4 turn on the axis of class.

In chapters 5 and 6, I show how black gentrifiers seek to reconcile their dreams for racial community with impulses as property owners. I spent time in their houses and accompanied these residents on neighborhood strolls. I caught them and watched as they joined others at Little League games, stores and commercial spaces, museum openings, and community meetings. The chapters examine their private behavior and public actions that define their efforts at becoming community insiders. I conclude that there are no easy answers but suggest that in this modern period, the tricky business of constructing race identity is negotiated as a public *and* private, individual *and* collective matter.

Modern-day issues of race policy, identity, and politics have become increasingly complex but at times are collapsed into and framed by an older set of categories that appear to be straightforward and monolithic. Contemporary discussions about race often bog down or are avoided as the source of tension, unease, and confusion. When Rodney King, Clarence Thomas, and O. J. Simpson were thrust into the glare of the national media eye, they each helped reveal the distance between racial meaning in the past and present of America. These race dramas and the arguments and conversations they opened up within black America revealed a black community that was splintered along messy lines of class, gender, generational, and sexual racial identities.

This book illuminates the tentative coexistence of conflicting forces today in mainstream and black America: hopeful signs of assimilation and integration accompany a persistence of negative experiences of racism. From the perspective of middle-class blacks in Harlem, readers gain a chance to listen and learn from their personal narratives the more subtle forms that racism takes. We also gain insight into the ways that the specifics of this historical moment give rise to individual and collective racial identities simultaneously.

Efforts to promote and sustain racial integration in America are hindered because a lot of information is not revealed across the racial divide. We may learn in integrated classrooms, work in integrated offices, and shop in integrated stores, but when we shift from public settings to the more private worlds we inhabit, our most intimate relations with family, friends, and community are still remarkably segregated.

Today, Harlem residents become more like the rest of America, with a range of fresh shopping choices, courtesy of Starbucks, Old Navy, and Blockbuster Video. But as Harlemites engage in shared rituals of consumption, they do so within a community defined by racial difference. That America's increasing integration is also accompanied by voluntary segregation on the part of a group of middle-class black professionals gives pause. The haven found by moving "home to Harlem" may be an unusual and even isolated event. But to the degree that it provides insight into continuing feelings of isolation, invisibility, or marginality, it offers a lens through which to more critically evaluate race and class in integrated America.

chapter 1

Harlem between Heaven and Hell

A Harlem-bound express train pulls into the Ninety-sixth Street subway station on Manhattan's Upper West Side. A rider promises a trick guaranteed to dazzle an "alien brother," star of John Sayles's film, *Brother from Another Planet.* In an instant, predicts the brother's traveling companion, he can make the white passengers disappear. The train glides into its destination on an ear-shattering screech of brakes, its doors swoosh open, and sure enough, the white riders scatter. What magic is it that leaves the Harlem-bound train absent of white passengers?

Moviegoers attuned to New York's racial geography will see through this not so mystical sleight of hand. Whites and blacks historically have inhabited two separate uptown worlds. The joke works from a subtext that weds history and geography to race: above Ninety-sixth Street, the 110th, 116th, and 125th Streets serviced by this train will drop you into the very heart of Harlem—and woe unto the white rider who forgets to transfer.

While doing fieldwork and living in Harlem, I was an uptown subway regular. I recognize this "anticipated fear" of Harlem as both a reel and real occurrence. It is a look of too-late recognition that reveals itself in alarmed faces and darting eyes. Sometimes it is the student new to neighboring Columbia University, still unschooled in the racial geography of the urban campus perimeter. Or it could be the tourist—a U.S. or foreign visitor toting maps and guidebooks that suggest where and how to avoid the "dangers" of Manhattan/Harlem.

This is a scene that could be played out across urban America. The ghettos of Atlanta, Boston, Washington, D.C., Detroit, Chicago, Los Angeles are marginalized spaces where black/white boundaries reinforce a dualistic hierarchy of coded racial and racist meanings. Even beyond the days of rigidly codified residential segregation, a seemingly "invisible hand" of preference, money, and market forces continues to produce a de facto racial segregation throughout the United States.[1]

Conscious and unconscious "knowledge" about race and place joins actions to attitudes that are the end result of a complex discursive practice of "racial formations." An intricate calculus of awareness and avoidance adds up to a wide variety of practices that construct and reproduce racialized spaces over time. In urban America, the adherence to spoken and unspoken boundaries between black and white spaces translates social relations of racism into spatial terms. Expressions such as "the wrong side of the tracks" to refer to racial or ethnic neighborhoods, and local knowledge that "they" live up, down, or over "there" are indicators of this social production of racialized space.

David Sibley's studies about Gypsy communities in Britain and other European countries explore the consequences of these hierarchies of values when they are arranged in space. "In order to legitimate exclusion," argues Sibley, "people who are defined as 'other' or residual, beyond the boundaries of the acceptable, are commonly represented as less than human."[2] Sibley locates our awareness of marginal social statuses in boundary processes that reveal "distinctions [we acknowledge] between the pure and the defiled, the normal and the deviant, the same and the other."[3] When dominant society views outsiders as "polluting," exclusion, containment, and invisibility in the landscape work as strategies by which dominant groups can expel contamination. One consequence of these boundary practices is that marginal spaces confer outsider status on those who inhabit them. "A fear of the other," concludes Sibley, "becomes a fear of place."[4] Because landscapes of exclusion appear threatening, they are places avoided by members of the dominant society.

At Ninety-sixth Street in Manhattan, John Sayles brings "us" face to face with the stark fact of continued patterns of U.S. racial separation. Here we stand at "the edge of hell" before Harlem. Residential segregation and urban fear of minorities all but guarantee the disappearance of whites in his sight gag. But the success of Sayles's "magic" hides as much as it reveals about race in America. The white disappearing act cannot really show the alien brother the myriad social and historical forces that combine to produce this reaction to Harlem.

Further, if we, as an audience, assume that there is a shared vantage point for viewing Harlem, we miss the role that power and particular standpoints play in shaping our "social constructions of reality." We (wrongly) assume that shared spatial vocabularies order space into front/back, high/low, and center/margin dichotomies whose meanings stem from natural or commonsense ideas. To deconstruct these assumptions of neutrality and natural meanings, as Edward Soja argues in *Postmodern Geographies*, a "spatial imagination" must be placed alongside historical and sociological analysis.

> We must be insistently aware of how space can be made to hide consequences from us, how relations of power and discipline are inscribed into the apparently innocent spatiality of social life, how human geographies become filled with politics and ideology.[5]

When "our" space is made distinct from "theirs," the two are pairs in hierarchically coded series of relations—good/bad, light/dark, clean/unclean, safe/unsafe, and so on. Familiar sets of binary symbolisms affix dominant social norms and values onto places. This process also reveals how racism is embedded in space and spatial practices. These relational and value-based interpretations must be seen within the context of social relations. If we trace the roots of these symbolic meanings to positions and persons of status and power, it is clear how one meaning can be taken as the "official or widely shared reality" of a place.

But within the borders and margins of such spaces are alternative worlds of meaning that contest through reinvention these terms of exclusion and containment. Rather than being fixed or anchored, symbolic meanings attached to physical places reveal the competing vantage points and values of different groups. Oppositional meanings of space emerge if "outsiders" are repositioned as "insiders" who become agents in a process of place making. Through this inversion, according to Soja, spaces of representation embody complex symbolisms, linked to the "clandestine or underground side of social life and to art." These "lived spaces of representation are thus the terrain for the generation of 'counterspaces,' spaces of resistance to the dominant order arising precisely from their subordinate, peripheral or marginalized positioning."[6]

This chapter explores Harlem as a counterspace whose meanings also arise from its symbolic construction by blacks. I loosely follow a chronological account of Harlem's history from the 1920s to the present. Drawing from a blend of historical, literary, and social science works on Harlem, I am primarily interested in directing readers to the onset and recurrence of three thematic dichotomies that will later help make sense of the swirl of interpretations around Harlem's modern redevelopment struggles. Between the extremes of insider and outsider, black and white, and heaven and hell, it is clear that, even within the black community, a unitary construction of Harlem has never existed.

As a site of opposition to dominant (or hegemonic) discourses, Harlem is an important historical site that functions as a staging ground for "rituals of reversal" used to counter racism. Matters regarding *who* could speak for Harlem were not without complication, though. As repositioned "insiders," black leaders, or "race men," would stress internal community control as a necessary strategy. It would be a black voice of self-representation, not a white one, that the "New Negro" used to challenge marginalization in broader American society.

Wrangling over *how* these strategies of "ritual reversal" would be used illuminates another longstanding conflict over Harlem's symbolic representation. In contrast to its earliest depictions as heaven, and other positive idealizations, the chapter shows a Harlem depicted, by blacks, using a terminology of sexuality, deviance, mental illness, disease, and bodily functions.

Most important, I want here to provide a starting point for a critical examination of the limitations of essentialized race thinking. Stepping into the historic space of the "black Mecca" or "promised land" shows that even an era defined by more absolute black and white territorial segregations produced an illogic behind "race" thinking as an "antiracist" strategy. Overshadowed by the challenge of confronting racism, Harlem Renaissance leaders often sidestepped problems inherent with equating a black voice and experience with an insider perspective. This chapter should provide a historic starting point that will assist us later in seeing beyond simplified categories of race community, identity, and position that characterize, but are not unique to, Harlem's urban renewal and gentrification struggles during the past three decades.

Viewed side by side, the Langston Hughes poems that open this book suggest a magic of black Harlem—then and now. The association of Harlem with heaven and paradise reminds us that there was a hopeful optimism amid a racial pride that surrounded the community's birth. With his later lament Hughes poses a question about the downfall of Harlem, and perhaps of black America, that is equally relevant to Harlem's current redevelopment struggles. Where he situates a collective "we" on the edge of hell *in* Harlem, he created a collective body that looks *outward*, asking "What are we gonna do?" First, though, Hughes's lament invites another question: "What do we remember?"

The Great Subway Proposition: The Real-Estate Market and Harlem's "Negro Invasion"

At the turn of the century the physical segregation that dictated residential separation between blacks and whites provided a context for the development of black Harlem. The "great subway proposition"—the plan to extend a streetcar line to Manhattan's upper reaches to connect outlying areas to downtown—spurred wild real-estate speculation in Harlem, leading to inflated prices and artificial market values.[7]

The bust came in 1905, as many speculators realized that too many houses had been constructed, prices were too high, and the completion date for connecting this part of Manhattan to downtown by subway was uncertain. To save themselves from financial ruin, many landlords were willing to rent properties to blacks.[8]

Some realtors used the threat of renting to blacks to frighten white neighbors into buying them out at high prices. Others shrewdly took advantage of white fear and prejudice. The hope was that by placing blacks into certain properties, neighboring whites would vacate their properties and free them up at extremely low prices.[9]

For the first time in the city's history, blacks were offered decent living accommodations, and they flocked to Harlem. Many white tenants and realtors unsuccessfully fought what they called a "Negro invasion." This notice appeared on an apartment building in 1916:

> We have endeavored for some time to avoid turning over this house to colored tenants, but as the result of . . . rapid changes in conditions . . . this issue has been forced upon us.[10]

Rather than live with blacks, whites at first resisted, then fled as quickly as possible, contributing to the emergence of a newly segregated portion of the city. While blacks had been concentrated in other areas of New York—most notably in San Juan Hill and the Tenderloin district in lower Manhattan, for example—they had until this point occupied only one or two streets or blocks. The consolidation of the black community in Harlem was the first time blacks in New York had occupied a sizable area as their own.

Amid a wave of mass south-to-north migration at the dawn of the twentieth century, Harlem was but one of the newly urbanizing communities whose racial boundaries reflected the rigid segregation of the day. Studies such as James Weldon Johnson's *Black Manhattan,* Gilbert Osofsky's *Harlem: The Making of a Ghetto,* and Seth Scheiner's *Negro Mecca* locate the formation of black Harlem at the spatial intersection of race relations and the demographic transformation of urbanizing America. While other segregated black communities sprang up in northern cities at the time, Harlem became a lasting symbol of black cultural identity and maintains a unique role as a symbol of black cultural expression.

It was almost inevitable that some portion of New York City was to become a "black belt" due to the large migration of blacks to northern industrial centers. "The most important factor underlying the establishment of Harlem as a Negro community," wrote Osofsky, "was the substantial increase of Negro population in New York City in the years 1890–1914."[11] By 1914, some fifty thousand Negroes lived in Harlem.[12]

Writing at the end of Harlem's consolidation as a black ghetto, sociologist E. Franklin Frazier noted that within Harlem's boundaries, five concentric zones gave shape to a radial pattern that mirrored ecological patterns of a self-contained city.[13] The black population within these five zones of Harlem rose from 27,827 in 1910 to 203,482 by 1934.[14] With its own central business district radiating out toward distinct residential areas, a spatial ecology accounted for one of the many monikers by which Harlem was known—it was a "city within a city," some proudly declared. Within the boundaries of Harlem, a spatial logic unfolded such that the community, as a center space for blacks, had its own front and back, high and low regions.

"Hill" and "Valley," for instance, became geographic distinctions that accompanied the separation and stratification of the community into middle-class, poor, and working-class Harlemites. Sugar Hill, which ran from 145th Street to 155th Street, between Amsterdam and Edgecombe Avenues, was literally a community on a slope. By the late 1920s, a black elite had displaced Jewish, German, and Irish families fleeing racial integration there.[15]

Central Harlem, also known as the Valley, was the heart of Harlem's institutional and social life. Home to the more affordable apartments occupied by the masses, it was also the location of another well-known black elite neighborhood, between Seventh and Eighth Avenues on 138th and 139th Streets. With its prized Stanford White townhouses, Strivers Row was a middle-class enclave denoting ascension and mobility.

Even with its own class and status divisions, the restrictive confines of the ghetto gave rise to a Harlem within which there was a racially defined local community life that followed the pattern of larger urban areas. While the "physical ghetto was a product of white racism," writes Allan Spear, "the institutional ghetto was the creation of black civic leaders and entrepreneurs determined to make the black community a decent place to live."[16] This was certainly true in Harlem, where institutional support for the economic, political, and cultural life of Negroes was everywhere in evidence. To serve the community, black cultural and political institutions found a home in Harlem.

Black churches and realty offices initially played a central role in developing the institutional life of Harlem. The Abyssinian Baptist Church, Bethel African Methodist Episcopal, African Methodist Episcopal Zion, and St. Philip's Protestant Episcopal Church followed their congregations to Harlem. Those with some wealth invested in Harlem and, as landholders, helped "transform Harlem into a Negro section."[17] Today, black churches in Harlem continue to play a role in the development of the community by financing affordable housing and providing needed social services.[18]

Real-estate investors such as John E. Nail, Henry Parker, Philip Payton, and John Royall profited financially as middlemen who eased the transition of blacks into Harlem housing. Payton, who established the Afro-American Realty Company, for example, specialized in "managing colored tenants" for white landlords.

Following the black migration uptown, major black organizations in the city also began to relocate in Harlem by 1920, lending it an institutional importance that would add to its distinctiveness as a ghetto. The black YMCA and YWCA, black branches of fraternal organizations such as the Masons, the Elks, and the Oddfellows, and black insurance companies moved to Harlem to serve the black community. Two important black newspapers, the *Amsterdam News* and the *New York Age*, also joined the trek uptown.

The NAACP opened an office in Harlem, and the National League on Urban Condition Among Negroes, which would later become the National Urban League, moved its headquarters there in 1914. Harlem became the international hub for Marcus Garvey's black nationalist Universal Negro Improvement Association (UNIA); the mass movement was founded in Harlem in 1917.

As Harlem consolidated its role as a "black belt," it took on a powerful significance for writers and artists. From 1919 to 1929 the cultural movement defining the neighborhood's heyday took place: the Harlem Renaissance. Those were the years, wrote Langston Hughes, when "Harlem was in vogue." The philosophy and art that came out of Harlem at this time have had a lasting significance for the development of modern black consciousness.

Thereafter, this black "city within a city" exerted a magnetic pull for blacks from all over the world. Harlem loomed large as the "symbol of liberty" and a "promised land" in the black imagination.[19] In "Nigger Heaven"[20] as Harlem was called in a controversial book of the time, an emerging artistic community formed the nucleus of a black artistic movement that generated a whirlwind of creativity. Some of the most famous political and literary writings, plays, and music by American blacks emerged there, spawning a lasting symbolism.

The New Negro and the Harlem Renaissance

Now a space existed in which black artists and intellectuals participated jointly in the creation of a new urban collective identity. Thus, despite the racist underpinnings—political and economic restrictions in housing and employment—that explain when and how Negroes came to occupy the northern reaches of Manhattan Island, they would attempt to create a social and cultural life of their own.

The derogatory "Nigger Heaven"[21]—a term used to describe segregated theater balconies—captured the marginality of Harlem and its residents that would play a central role in shaping the form of cultural expressions that came out of the ghetto during this period. In Harlem, it was also a conscious strategy that these cultural expressions would be a matter of *self*-definition.

As Jervis Anderson notes in his cultural history of Harlem, Carl Van Vechten's title *Nigger Heaven,* which was hotly debated, was taken from words spoken by a *black* character in the novel:

> Nigger Heaven! That's what Harlem is. We sit in our places in the gallery of this New York theater and watch the white world sitting down below in the good seats in the orchestra. Occasionally, they turn their faces up towards us, their hard, cruel faces, to laugh or sneer, but they never beckon. It never seems to occur to them that Nigger Heaven is crowded, that there isn't another seat, that something has to be done. (149)

The value of "Nigger Heaven" as a colloquialism is in its clear reference to a spatial distinction between blacks and whites. This stark separation draws our attention not only to how front and back space reinforces high and low status but also to how the relative positions of center and margin shape black racial consciousness as well.

Van Vechten's use of the term situates us in the theater as a space in which differently positioned viewers watch the race problem as a social drama. Van Vechten's character is offering a harsh indictment of whites who would turn their gaze from center stage and, looking back, still not see what was before them. Seen from the backstage position of blacks, this view suggests that disdain on the part of whites, even when they do notice blacks, means they do not see in segregation a problem demanding joint action.

But this is the view of Van Vechten, a white writer, who can only adopt the gaze of a black observer through his fictional use of Harlem. The controversy surrounding Van Vechten's use of Harlem material to write about race relations highlighted a fundamental political view that Harlem writing should come from insiders. When Harlem's image and identity were so possessively guarded and policed, purportedly as protection against outsiders, an authoritative voice about Harlem was, for its renaissance leaders, appropriated by and for blacks themselves.

The marginality of Harlem and its residents would play a large role in shaping the cultural forms and indictments of racism that came out of the ghetto during this period. As the site of a flowering of black artistic and political expression, Harlem at the time represented black America's hope to create a "New Negro" reborn from the "social death" of slavery. This was a strategy meant to move black America beyond racist stereotypes of aunties, uncles, mammies, Uncle Tom, and Sambo.

As the most famous of the Negro ghettos of the time, Harlem exerted a profound influence in the creation of America's newest cultural voice. Here a group of black Americans, striving to create a cultural consciousness, attempted to forge a new identity for blacks. Thus entered into our culture the "New Negro" of the Negro Renaissance, an artistic movement that could even claim its own midwife, as Alain Locke was known. Images of birth and rebirth are rife in the accounts of the cultural imagery and race symbolism developing in Harlem during the early 1900s.

Locke, author of the essay "The New Negro," pointed to Harlem's crucial role for blacks in the emerging cultural movement. Locke wrote:

> In Harlem, Negro life is seizing upon its first chances for group expression and self-determination. It is—or promises at least to be—a race capital. That is why our comparison is taken with those nascent centers of folk expression and self-determination which are playing a creative part in the world today. Without pretense to their political significance, Harlem has the same role to play for the "New Negro" as Dublin has had for the New Ireland or Prague for the New Czechoslovakia.[22]

Locke's essay, which functioned as a manifesto of the Negro Renaissance, reveals the goals and purposes of the movement as a twofold task. According to Locke, while the "New Negro" must be a "collaborator and participant in American civilization," at the same time he must "preserve and implement his own racial traditions."[23]

This duality echoed philosopher W. E. B. Du Bois's concern with the double consciousness of the Afro-American:

> [T]his double consciousness, this sense of always looking at one's self through the eyes of others, of measuring one's soul by the tape of a world that looks on in amused contempt and pity. One ever feels his twoness—An American, a Negro; two souls, two thoughts, two unreconciled strivings; two warring ideals in one dark body, whose dogged strength alone keeps it from being torn asunder.[24]

The New Negro movement was an ambitious attempt to resolve the black American dilemma with which Du Bois had grappled, although it was judged later as misguided. In essence, its aim was racial equality through a rehabilitation of the Negro image. The Harlem Renaissance promoted the talents of an elite group of artists and intellectuals, dubbed the "talented tenth" by Du Bois. He believed this group was capable of outstanding achievement and of shouldering the responsibility to represent race to the entire world in a positive light.

A built-in failing was the naïveté and a reliance on whites, who were both the chief audience and patrons of this cultural makeover. White publications such as *Survey Graphic* and Max Eastman's *Socialist Liberator* devoted issues to writings by Locke and other blacks. Other whites, such as Van Vechten (whose novel sensationalized a seamy side of Harlem nightlife), promoted black theater, music, and writing through articles. Charlotte Mason, who gave financial support to writers Langston Hughes and Zora Neale Hurston, has been depicted in Harlem autobiographies as a strict and unyielding, if generous, benefactor.

The sheer volume and quality of literary and other works created during this period drew attention from all over the world. Political, economic, and social advancement were seen by renaissance leaders as tied to cultural expression directed outward from this geographic and spiritual center. The renaissance artists "saw art and letters as a bridge across the chasm between the races," wrote Nathan Huggins. "The time and the circumstances of its creation made Harlem symbolize the Afro-American's coming of age."[25]

At their most optimistic, boosters thought such an approach would lead all Negroes to a new stage. Locke ambitiously proclaimed that "the Negro . . .

can at least . . . celebrate the attainment of a significant and satisfying new phase of group development, and with it a spiritual Coming of Age."[26] This transitional racial attitude as one of resistance would become an enduring symbolism for reimagining Harlem during later periods of community crisis.

Harlem-based publications such as the radical *The Messenger, Harlem,* and *Fire!!* provided a voice for young black writers and a forum for the rough-and-tumble political debates among leaders such as Du Bois and Garvey. *The Crisis,* the Du Bois–edited monthly journal of the NAACP, enjoyed a peak circulation of 116,000. *The Crisis* and the lesser known Urban League bulletin, *Opportunity,* focused attention on politics and the economy in attempting to break down prejudice and research social issues affecting Negroes. They also published the organization's sponsorship of competitions, prizes, and fellowships to further encourage creativity and production of the arts.

The more cultural and artistic activity flourished in Harlem, the more Harlem exerted a powerful attraction for blacks from all over the world to come and join this vibrant racial community. The magnetism of Harlem as a communal space denoting racial pride would be another of its enduring legacies. As a sacred center, Harlem was made literally and metaphorically into an essential location for a strategic and ritualistic reversal of a profane Negro identity.

Here's to Harlem! Harlem as Heaven

Writers such as Rudolph Fisher, Langston Hughes, Nella Larsen, and Claude McKay were able to bring the Afro-American experience to the world through the arts. In their works, many of the Harlem writers employed Harlem as both setting and symbol. Within the boundaries of the community, black writers were able to imagine alternative racial identities that challenged the outsider and marginal status of the race as a collective body.

As Langston Hughes revealed in his autobiography, Harlem played a central role in the developing racial consciousness of a young adult:

> I had come to New York to enter Columbia College as a freshman, but really why I had come to New York was to see Harlem. I found it hard a week or so later to tear myself away from Harlem when it came time to move up the hill to the dormitory at Columbia. That winter I spent as little time as possible on campus. Instead, I spent as much time as I could in Harlem, and this I have done ever since. I was in love with Harlem long before I got there, and still I am in love with it. Everybody seemed to make me welcome. The sheer dark size of Harlem intrigued me.[27]

Hughes's autobiographical recollection of Harlem and its physical relation to Columbia University—the college on a hill—juxtaposes two distinct worlds within Manhattan. Hughes inscribes his own inverted meaning to these high and low spheres through a sentimental attachment to Harlem and its residents. Hughes's attraction to Harlem is illustrated through the contrast between being an outsider "up the hill" and feeling welcomed in the "sheer dark" down below in Harlem. At this point, at least, "down below" was not a space equated with hell. Indeed Hughes, who was to become known as the poet laureate of Harlem, often used the community as an idealized symbolic referent.

For Hughes, writes Arthur Davis, "Harlem was place, symbol, and on occasion protagonist."[28] In "A Toast to Harlem," Jesse B. Simple states a love for Harlem that echoes Hughes's own:

> Anyhow Harlem is the place I always did want to be . . . That's a fact, I love Harlem.
>
> What is it you love about Harlem?
>
> It's so full of negroes. I feel like I got protection.
>
> From what?
>
> White folks . . . Furthermore, I like Harlem because it belongs to me.[29]

Simple, Hughes's Everyman, is Harlem. Placed within this context he, like Hughes, thrills to the darkness that surrounds him in Harlem. Given the larger meaning found in Harlem's clear opposition between black and white, Hughes recognizes the community as a place that provides blacks—"stolen from Africa," to quote Bob Marley—something they can claim as their own.

In the literature of the time, Harlem provided a symbolic space upon which the writer could reflect and present the conditions of black Americans to the rest of the world. In *Quicksand,* Nella Larsen masterfully employs Harlem as a setting in which to work out protagonist Helga Crane's racial identity struggle. The wanderings of Helga, a tragic mulatto uneasy in her relationship to both blacks and whites, take her from the American South to Chicago and New York and abroad to Copenhagen in order to find a place where she will fit in. It is when Helga arrives in "Harlem, teeming black Harlem" that she feels at home:

> Helga Crane now meant to have a home and perhaps laughing, appealing dark-eyed children in Harlem. Her existence was bounded by Central Park, Fifth Avenue, St. Nicholas Park and 145th Street.[30]

The use of Harlem's physical boundaries in this fictional work mirrors the way Harlem functioned as a metaphor for explorations of race and identity for other renaissance writers. With her desires for "dark-eyed children" who will be born here, Larsen also stakes a claim for later generations of black America. For Larsen's Helga Crane, residence and birth in Harlem echoed a shared strategy of making the community function as a ritual space of birth and the creation of life. The promise of Harlem is one alternative to pitfalls that threaten to mire Helga as she moves through a number of American and European geographies.

In *Passing,* Larsen employs Harlem's boundaries in a similar fashion. The story's shifting in and out of Harlem serves as a frame for exploring the slippery terrain of black and white boundaries that confront those light enough to pass. Harlem's boundaries mark Clare Kendry's shift from a white world to a black one as she grapples with feelings of alienation. Clare's movement in and out of Harlem comments on passing as one resistance strategy to racism. As an individual act, however, passing does little to subvert negative identities that are imposed on collective groups. The novel's continued juxtaposition of being "inside" and "outside" Harlem uses its repeated moments of boundary crossing to point to the difficulties of the color line—even for light-skinned blacks.

Larsen's critique of passing is implicit in her use of a fair-skinned character who is light enough to pass but continues to be drawn to Harlem even when it could jeopardize her "successful" marriage to a white businessman. Despite her own ability to pass, Clare is an outsider in a white world whose racist remarks, while not intended for her, still sting. In the novel, the boundaries of Harlem are used to bring Clare back into a black world where communal belonging is an antidote to unspoken shame.

Similarly in Claude McKay's picaresque novel *Home to Harlem,* the main character's wanderings take him in and out of Harlem—a strategy employed by other renaissance writers—as a place through which to explore race and identity as a philosophical and existential concern. What is noteworthy about McKay's novel was its reception by the leading intellectuals of the Harlem Renaissance. *Home to Harlem* was condemned because of its portrayal of a lower class and a "lower side" of black life.

A leading critic of McKay's work was Du Bois, advocate of the position that an intellectually gifted "talented tenth" would lead the way in replacing negative images of blacks through a more positive mission to "uplift the race." From this standpoint, Du Bois recoiled at McKay's imagery of what he labeled the "debauched Tenth." Writing about McKay's *Home to Harlem,* Du Bois remarked that the book "nauseated" him and that "after the dirtier parts of its filth I feel distinctly like taking a bath."[31] This critique reveals Du Bois's concern that racial representation needed to be protected from polluting influences, even by black writers who ought to have been "insiders."

Clearly, Harlem was to be used to explore issues of race and representation, but renaissance leaders strictly policed the borders of what constituted an acceptable representation of race. At times this meant that themes of class, gender, and sexuality went unaddressed or were pushed aside, as renaissance leaders deliberately contributed to their silence and marginalization. Because Harlem and its *racial* image were central features of the ritual reversal of meaning black leaders hoped to accomplish, an uncomplicated relationship between insider status and race was assumed to guarantee a unified voice and similar perspective. This did not always happen, though. Harlem's artists did not, in fact, speak with a collective voice or from a shared perspective.

Rudolph Fisher, a writer who saw himself as an "interpreter" of Harlem,[32] made use of Harlem as a physical space to explore the contradictions of black American life brought about by the great migration. "Fisher succeeded," writes Leonard Deutsch, "in charting the physical and moral topography of Harlem during the Harlem Renaissance." He offered us "rigorous realism of place."[33]

In stories such as "The City of Refuge" and "The Promised Land," Fisher wrote about Harlem in ways that went beyond revealing its symbolic importance as a sacred center. Fisher's stories also struggled with the complex and often contradictory meaning Harlem held for blacks. Harlem may have been a race capital and a Mecca, but it was also, according to Fisher, "that great noisy, heartless crowded place where you lived under the same roof with a hundred people you never knew; where night was alive and morning dead."[34]

In "The City of Refuge," for instance, King Solomon Gillis has moved from North Carolina to Harlem. As the title suggests, Harlem is a place filled with promise and hope. Yet despite the freedom associated with Harlem—it's "even got cullud policemans"—a string of bad associations and hard luck surrounds Gillis. When Gillis is arrested in Harlem, it is because he, as many others would, "falls victim to the myth of Harlem."[35]

In several of his stories, Fisher portrays characters who fall to this myth. The hope of Harlem as a promised land dissolves for many Southerners who chased elusive dreams in this great northern city. In Fisher's story "The Promised Land," a character laments:

> New York. Harlem. Thought all along 't was d' las' stop fo' Heaven. Canaan hitself. Reg'lar promis' lan'. Well, dats jes' whut 't is—a promis' lan'. All hit do is promise. Promise money lak growin' on trees—ain' even got d' trees. Promise wuk fo' dem whut want wuk—look at my boy, Wesley. Promise freedom fum d' whi' folks—white man be hyeh to-day, take d' las penny fo' rent....[36]

Fisher reveals the paradox of the trek to that "ever elusive Canaan"[37] many Southerners believed would greet them in Harlem. In storied Harlem, dashed hopes—for jobs, money, and freedom—were ignored in the mythmaking. Fisher, though, was one writer whose characters and Harlem imagery depicted the disappointment found in the real tensions between image and reality. Fisher characterized Harlem as a promised land and Mecca, but in stories that are tinged with sad ironies. "The Promised Land" ends with Mammy's mournful hymn: "Bow low!—How low mus' I bow to enter in de promis' land?"[38] Fisher situates Mammy between a state of high and low where, even from within Harlem, the black promised land can frustrate with its unrealized dreams.

The myth of Harlem knew many forms. In music as well as literature, Harlem's cultural image resounded worldwide. Duke Ellington's jazz composition "A Tone Parallel to Harlem (The Harlem Suite)"[39] is another example of the black experience presented through Harlem as a symbol. Even in music, there is a concern for making the spatial geography of Harlem a more highly visible space in the American cultural landscape. "A brisk tour of Harlem"[40] is what Ellington intended in this piece, according to the CD liner notes:

> Like a kind of film montage, scenes follow one another with bewildering rapidity, overlapping and dissolving as Ellington's musical images illustrate the different facets of the city within a city.[41]

Other songs about Harlem, such as Ellington's "Take the A-Train" and Louis Armstrong's "Drop Me Off in Harlem," lyrically celebrated the community. Riding the sharp staccato of a trumpet or under the spell of the piano, listeners were connected to the rhythms of life in the queen of the black belts.

As the Jazz Age of the 1920s progressed, the music scene in Harlem became a major attraction, even drawing whites from around the globe to a hotbed of black American innovation. As the site of a plethora of black art and entertainment, Harlem seemed to offer an invitation to join in the "authentic" black experience. As critics would argue, much of this experience was aimed at whites and constructed for white consumption.

Harlem's most famous nightclubs—the gangster-operated Cotton Club, the elegant Savoy Ballroom, and the trendy Apollo Theater—became required stopovers for top black performers such as Duke Ellington, Cab Calloway, Ethel Waters, Count Basie, and Ella Fitzgerald. Ironically, while the entertainers were black, the color line kept many of Harlem's own residents from patronizing many of these establishments. At some clubs, black performers and customers were required to use the back door.

Part of the draw for the well-dressed white "slummers" who flocked to Harlem for its nightlife was the powerful sense of its foreignness. Harlem was, for them, a "primitive" and "exotic" place—the whites-only Cotton Club bore a jungle decor—where whites could leave behind the stiff-collar world for a "moral vacation," as one commentator of the time noted.[42] These white "slummers," however, could slip in and out of the marginal space of Harlem, merely going there to enjoy the benefits of the clubs and the good times. In no way did they assume an "outsider" status that marked a permanent stigma. As such, not only was passage in and out of the community a luxury to be experienced, whites even had access to spaces off-limits to blacks. Thus, the privileges of whiteness guaranteed an unequal amount of unrestricted passage.

But when the Great Depression came, the golden era of Harlem came to an end. As if waking from a dream, observers suddenly came face-to-face with a darker reality of Harlem largely ignored during the renaissance, save for the writings of critics such as Claude McKay and Rudolph Fisher. "Negro Harlem, within the space of ten years, became the most 'incredible slum' in the entire city,"[43] wrote Gilbert Osofsky. Further years of poverty and suffering soon rendered Harlem one of the most depressed slums in the United States.

According to David Levering Lewis, "when social scientists during the Depression poked behind the Harlem facade, they found evidence of decay that had existed, unrecognized, for years. . . ."[44] By the mid-1930s, unemployment was running at about 50 percent in Harlem, and according to sociologist E. Franklin Frazier, nearly half of Harlem's fifty-six thousand black families were on home relief. Tenements were overcrowded, and many lacked sanitary facilities. Wages dropped for those who worked, and blacks found themselves paying 40 to 50 percent of their income on rent, compared with 20 to 25 percent for white families.

The blister burst open in 1935, when the rumor of the white beating of a black teen prompted mobs to burn and loot businesses in Harlem, causing damage in the hundreds of thousands of dollars. A mayoral commission concluded in its preliminary findings that "this sudden breach of the public order was the result of a highly emotional situation among the colored people of Harlem, due in large part to the nervous strain of years of unemployment and insecurity."[45]

Now another truth was out. Harlem—Nigger Heaven, Negro Mecca, Promised Land—was "just another festering black ghetto, which all the frustrations [of] poverty and or the lack of employment foster."[46]

Beyond the Renaissance: Nigger Heaven as Hell

Harlem stubbornly maintained its role as a symbol of race and the black American condition. Only now it was more clearly identified as a ghetto where poverty, crime, and drugs took their toll on the "manchild in the promised land." The artistic voice that trumpeted Harlem to the world also became more edgy, angrier, less accommodating, and more interested in autonomy.

In contrast to the more spirited toast Langston Hughes had offered up to Harlem, praising it as heaven, his "Puzzled" would lament:

> So we stand here
> On the edge of hell
> In Harlem
> And look out on the world
> And wonder
> What we're gonna do
> In the face of
> What we remember.[47]

The poverty and despair of Harlem came to symbolize the condition of blacks in all the Harlems throughout the United States. A defiant response to the mayoral report on the 1935 Harlem riot came from Alain Locke, who championed Harlem's continuing role as a race capital that stood for Negro self-determination. This renaissance ideal, he argued, would be a necessary ingredient of post-riot rebuilding.

Many writers still found promise in Harlem as a symbol. After all, the important black institutions—the churches, newspapers, social organizations—that took root in Harlem during more hopeful times still offered a heart for the community. In *Harlem: Negro Metropolis*, Claude McKay wrote that in spite of its "grimy misery" and its "slum features," Harlem

> does not exude the atmosphere of the slums. It remains the queen of the black belts, the Negro capital of the world. It has achieved a remarkable political

> maturity, a movement of the Negro people towards greater self-development and community autonomy. . . .[48]

Just as Harlem had been an important symbol for the artists of the Harlem Renaissance, its role as a metaphor continued. McKay is able to elevate the status of Harlem even in its low-down condition. In part, he assigns this regal status to the increasingly troubled community through a reworking of the inward- and outward-looking political ideology that was established during the renaissance. In his call for self-development and autonomy, McKay's response to the demise of Harlem would suggest that blacks in Harlem could not afford to continue their reliance on others.

It was 1940 when McKay was calling for a more inward-looking view. However, the segregated conditions that contributed to Harlem's growth and glory, as well as its misery, eased as the 1950s and 1960s ushered in a new age of race relations. As Harlem's existence was less and less determined by exclusion and the restrictions that confined blacks to shared spaces, the community was abandoned by many. As clubs and businesses opened their downtown doors to black musicians and patrons, Harlem lost its grip as a center of artistic activity.

Integration and a black exodus led to more recent images of Harlem not as a place full of promise, but as a hell. This image emerged not only in the artistic community but in the social sciences as well.

In a 1948 essay titled "Harlem Is Nowhere," Ralph Ellison drew on Harlem's despair to speak of the condition of poverty in black America. The essay begins with a descent into a basement psychiatric clinic. We are pulled down into Ellison's metaphoric space (made famous with *Invisible Man*). Here, Harlem is equated with madness:

> To live in Harlem is to dwell in the very bowels of the city; it is to pass a labyrinthine existence among streets that explode monotonously skyward with the spires and crosses of churches and clutter under foot with garbage and decay. Harlem is a ruin—many of its ordinary aspects (its crimes, its casual violence, its crumbling buildings with littered areaways, ill-smelling halls and vermin-invaded rooms) are indistinguishable from the distorted images that appear in dreams, and which, like muggers haunting a lonely hall, quiver in the waking mind with hidden and threatening significance.[49]

The Harlem Ellison describes recalls depictions of Harlem life by painters such as Jacob Lawrence and Romare Beardon during the Depression. Ellison's "exploding streets" and stretched spires and crosses color and leap from the page. The passage also evokes the sonorous notes of Ellington's "Harlem Airshaft" and "Harlem Speaks," which made a symbolic space from the fusion of art and geography.

But the Harlem Ellison describes is also a far cry from elevated renaissance and Jazz Age images. Depicting Harlem as a low and profane space, Ellison's imagery of defecation, disease, and danger is an inversion of Harlem as heaven. Symbols that once helped along the community's project of ritual reversal give way to an imagery more befitting hell.

"This is no dream," Ellison points out, lest we equate this Harlem with the Harlem of a surrealist artistic imagination,

> but the reality of well over four hundred thousand Americans; a reality which for many defines and colors the world. Overcrowded and exploited politically and economically, Harlem is the scene and symbol of the Negro's perpetual alienation in the land of his birth.[50]

Despite the title "Harlem Is Nowhere," Ellison uses a vivid imagery in the essay to construct a landscape that casts us into a place that is very real.

Now, to voice the anger of black America through Harlem—its most prominent symbol—required an alternative symbolic construction of the ghetto as hell. By the 1960s, Harlem is associated with representations that range from decay to violence to disease. These images are seen in constructions of insiders and outsiders alike.

"Harlem: A Community in Transition" was the topic of the summer 1963 issue of *Freedomways—A Quarterly Review of the Negro Freedom Movement.* The editors' note introducing the issue relies on a negative image of Harlem to project a broader concern. "Harlem is home for more than one-third of the Negroes of New York," they begin. But its significance is larger:

> Harlem is a condition of life for the overwhelming number of the two-thirds of America's twenty million Negroes who live in its cities. Harlem is a community of New York but Harlem is a euphemism for the most deprived areas in every city in the country which are assigned to Negroes in the United States. Negro citizens live in the Harlems of her cities not out of choice but from the absence of choice. Poverty more than the distinctiveness of color hold *[sic]* Negro Americans fast in the Harlems of America and set *[sic]* us apart from our fellow Americans.[51]

The editors then use Harlem metaphorically to voice a collective complaint of all blacks: "Harlem has grievances. Harlem is angry. Harlem is determined."[52]

This attitude is also apparent in the angry tone of the essay "Talking about Harlem." The essay, written for the Harlem issue of *Freedomways* by writer Sylvester Leaks, imposes on Harlem symbols of a damaged physical body:

> I'm talking now about Harlem: A six square mile festering black scar on the alabaster underbelly of the white man's indifference.
>
> HARLEM: A bastard child, born out of wedlock, baptized in the gut bucket of life, midwifed by oppression and fathered by racial hate, circumscribed by fear and guilt-ridden detractors.[53]

In this passage, Leaks reverses the imagery of rebirth that surrounded the Negro Renaissance as an era of hope. The lofty depiction by cultural midwife Alain Locke of the "New Negro's" glorious arrival into the world is supplanted by a harsher image.

While Negro Harlem once had a role to play in the development of a New Negro and his culture, it now came to represent the lingering frustrations of blacks in white society. The message carried through Harlem by artists, poets, and social scientists was that blacks were still oppressed a century removed from slavery. Harlem symbolized broken dreams, and much of its reputation was linked to rioting, poverty, crime, and hopelessness.

Claude Brown's autobiography, *Manchild in the Promised Land,* was hailed by white critics upon publication in 1965. It was praised not so much for its artistic merits but for the portrait of life in the ghetto—the Harlem ghetto—which directed attention to similar conditions of poverty in other ghettos. But then voguish social science explorations of the black condition in Harlem often threatened to blur what many held to be an important boundary between art and science.

Albert Murray, for one, leveled criticism at Brown's artistic use of Harlem as a universal symbol of the sociological condition of the ghetto. *Manchild in the Promised Land* was a work, according to Murray, that purported to be a personal memoir but was, in fact, closer to what he called the "social science fakelore of black pathology."[54] In a scathing essay titled "Image and Unlikeliness in Harlem," Murray criticized the "images of Harlem that could have been derived only from the current fad in psychopolitical gossip about Negro self-hatred."[55] It is imperative, Murray argued, that "those who would help Harlem achieve its aspirations . . . disentangle themselves" from the "folklore of condescension" he read into this approach.[56]

As a symbol, Harlem's boundaries extended to the scientific examination of the black community as well. Social science studies conducted during the 1960s also treated Harlem as representative of the black ghetto condition.

Discussions over precisely what were, for the black community, its problems and solutions, however, revealed divergent attitudes about how Harlem should be represented. Even those who employed a precise language that peddled the scientific pretense of objectivity did not escape criticism.

Kenneth Clark's *Dark Ghetto* and a study of Negro youth in the ghetto by Harlem Youth Opportunities Unlimited, Inc., or HARYOU, exemplified the use by social science of Harlem as a universal representation of the ghetto. Clark's study grew directly out of his work on the HARYOU-ACT project. Rejecting the detached stance of an objective social scientist, Clark, a long-time resident of Harlem, described his work as that of an "involved observer."

The HARYOU project was, according to Clark, "an experiment in community psychiatry."[57] Clark and a team of researchers sought to study the pathology of ghetto youth by focusing on larger societal problems that create ghettos such as Harlem. Clark likened Harlem to a laboratory for his community research. As such, Clark was working in a tradition established in the 1930s with James Weldon Johnson's *Black Manhattan.* "Harlem is more than a community," wrote Johnson, "it is a large scale laboratory experiment in the race problem and from it a good many facts have been found."[58] Continuing in this tradition, Clark wrote:

> All the youth associated with HARYOU formed a valuable natural laboratory for direct observation and study of the human forces at work in the larger community. They were a microcosm of the Harlem community, though in a technical sense not totally representative of the people of Harlem.[59]

Clark noted that Harlem was useful as a social science laboratory because the feelings and attitudes residents expressed about themselves were more accurate and therefore more reliable than statistics. But using the language of science, Clark points to accuracy and reliability, standards that are used to guarantee validity, to provide an authority for his Harlem subjects.

In *Dark Ghetto,* Clark uses voices of Harlem residents to serve as a poignant prologue, titled "Cry of the Ghetto." Not only do these ghetto residents speak for themselves in ways that statistics could not, but as residents of Harlem, they purport to reflect concerns arising from all the dark ghettos Clark seeks to explain.

Albert Murray was outspoken in his criticism of the Harlem found in Clark's HARYOU-ACT work. Calling Clark's "Youth in the Ghetto" monograph a "monument to social science nonsense and nonsensibility," Murray pointed out that its "unfounded and flimsy statistics" merely proved that as long as scholars offered up degrading images of blacks, shoddy methodology would be overlooked:

> [T]he HARYOU-Act Program was ostensibly initiated as a measure to accelerate the movement of Harlem youth into the mainstream of national activity. But what its built-in racism has actually stimulated is a . . . so-called community development program that bunches young Negroes even closer together in Harlem and provides even less contact with other areas of the city than they *normally* have. . . . most of the plans and programs for the rehabilitation of Harlem and Watts . . . begin with studies that find such places are "ghettos" which suffer, as a result of being somehow blocked away from the rest of New York and Los Angeles. Every failing of man and beast is attributed to the inhabitants of such places; *and then the programs promptly institute measures that could only have been designed to lock the inhabitants even further away from the center of things.*[60]

Murray's criticism of studies like *Dark Ghetto* does not stop simply at disagreement over degrading images. Murray also takes issue with the idea that by maintaining Harlem (or Watts) as a space apart from the real center of economic activity, the notion of community self-sufficiency reinforces the very marginality reform programs are meant to eradicate.

Murray's critique points to a problem with the logic that associates the promise of a collective consciousness with separate racial "centers" for blacks and whites. But as we have seen throughout this chapter, black intellectuals in Harlem played a defining role in a reconstruction of marginality, identity, and space that upheld precisely such a logic. Harlem's history reveals that from a black perspective, the marginal space of the balcony could provide a shared point of observation and a collective space of resistance. By inverting the values of a racist logic, pride, and not shame, was to be found through an attachment to such spaces.

Alternately though, Harlem's marginality embodied for many black writers a dark despair that defined the space of "the other" in negative terms. By extension then, racial minorities, when they were seen as being limited or restricted by such spaces, needed to cast off the identities that marginal arenas reinforced. In fighting for a place at the core of American life, the struggle for many blacks was marked by increasing demands to move from the margins to the center. With a "vocabulary of spatial organization" that privileged a front and center away from racially defined exclusionary territories, this integrationist strategy called for the dissolution of marginal spaces and by extension marginality. Let us into the theater and out of the balcony, went the call. We demand seats at the front, not the back, of the bus.

Seen this way, escape from the ghetto was viewed as progress. By embracing mainstream spatial values of front and back with their respective positive and negative meaning, advocates of integration moved away from the idea that a group could create in its own spaces an inversion of values or meanings.

In an essay titled "Harlem, ou le cancer de l'Amerique," Chester Himes declared Harlem to be "like a cancer on the body of a nation," and concluded that "the most important thing to many Harlem Negroes is how to escape from it."[61] In associating Harlem with a diseased body, Himes's essay was yet another move away from the rituals of symbolic inversion that defined the Harlem Renaissance project that gave Harlem a central and sacred position.

Escape and Return: But Whose Harlem Is It?

Years of flight from Harlem by the black middle class was offered as an explanation for the despair and declining social conditions in the community. And as slum conditions worsened and political frustrations grew, Harlems throughout the nation burned. Newark, Watts, and Detroit were ablaze with racial anger.

But as rioting broke out across the country, many in black America, rejecting integrationist strategies, increasingly moved toward a nationalist identity in which culture and place continued to play a central role. The rise of the Black Power movement was accompanied by the development of a Black Arts movement—a nationalist cultural movement. Harlem was a wellspring as the Negro continued his search for identity.

Underscoring Harlem's role in this shift toward a nationalist stance, Leroy Jones, a significant player in the nationalist Black Arts movement, traveled between Greenwich Village, home of the Beat scene, and Harlem. Jones's rebirth as Amiri Baraka paralleled his downtown-to-uptown transition. His rite of passage plays on Harlem's function as a space in which a crossing between a bohemian and nationalist identity can happen.

Theodore Hudson's literary biography of Jones points out that Jones ostensibly went to Harlem to run the Black Arts Repertory Theater/School (BART/S). He founded BART/S to "reeducate the nearly half a million Harlem Negroes to find new pride in their color."[62] According to a BART/S handbill, the theater was "dedicated to the education and cultural awakening of the black people in America." An Associated Press news report of November 30, 1966, noted:

> each night in a makeshift Harlem theater a group of young Negroes give vent to their hatred of white people. They act out their dreams of a day when the Negro will stand apart from the white world, and Harlem will be an independent nation.

BART/S brought Baraka to Harlem as the center of his contribution to a burgeoning cultural nationalism. In an interview with the scholar Werner Sollors, Baraka discussed the relationship between community identity and New York versus Harlem:

> I remember when we were in New York they used to say when you talk about Black people you had to talk about Harlem. That people who didn't live in Harlem didn't know anything about Black people. Fantastic. That was where black folks were. Fantastic! In the world! If you didn't have much to do with Harlem, you really didn't have much to do with Black people.[63]

Jones's earlier association with the Beats and their bohemian lifestyle had placed him squarely in the Village. His remarks to Sollors closely link his black nationalism with the "black masses" in Harlem.

This link is ironic in light of Baraka's earlier antagonistic feelings toward Harlem, which he felt was the "veritable capital city of the Black Bourgeoisie."[64] "The Negro Bohemian's flight from Harlem," Jones wrote, "is not a flight from the world of color but the flight of any would-be Bohemian from . . . the provinciality, philistinism and moral hypocrisy of American life."[65]

Writing in *Blues People,* Jones had made clear his disdain for the elitism associated with Du Bois and his "talented tenth":

> There is still for all the race pride and race consciousness that these spokesmen for the renaissance claimed, the smell of the dry rot of the middle class Negro mind.[66]

As an elite group who had little knowledge of or appeal to the masses of poorer Negroes in the community, Jones wrote, the talented tenth only succeeded in a "strained appreciation for things black."[67]

Later Jones reversed his position on Harlem in order to make a cultural association with the black masses. Jones's uptown move and the establishment of the theater/school greatly influenced theater and art in the black nationalist phase of 1960s culture. "In a very real sense," wrote Jones in a 1962 essay, "Harlem is the capital of black America."[68] "Looking back at BART/S," wrote Hudson, "Jones claimed, 'We went uptown to Harlem and opened a theatre, and blew a billion words into the firmament like black prayers to force change.'"[69]

Even today, Harlem plays the role of a black capital. Controversies over race and representation continue to draw on the power of Harlem's racial symbolism. Popular culture—television, film, and print media—makes use of Harlem's name and its boundaries to signal blackness and its distinctive, oppositional role in relation to whiteness. These images are not neutral, however. Whether Harlem is constructed by insiders or outsiders, its meaning shapes and is shaped by multiple versions of reality for creators and consumers of its imagery.

As late as the mid-1990s, Sydney Lumet's film *Night Falls in Manhattan* showed how often, even as a throwaway reference point, Harlem's image is reflected through white eyes as simply no good. Lumet's film, which is really about a hero's internal struggle over his own place in a crooked criminal-justice system, is set in motion by the murderous rampage of an unrepentant black crack dealer. While the rest of the film is centered downtown, the crack dealer in this introductory sequence is from Harlem.

In contrast, Eddie Murphy's 1989 film *Harlem Nights* presents a strikingly different film construction of Harlem as a symbolic space. Harlem is shown as a place in which commonly held racial meanings are inverted. The film undermines stereotypic associations of white as basically good, and black as evil. In this film blacks are the good guys. The whites in this story, even though they are cops, are cast as bad because they are crooked blackmailers.

In Murphy's Harlem, blacks are triumphant. At the end of the film, having outwitted the crooked cops, the gang of Harlem (K)nights flees the city with a sack full of money. As they stand in New Jersey and look across at the lights of Manhattan, one of the group, played by Richard Pryor, notes that they must move on. His son, played by Murphy, reasons that surely they will find someplace else to go. But the Pryor character, offering a father's wisdom, reminds him "there's no place like Harlem."[70]

But it is not just black versus white insiders and outsiders who have differing interpretations of black racial identity and engage in conflicts over Harlem's meaning. Michael Smith uses an exchange between Spike Lee and Amiri Baraka, discussing the film rights to interpret the life of Malcolm X, as an illustration of the problems with giving voice to "authentic" marginal sensibilities. Part of this problem, argues Smith, lies in a conflation of race, class, and culture, that is, a general failure to recognize the diversity of the experience of being black.[71]

Lee's and Baraka's struggle took place literally and symbolically in and out of Harlem. Baraka's attack on Lee as a "middle-class Negro" happened during a political rally in Harlem. Lee's response, in a *Newsweek* column, in turn challenged Baraka's relationship to Harlem itself:

> In fact when Malcolm was alive, Amiri Baraka was down in Greenwich Village running around with Allen Ginsberg and living that "Jungle Fever" beatnik-bohemian life style. . . .

Lee does not merely challenge Baraka's past relationship with Harlem. Lee also charges that Baraka has no current credibility as a spokesperson for the race:

> After the rally to protest the film, Baraka, the Black Marxist Revolutionary, jumped into a black limo and sped off down Lenox Avenue, past the lumpen proletariat of Harlem.[72]

It is noteworthy that both Lee and Baraka waged their struggle over the film rights to Malcolm X—an image and an icon in his own right—by invoking Harlem as place and idea. In the way that Harlem has long stood in for black America, the way it is viewed becomes a metaphor for a broader segment of society. Yet, as we have seen, it is problematic to accept any single version of what Harlem stands for and to whom it belongs. In efforts to counteract negative stereotypes of Harlem (or race for that matter), image makers, race men, and renaissance leaders often went too far in the other direction. This has resulted in censorship, distortion, and a limited range of meanings for symbolic and real Harlem.

A vision of Harlem as hopeless is likely to be prone to remedies that disregard parts that are "healthy" in favor of a wholesale overhaul, such as in the form of slum-clearance policies. Understandable efforts to combat a negative public image, on the other hand, tend to overcompensate in the form of selective memories that fail to note that the glories of the renaissance were accompanied by poverty, slum conditions, and a limited black elite participation in that movement.

As we will see, the weight of nostalgia over the years has played a role in influencing, some would say inhibiting, the pace of Harlem's contemporary redevelopment. The past is also used to determine who is welcome and who is not, preventing a critical look at the specific motives and behaviors of those who would move into the community during the 1980s and 1990s.

LEAVE

chapter 2

Insiders and Outsiders

Property of the City of New York: NO TRESPASSING

—sign on boarded-up brownstone

LEAVE

—graffito on Harlem brownstone

A tall white tower dominates the corner of 125th Street between Seventh Avenue and Lenox Avenue. This structure, the New York State Office Building, is named for one of Harlem's heroes—Adam Clayton Powell Jr., New York's first black congressman. Like many buildings here, its name is a connection to the black history still alive in Harlem.

The Adam Clayton Powell Building is testimony to the fact that, in this part of town at least, blacks have a symbolic claim to a collective past. But this black hero's name was not added until six years after the structure came to dominate the corner in the heart of Harlem. Some would later claim that the name was offered in appeasement for a battle the community had lost.

In 1969, Governor Nelson Rockefeller moved to build at 125th Street and Seventh Avenue—an action seen by many Harlemites as the first step in a "white reclaiming," and one demanding defensive action.[1] The construction site became freighted with importance as the building controversy became a broader battle for community control.

A flyer distributed at the protest site gave voice to what some depicted as a life-and-death struggle:

> There is no reason in the world
> for us to believe that that building
> is in the interest of the people of Harlem.
> That building is like a dagger
> pointed at the heart of the community.[2]

In the language of the protesters, the construction of the State Office Building, or SOB, was portrayed as an act of physical violence against Harlem by the state government. Invoking the body as a symbol of the community, its heart threatened, protesters provided justification for battling against this interloper.

Speaking a language loaded with war imagery, protesters occupied the building's proposed location and dubbed it Reclamation Site #1 on June 30, 1969. Some four hundred Harlemites, "many of them armed with machetes," declared the land at 125th Street, between Seventh and Lenox Avenues, the "first piece of land reclaimed by black people for the use of black people."[3]

This attitude represented one current of thought in the community, namely, that urban revitalization in Harlem posed a choice: "whether to build *in* Harlem or *for* Harlem." In essence, the controversy surrounding the SOB became a "burgeoning symbol of community control."[4] By laying claim to Harlem in defense of its cultural past and its role as a cultural Mecca, those who opposed this project and the destruction of other property on the site took on the government, protecting territory as warriors in a battle.

In this same period, Harlem waged fights with the city over neighborhood destruction on a number of fronts. These conflicts over the fate of city-owned properties would presage community struggles over gentrification. Here, as in cities elsewhere, urban renewal programs were viewed derisively as tantamount to "Negro removal." Slum clearance policies that brought bulldozers to Harlem seemed to provide solid evidence of this.

In my conversations with residents about contemporary gentrification, the controversy surrounding the SOB was often one of the first topics mentioned. The battle stood out in many minds as a watershed moment. The struggle at the SOB construction site foreshadowed the community's showdown with the city over subsequent redevelopment plans. It also put firmly in place a rhetoric of community control. In the aftermath of the SOB struggle, a logic pitting insiders against outsiders would reemerge as a framework for depicting the community's struggles over preservation and housing redevelopment.

Today, history and collective memory are thick in the air around the large plaza where the SOB was ultimately built, despite noisy community opposition. A hot dog vendor is busy under a street sign designating the space as African Square. Beyond the plaza, 125th Street stretches east and west as Martin Luther King Boulevard. Flanking the plaza, Seventh and Lenox Avenues have been rechristened Malcolm X and Adam Clayton Powell Boulevards. For the moment, this is still the heart of a black Harlem.

City buses wheeze and grumble past. Cabbies squeal brakes. Cars and horns and engines create an urban symphony. At this busy crossroads, the past, present, and future tenses of Harlem rub shoulders.

When the workday is done, the bustle of subway and bus commuters takes over. Toting briefcases, umbrellas, and folded newspapers, commuters heading home zigzag across the plaza. A fast-moving passerby sets pecking pigeons in motion; as if blown by wind, the birds rise, rearrange themselves, and drop back to their work on the ground. A brown child, happy to be reunited with Daddy, home from work, swings on the end of a cuff-linked sleeve.

Across 125th Street sits the famed Hotel Theresa. Residents proudly remember this as the spot where Fidel Castro stayed when he came to New York City in 1960. Decades later, black pride fills this space again, loud with its cheers and applause for Nelson Mandela. Old-timers will tell you that further back, Adam Clayton Powell led the boycott to open up jobs on 125th Street—"DON'T SHOP WHERE YOU CAN'T WORK." Race riots in 1935 and 1943 had secured the unsavory reputation 125th Street would carry for decades.

Around back, in the shadow of the SOB, lies a stretch of cleared empty lots. Several red-eyed partyers look into my camera lens. Behind a chain-link fence they have set up an outdoor party. The top of a wooden cable spool is a makeshift table. Its surface is covered with a clutter of plastic cups, a forty-ounce beer, a bottle of generic vodka, a few empty beer bottles. The three are sitting on an old kitchen chair, an armchair that has lost its legs, and a car seat. The men appear to be in their early thirties; the woman looks fortyish. Their smiles are endless as they enjoy themselves on this sunny afternoon.

Arnold Roberts, a self-described community activist, steps from behind the chain-link fence. He offers an outstretched hand and volunteers that he is collecting signatures on a petition. He waves a clipboard of fluttering pages lined with names, addresses, and signatures. Roberts is angry. He grouses about a housing complex that a Harlem church is slated to open this spring: "Why you gonna build condos in a community full of housing projects?" he asks.

Roberts eyes me suspiciously but keeps on with his speech while I focus my camera on a mural:

SUPPORT COMMUNITY STRUGGLES

BETTER HOUSING EDUCATION UNITY EQUALITY

The mural looms large, creating a three-dimensional effect. The small crowd of protesters it depicts seems to march straight out of the wall. A caramel-skinned woman, her fist raised in the air, leads the bunch. A dark, smiling child in a blue dress is at her side, followed by a toffee-colored priest, an alabaster man with hammer and hard hat, and a mahogany woman whose orange head wrap picks up the flower-print pattern on her blue dress. In the rear, another brown arm holds a torch aloft. The determined-looking group is the mural's foreground. On both sides, the marchers are flanked by a painted streetscape that includes a church, a brownstone, a high-rise apartment building—and a bulldozer.

In the 1960s, the bulldozers arrived in the middle of the night. Many of Harlem's abandoned buildings, including brownstones that represented the community's architectural treasures, fell to the wrecking ball. Some residents saw the city's urban renewal programs as a deliberate attempt to destroy not just buildings but the vitality of the community as well. From its renaissance legacy, Harlem already had given a "once upon a time moment" to black America. As we shall see, from the 1960s through the 1990s, urban renewal and subsequent gentrification would push middle-class Harlemites back onto the stage of black history-making. Because of their elite status, this group has exercised power privileges that reveal the disparate ways that race can be used to shape a black community's future by wielding emblems of the past.

"SUPPORT COMMUNITY STRUGGLES" the mural's marchers remind. "SUPPORT COMMUNITY STRUGGLES," the community responds. Past struggles have imparted the value of local control, social activism, and self-empowerment. "Support for community struggles" is part of a familiar liberal rhetoric, closely knit to the 1960s notion of racial justice and fair play.

But how does one support a community's struggles? In the aftermath of the SOB struggle, support for Harlem would come in a variety of forms and would give rise to a range of conflicting positions from inside the community. Beyond questions about what constitutes support, though, a trickier set of questions arises: What is the community? Who makes up this community? Who speaks for its needs?

Despite a story line that depicted the poor as the sole victims of urban renewal, the SOB proposal drew wide opposition from middle-class residents, who worried about displacement of a different sort. Their concerns were history and the availability of housing for the middle class. This middle-class component of resistance to urban renewal would produce redevelopment-agency policies that placed a premium on the preservation of history and on class diversity among blacks in Harlem.[5]

This policy provided an official means of inducement for middle-class blacks who would arrive in the 1980s and 1990s as gentrifiers. There was also a strong informal aspect of "recruitment." Longer-term residents would tell friends and relatives—some of whom may have lived in Harlem years earlier—about available properties there, turning their network of kin and acquaintances into a source of newcomers to the community. This is one feature that makes Harlem's black gentrification unique and is important for explaining the arrival of newcomers, and their motives.

Scholar Robert Beauregard points to a layer of meaning articulated by gentrification's "boosters: redevelopment bodies, local newspapers, 'city' magazines, mayors' offices, real-estate organizations, financial institutions, historic preservationists and neighborhood organizations comprised of middle class homeowners."[6] Community "boosters," as Beauregard defines them, have "an interest in increased economic activity within the city and an affinity for the middle class who function as gentrifiers."[7] Thus, we supposedly get from these boosters a perspective that gives rise to a language of gentrification that is often uncritical of the process since "they convey an ideology meant to foster continued gentrification."[8]

Beauregard introduces this idea to caution against this group's limited, and self-interested, presentation of gentrification. Here in Harlem, though, we see a twist. Gentrification studies often identify power with whites and thus cannot completely account for groups such as these middle-class power brokers in Harlem. While they fit Beauregard's definition of community boosters, this group should not be dismissed too quickly or characterized one-dimensionally merely for pushing predictable class interests.

What sets them apart in their position and in this context is also tied to blackness. They defy a conventional picture of a white booster class imposing its will on (poor) minority communities. In this chapter, we will see that there was not absolute consensus among them over basic considerations of what type of development should occur in Harlem. Shaped by race, their comments and actions—such as opposing free-market sales of brownstones—would seem illogical if viewed purely through a prism of economic self-interest. In Harlem, the intersection of race and class contributes to the creation of a wholly new variety of community booster.

The actions of Harlem's black insiders during urban restructuring also challenge an overly simple understanding of "community struggle" that was bandied about during urban renewal. Through interviews, this chapter considers urban renewal, community preservation, and the onset of gentrification from the point(s) of view of long-time, middle-class Harlemites, real-estate brokers, planners, development agency officials, and community activists.

A number of "insider" opinions arose and coalesced around the dichotomies of insider and outsider, black and white, and heaven and hell, discussed in the previous chapter. During the 1960s and 1970s, black middle-class Harlemites employed Harlem's established symbols anew. We will see that for these black middle-class participants in the battle to slow and define urban renewal, a collective community struggle was expressed in very middle-class considerations, such as preserving architectural features and historical properties, but with race in mind, too.

Support Community Struggles: Insider/Outsider

Allison Carson, who was born and raised in Harlem, was active during the 1960s struggle to preserve brownstones and designate landmark areas within the community. We talk as she guides me up and down the sidewalks of her neighborhood, rows of brownstones mirroring each other on either side. These are her streets. And they are the historic setting of another dramatic slice of a community struggle that lingers as part of the memory of Harlem's recent past.

Carson's words rush out, a combination of urgency and excitement, as she recalls the late nights when she joined other neighbors united against the city:

> In the late sixties the city was trying to raze all of Harlem. They would come up in the middle of the night with bulldozers, no permits, and demolish buildings. In the beginning, we just stood in front of the bulldozers at four o'clock in the morning. We had this group that would get on the phone: "They're on 118th Street!" Then, like the fire department, we would get on our clothes and run out and stop these demolitions.

As in the struggle against the construction of the SOB, the resistance to the brownstone demolitions was played out in oppositional terms of territorial control. The city, in Carson's recollection, showed complete disregard for the community's commitment to the place, despite its sagging appearance and deterioration.

"We had a huge percentage of people who were here by choice. They had been here a long time," recalled Carson. "They wanted to stay," she continued, explaining the residents' sentiment about Harlem:

> They believed in the community, and they did not think of it as completely negative. They liked living in the community. They liked the fact that it had an international profile as being a black community. You would hear people say, "This is our Israel."

Central to resistance against urban renewal was an implicit fear that whites would take over eventually. Harlem residents used that concern to pressure the city. This resulted in a cautious tone on the part of the city, evident in public documents on Harlem revitalization. This community pressure would also be instrumental in how the city would disburse residential properties it owned in Harlem.

A pressing question for the city was how to get much of the abandoned and empty real estate in Harlem back on the tax rolls at a time of declining public moneys for community redevelopment. But within the community, the specific details for filling Harlem's empty brownstones raised thorny questions of community control. Residents wondered about the city's intentions for their territory and questioned exactly to whom Harlem would become home. One official told the *New York Times:* "We have very deliberately tried to make it clear that what is going to be done with city-owned property in Harlem will be a joint decision of the city and the community. That has meant we've had to go slowly."[9]

The city took the position that, ideally, relatively well-off blacks would play a major role in the redevelopment of Harlem. "No one is going to stop whites from moving in," a New York City official was quoted as saying in *The Economist,* "but our goal is not to bring them in."[10] Throughout the 1970s and 1980s, city and other public officials would continue to sound a note of caution in a media discourse built around redevelopment in Harlem. Not all (middle-class) residents were opposed to a white component. In a neighborhood association newsletter, the president of Harlem's Consolidated Block Associations said, "We don't care if they are black, white, or from outer space, just as long as they renovate and pay their taxes."[11]

During the 1980s, two open-market auctions were held in Harlem. In 1982, 12 of 300 brownstones were auctioned. A formula was devised whereby 65 percent of the properties available in the auction would go to Harlem and Manhattan Valley residents. Mayor Ed Koch was opposed to a system that gave Harlem residents an advantage over nonresidents. While Koch ultimately went along with the plan, he labeled it discriminatory and said it would be scrapped after the brownstones were sold. Five of the homes went to Harlemites. In 1985, 149 vacant buildings were offered as part of a second auction of city-owned brownstones.

These community skirmishes show how and when determinations of the future of Harlem's real estate shifted into a cultural, as well as material, realm. Out of land-use and building confrontations between Harlem and the city came a position that argued for "community" empowerment, meaning that Harlem's fate was not left entirely to the free market. And the position that redevelopment, to some extent, should be controlled from the inside was partially successful. Some Harlemites praised the city for the caution it exercised in the redevelopment effort.

But others wanted less intervention in Harlem's real-estate market. Community pressure to maintain control over empty brownstones, charged these critics, led paradoxically to further deterioration by slowing redevelopment. The furor caused by fear of an onslaught of whites in part created this problem, said Spencer Thomas, reflecting back:

> Community Board 10 and Community Board 9 decided that they weren't going to allow them to do anything until they could control who could buy and make sure that people who were living in Harlem had opportunities to get the buildings. The problem with that is, it took them so long to do that that the very structures they were trying to save became destroyed in the process. Just normal destruction—time and weather. But some of it was deliberate—drug problems, folks taking the copper and fireplaces out of the buildings. They'd lift things like that. And we're trying to solve some of those problems now. We and a lot of folks created some of that situation ourselves.

To many, the dilemma over dispensing with remaining buildings is reduced to a community view that there is a desperate need for capital, in the form of an increased tax base and reinvestment. Allison Carson agrees that the issue was sensitive. But, she declares: "I think the brownstones ought to go out on the open market."

> I think that the notion the community should control it from the inside is certainly one I can understand and subscribe to. But I think that the one thing Harlem does not have that it would need is an infusion of capital. It's cut off from the capitalist system. It's not participating in the economy, and so my sense is what would we lose if every city-owned property went to the public sector? To my way of thinking the very worst thing that could happen is that

> buildings that are now vacant would be improved. You want a population to come in here that's gonna support services, so that you can start to rebuild the economy. There's no economic base in this community.

As one who had taken positions and even actions that run counter to city plans, Carson admittedly is sympathetic to the view that Harlemites want to control the redevelopment process from the inside. But her acknowledgement that an infusion of capital was necessary for community redevelopment also points to the fact that in their struggles for internal control, community activists, by staking a possessive claim for the community, had cut themselves off from a needed tool of development.

The idea that Harlem's empty brownstones should be placed on the open market is shared by some realtors and developers. Nicole Johnson is a third-generation Harlemite who works with Beebee Family Realty, a family-run business on 128th Street. Johnson is a tiny woman. A neat pile of curls tops her head. Her suit is old, threadbare but sensible. She shares her opinions about what should be done in Harlem. On this topic she talks fast and with force. It is as if she has decided she knows the right position—she is just humoring anyone who takes a contrary stance.

We shrink our shoulders, lower our heads, and step down into the office space where I will talk to her. Mounds and piles from the family business stuff the room. Against the far wall, three file cabinets support a stack of legal pads, file folders, and empty boxes. The office is dingy. Its carpet is worn and stained, and the room has a musty odor. A tower of phone books sits beside the desk.

Johnson settles comfortably behind her desk, with both the phone and her bulging Rolodex within arm's reach. She draws a haul off her cigarette and exhales. She waves a hand through the smoky air signaling something to someone, her shoulder clutches the phone to her right ear, she leans forward across the desk, urging me to write down that man's phone number, and she is ordering a cab.

Johnson is frustrated by the lack of activity in the community's housing market. Pushing for intervention that will realign a "stable" marketplace, she argues that "because the city owns about half the townhouses in Harlem, the market here isn't functioning like a normal marketplace. You can't have a genuine supply-and-demand dynamic if a large portion of the supply has been removed."

Guided by dollars and cents, Johnson also speaks of the need to increase the middle-class residential population in Harlem:

> I personally think in terms of the community being able to survive, there has to be people coming in, particularly people with some means. That should be people who have money in the bank—blacks or whites. As it is, the community is not going to survive. I mean, just to have a community of poor people who have nothing, there's no mechanism for growth.

Leaving her office, we move out into a humid summer night. We are headed to a meeting of the Harlem Homeowners and Taxpayers Association, where Johnson wants me to see firsthand just how heated and emotional discussions about Harlem brownstones can be.

Support Community Struggles: Harlem as Heaven/Harlem as Hell

The vigilance of Harlemites who through the years have challenged the city's motives and actions, pressured elected officials, and often criticized the Harlem Urban Development Corporation, founded in 1971 as an internal redevelopment agency, for going too fast or too slow, is an indication that residents are aware of Harlem's unique cultural importance. Talk of change prompts a defense of the past.

The symbolism attached to the cultural capital of black America is still alive, they argue, in the community's remaining institutions. Preservation of these traditions and institutions is cited as a top priority of many residents.

But one hears in the reflections of older Harlemites accounts of a place that, in many ways, no longer exists:

> Harlem was a beautiful place, a clean place. And it was a proud place. There was not a city in the world could touch it. Seventh Avenue, there wasn't a house out of place. On Saturdays and Sundays in the afternoon, you see the people just walkin' the streets. How well dressed they were, just to parade around and walk down the street. Plenty of night clubs and entertainment and restaurants and things of that nature. There wasn't no fighting, no stealing, nobody snatching pocketbooks. If somebody snatched a pocketbook, it would be on the front page. That was big news. I talk to some older people and I say, you know, it's a shame that our children cannot really see what Harlem used to be. If they ever saw it, they'd love it to death.

> My favorite beautician was Frenchie. Frenchie was an institution. Frenchie was a character. And you had as much fun going to the salon as you did what he used to do to your hair. He was a lot of fun. But we came down one day and the sign was there, you know. The whole building is now empty.

> In Frank's—the old Frank's now, to those of us who were here from Year One—you kind of resent the fact that it's now a fried-fish joint run by Asians. And it just does something to my gut when I see what used to be, I mean the most elegant restaurant up here.
>
> And the Red Rooster closed. Now that really upsets me. And Johnson's was next to it. They're both gone. When you came to New York, everybody who was anybody spent some time in the Rooster because that's where you saw everybody who was anybody, from Adam Clayton Powell right straight down. Oh, it was great. They had something in the back that they called the family table, and you weren't in if you didn't sit at the family table. Well that's where my seat was. At that time I was editing a magazine out of Washington, and I'd go to the Rooster once or twice a week. And you'd just sit there and the information just came. I could write the whole magazine, you know, just being in there. Because everybody who came to Harlem came to the Red Rooster at some point. And of course, Adam would be in just every other night. And he was an institution all by himself. They're both gone. I don't think anything hurt, though, as bad as Small's. Small's was the last to go, and that just about did it. So you miss that kind of thing. It's a flavor of Harlem that disappeared.

There is wistfulness in these comments. By evoking images of life on the avenues and in institutions like Small's, the Red Rooster, and Johnson's, this woman depicts a portrait of social life in old Harlem. But these places were a part of a business and economic community tied to the needs of a segregated black community. Aside from conjuring the names of these businesses, the speaker also evokes a time when communal ties sprang from the shared spaces of segregated Harlem, creating networks of information and support.

Still, the speaker also suggests the important function this collective past might play for a younger generation. Seen this way, Harlem's past is held up as an inheritance for later generations. And beyond merely designating institutional sites as inert markers of the past, older Harlemites struggle to present the symbols of the historical black community as useful and relevant for today's world. The promise, hope, anger, defiance, marginalization, and collective unity that Harlem has come to symbolize should, residents argue, play a role today:

> There is a resource in Harlem in history as well as a culture that's passed on. I think there's a community here that needs to be preserved and protected. People want to stay here. They want to continue to build on it. People want to be able to build something and make it last. People want to have institutions

survive and pass on values and history and tradition. This is what human culture is all about. And I think there is something to be said for that. It's very important.

There has to be a celebration of culture. The strength of any people comes from within and the celebration of ourselves and our culture. And that's what Harlem really is, you know, keeping that strength, generating that spirit so that eventually there is a stronger sense of self. Because the whole thing is about self-esteem. We know that. It's about how I feel about myself. I think it works because otherwise we would have self-destructed a long time ago.

A lot of people have been worried about Harlem coming back. It is coming back in the sense that we have many solid institutions here. We have Harlem Hospital. We have Studio Museum. We have the Dance Theater of Harlem. We have the Harlem School for the Arts. We have a lot of things going for us. And I have felt for the last five, ten years, there has been an upsurge, a sense of renewal and a sense of more consciousness in our people of black culture, and an appreciation of ourselves, confidence in ourselves.

These three Harlemites see in Harlem a resource for blacks that stems from shared culture. A movement for community preservation, alongside the housing and real-estate battles, is necessary, they each argue, to counter destructive forces, inside and outside. One strategy for continuity with the past is to designate landmarks and erect monuments:

There are a lot of places that should be made landmarks, like the Schomburg and Wells. Wells is just a bar, but it was very famous. Everybody went there for chicken and waffles at the early hours of the morning. We haven't done that job as well as we could. There are a lot of structures and buildings that should be preserved.

Barbara Ellis, a Harlemite since the mid-1960s, feels that it is especially important to foster an awareness of the African American past among a younger generation of blacks. For instance, Ellis supported renaming Harlem's streets:

I wanted them to rename the streets, like Frederick Douglass Boulevard and Adam Clayton Powell Jr. Because even now you stop and ask them [the younger generation], well, who was he? And the child is going to ask, well, what did he do? And someone will tell them that he's the one that opened up all the stores here that blacks weren't able to work in, and the subway and things like that. So then they will say, "I wasn't here for Martin Luther King

> and I was too young for Malcolm X but I'm here." It's our history—Harlem. They've got to stop and think.

Equating "our" history with that of Harlem, Ellis links symbolic historical markers to the intergenerational transmission of culture.

This is not a shared view, though. To some, it even seems foolish to focus on such things as history and symbolic markers when more pressing material needs confront the community. Paula Kimball suggests that neighborhood deterioration is an obstacle to such cultural transmission. Asked about pride in the neighborhood, she commented:

> I don't really see it. I mean, kids, when they walk around and see boarded-up buildings and buildings that are crumbling, and stores that are boarded up, and all the people who have stores don't look like you or speak your language, you don't get a sense that this is the area. Yeah, you know, you can wear a Malcolm X hat. But the idea that my area is special . . . you've got this charming neighborhood with all this historic housing. There were great things that happened here. [But] they can't put that together. Everything around them is dirty and disgusting. You can't translate that into a positive thing.

The idea that the history of Harlem is central in black culture does not necessarily result in shared images of a remembered past. Often the memories and images Harlemites hold, drawn on simple representations of Harlem's past, are based on a nostalgic, even mythical view of the place. So, for instance, historic memories contribute to the use of the "renaissance" as a metaphor characterizing hoped-for change. Critics of this language, however, argue for more unvarnished depictions of the past, stripped of the romanticism:

> I guess I look at it a little differently. Harlem has a lot of nostalgia. But that doesn't pay the bills, you know. Right now, all the things which Harlem has been famous for are not surviving.

Gus Sloan and Arnold Roberts also criticized nostalgic thinking as naive and neglectful of the limitations that race and class placed on blacks in Harlem's storied past:

> I disagree strongly with the feeling that there should be a renaissance. A renaissance is a stupid word because at the time I grew up in the late thirties, the renaissance, or cultural revolution, the creative forces were alien to the man on the street. And I thought myself a bright little boy, but I didn't identify with anything other than the music. I lived in a brownstone next door to Cab Calloway, and I used to see Ella Fitzgerald going back and forth to band

> practice. But the clubs on Seventh Avenue were frequented by whites who came from downtown in big cars. And we used to go and stand outside of Small's Paradise or the Cotton Club. The Savoy Ballroom was our local dance spot, you know. And anybody could go in there, but at Small's and a couple of other clubs, like the Cotton Club, blacks were only waiters and waitresses in there. So that period went by me completely.
>
> There was an almost Dickensian poverty in the side streets. You know at that time blacks were working as chauffeurs, doormen, elevator operators, the women were working as maids—all those low, non-skilled jobs. Now [that] we've come a long way, I think what we should have is a revitalization of Harlem. The hell with renaissance, rebirth. You cannot reborn anything. That word is redundant.

Other disagreements arise over creating symbolic imprints, such as with renaming streets and parks. "I will never call Lenox Avenue 'Malcolm X Boulevard.' And I will always call Seventh Avenue 'Seventh Avenue.' I don't call it 'Adam Clayton Powell Boulevard,'" Joan Sanders asserted defiantly. "I don't see the relevance in it."

> If the person, you know, lived and worked and died on the street, that may be a little more relevant. Right now there's a big thing about whether Dinkins will allow the Audubon Ballroom to be made a landmark, where Malcolm X was shot. And they want to tear it down. And people have gone to him and said, "Save this." To me, if there was some historical significance within the building, or they were making a museum out of it or something, then I'd say yes. Otherwise, what's the point?

Allison Carson, who supports landmark and preservation efforts, offers a possible explanation for the often divided thinking about these markers of the past:

> I think the real issue about the culture and how people feel about the culture is a very important one. But I'll give you an interesting example of some of the concepts. Are you familiar with Mount Morris Park? Mount Morris Park is now Marcus Garvey Park. Well there are a lot of very, very chauvinistic, proud black people who will still call it Mount Morris Park because that's part of history too. I mean there is this feeling that Harlem was part of the [American] Revolution and people are very interested in that.

Seventh Avenue, Lenox Avenue, and Mount Morris Park conjure images of Harlem's historic past that are no less important to some than Malcolm X,

Adam Clayton Powell, and Marcus Garvey are to others. But by selectively framing the history of Harlem within its racial past, the linkage between Harlem and blackness contributes to a racialized construction of the past that, in turn, is used to shape the future.

Arnold Roberts, a community activist, worries that the link between the past and the future was selectively used to justify redevelopment. Roberts's remarks suggest that class and status differences within the black community will necessarily complicate any effort to agree on a unified set of meanings:

> They talk about Harlem being a Mecca only when it's advantageous to be used in a meeting or proposal. It's an attractive historical word to use in conversation because Harlem is known as a Mecca, not only for its music and writers but doctors—a lot of great people came out of here. But people who remember that part of society don't realize what's happening here now.

When the past can be exploited for redevelopment projects, the optimism conveyed through the appropriation of language and terminology hides class interests at work:

> It is not being maintained as a Mecca, and it should. And the only way it can continue to be a Mecca as it was for the Paul Robesons or the Bumpy Johnsons or the Adam Clayton Powells is to continue to raise up those who are still here. They have a story to tell whether they live in the projects or a rundown tenement. That's what I'm afraid of. That's what I'm angry about. They are deciding what character this Mecca should take.

Because Harlem's symbols are mutable and vary, conflicts over who can wield the past as a resource are perhaps inevitable. These types of conflicts will surface in more detail in later chapters exploring the motivations and meanings borne by the recently arrived middle-class black gentry.

A lot is at stake. How the past is cast and then employed will affect the Harlem its residents know. Colliding images of the past also underlie disputes over the consequences of using symbolic markers:

> When they changed the name of the street to Martin Luther King Boulevard, I said, look at that now. This is Harlem and traditionally this has been 125th Street. Now people won't be able to find it. You know, that's our central business district, so a lot of people object to them changing it to Martin Luther King Boulevard, although it's supposed to be Martin Luther King/125th Street. That was the compromise, that they have both names. Just like Lenox Avenue, which is part of Harlem's history. Now we're going to say Malcolm X Boulevard? No, it's Lenox Avenue.

Development official Paul Morris places the larger significance of this controversy in the changing terms of race relations:

> I felt that Martin Luther King Boulevard should go from one end of Manhattan to the other. Why is it only in the black community? Martin Luther King saved America, that's my opinion. Why does Martin Luther King Boulevard go from river to river in Harlem when Martin Luther King is an American hero? He's a hero for everybody, not just for black folks. So that's why I say this should be 125th Street. Why must Frederick Douglass Boulevard end at 110th Street? You know what I mean?

The rigid boundaries that once defined Harlem confined residents and cultural heroes to the shared space above Ninety-sixth Street. Morris's argument echoes thinking that, today, black culture should not exist apart, marginalized from American culture.

Allison Carson also sees the culture of Harlem as a unique resource. But she, like Morris, wants it to be identified as an integral part of American culture—a shared resource not limited by restrictive racial boundaries:

> We've got to stop isolating Harlem from the rest of the world. You know the Dance Theater of Harlem is a symbol. It should be thought of as an international company that has its home in Harlem and not be thought of as a form of modern-day segregation. There are issues like that of trying to mainstream black institutions. Like the Schomburg, I mean. Spread that out. Let that be a resource for everybody.

Carson's hope is that the culture of the once marginal "Nigger Heaven" will be reimagined beyond racial lines. The "home" metaphor is appropriated by Carson in her description of the roots of the Dance Theater of Harlem. But her depiction of the Dance Theater as an international symbol is a sign of an approach that prefers mainstreaming to separation.

Whether the newest Harlemites will be black or white, some argue, does not take away from the past. For Carson, the survival of these symbols does not rest entirely on whether it is blacks or whites who join the community. Her hope is that *anyone* who comes will share in the collective process of rebuilding and preservation:

> For a lot of reasons, I don't care if 50 percent of the people who came into Harlem were not of African descent. What I do care about is that Frederick Douglass Circle be a real monument with flowers and a gorgeous statue. I really care that people know that the Schomburg exists. This is part of the history. We should repair the houses and do right by the monuments. We've got

> an incredible number of cultural institutions in this community. And I think that anybody who wants to come and contribute lifeblood, energy, good vibrations, and money is welcome here.

Also arguing for an integrated Harlem, Spencer Thomas, who was born and raised here, commented on the differences between Harlem then and now:

> What Harlem stood for and what it was and what it's going to be are two different things entirely: the view that we have of Harlem when we talk about the renaissance and the view of what Harlem ought to be. Look at the Apollo Theater and the National Black Theater on 125th Street. These things have been trying to re-create themselves in Harlem. But they have to re-create themselves in a different way. They can't be what was here before. It's a more outward-looking image than inward.

Support Community Struggles: Race and Class

An important component of my interviews with the long-term Harlem residents is what Harlem should look like. What emerges is a clear preference for a strong black presence along with a more solid base of middle-class homeowners. But there is an accompanying dilemma. What if this black middle-class influx evolved in such a way that it included, eventually, large numbers of whites? In other words, what if today's black newcomers are merely the leading edge of a more profound neighborhood transformation?

Some argue that whites belong in Harlem since altered race relations should induce the building of communities that are more racially integrated. But equally passionate arguments are made in favor of keeping Harlem's black majority. This is not new thinking in Harlem.

In a 1973 report, "A Survey of Leadership Attitudes toward the Quality of Life in Harlem," 77 percent of the community leaders surveyed said it was "very important" to find ways to keep middle-income blacks in Harlem as part of creating an economically diverse community, a goal of redevelopment. Two officials surveyed argued:

> We've got to keep our professionals because they are the only ones who can develop the community; they can provide for the community and give their time. While I don't believe in racial integration, I do believe in the integration of classes.[12]

> The middle-income families usually represent the leadership group that can get things done. Also, if they were there, there would be desirable housing, schools and living conditions. It is important to maintain their voting strength.[13]

While both respondents recognized the need for a higher-income group and more economic integration, they envisioned a mixed-income, stratified *black* community. The economic and political strength of the black middle class was seen as an asset for the larger black community.

Another official surveyed argued that prior abandonment by the black middle class "symbolizes their turning their backs on their heritage, denying their blackness, and having a lack of interest in the future of black people in general."[14] Similar criticism of the negative ways that integration has affected black communities through blacks' moving to traditionally white areas arose repeatedly in my interviews with Harlem residents. As previously segregated neighborhoods, stores, and restaurants opened up to blacks across America, the movement out hurt the residential and institutional life of black communities by stripping away an important caring and sharing found in the black ghetto, many interviewees said.

James Roosevelt was born and raised in Harlem but moved away as an adult. Roosevelt, the former vice president of the Harlem Cooperative, a community housing agency, talked about the role of middle-class blacks in the Harlem of his adolescence:

> When I was coming up, there were people who lived in Harlem who were judges, doctors, lawyers, show biz people, you know, who are now off in other places, who couldn't move out because it was segregated. And so they were role models who were present in the community. And they were also part of the tax base and part of the group that would come out and fight for better services and do all the things that are necessary for a successful community. And many of them moved out later. Not all of them, but many of them. And so I guess the issue is the right to go where you want to go. It was bad for the community in that sense.

Sociologist William Julius Wilson makes a related argument in *The Truly Disadvantaged*. "The exodus of middle- and working-class families from many ghetto neighborhoods," writes Wilson, "removes an important 'social buffer.'"[15] According to Wilson,

> [E]ven if the truly disadvantaged segments of an inner-city area experience a significant increase in long-term spells of joblessness, the basic institutions in that area (churches, schools, stores, recreational facilities, etc.) would remain viable if much of the base of their support comes from the more economically stable and secure families.[16]

Wilson's model suggests that middle-income blacks play a positive function in the black community.

Echoes of Wilson's position are heard in the comments of residents who have lived in Harlem for many years. Middle-class blacks who did not take part in the exodus describe as important their continued presence and involvement in neighborhood life. As many are quick to point out, they live in Harlem by choice—one that is accompanied by somber responsibilities. For some, it means serving as role models. For others, their contribution is as homeowners, purchasing, maintaining, and, on occasion, upgrading properties in Harlem.

Pat Mason grew up in Harlem. She left the community in the 1950s when she was married. She has since returned and taken over her father's medical practice in the 129th Street brownstone where she was raised. Mason suggests that middle-class visibility is needed to counteract the corrosive effects of the neighborhood's new "role models"—drug dealers. Mason reasons that the drug dealer's lifestyle could seem far more extravagant, accessible, and rewarding to today's youth:[17]

> It isn't true that everybody left Harlem. I've stayed in Harlem with my family. A lot of people stayed in Harlem. We hadn't been very visible somehow or other. But visibility is a funny thing. Some of us had Mercedes, but most professional people in Harlem lived rather modestly. At least externally. They were solid teachers and judges and politicians who had cars, but not extravagant cars. So, therefore, as role models to the average youngster in the street, we hadn't been very conspicuous. The conspicuous people and the flamboyant people were the drug dealers. So these kids, unless they have role models in school or some of the clubs after school, they're more aware of that than they are of the positive role models. Of course this is what we're trying to do more of.

Many Harlemites see personal relationships and closeness, such as acting as role models, as an integral part of the community's rhythm. This, in part, explains why some current residents, like community leaders in the 1973 Harlem Leadership Survey, are ambivalent about the arrival of whites, alongside, or in the wake of, black gentrifiers. This is a position that frustrates HUDC officials who advocate racial and class integration for the community. Paul Morris, the official at HUDC, noted that gentrification has been used as a "buzzword for white people moving into Harlem." This definition, he argued, obscures the positive effects of necessary economic integration:

> In the 1990s, I think it's passé to speak in terms of race. That's what I tell the white folks, too. Instead of talking integration on the racial aspect, let's talk about economic integration and attracting the black gentry. Otherwise it's always going to have low-level services.

But to move beyond racial segregation, and the negative effects of marginality and separateness, does not necessarily mean disregarding the past. Morris may respect Harlem's historical significance, but he nonetheless sees it as only part of the equation. In fact, Morris identifies the culture and history of Harlem as assets for attracting middle-income whites and blacks, "who for the most part come with their eyes open. They know what the place is about—good and bad."

To further explore these race and class issues, I asked long-term, middle-class residents whether they agreed that it is important to specifically recruit middle-class blacks to participate in the revitalization of Harlem. Many of these residents said they would accept economic change—as long as it was middle-class blacks who joined in the efforts to improve the quality of life in the community.

Discussion about attracting whites revolves around the question of whether white residents are compatible with preserving Harlem as an important black community. "They're coming. The sky is falling. These white people are coming," said Paula Kimball, mocking residents' trepidation about integration. "And yes," she conceded, "there were people who came. But there's so much space. So much potential," she argued.

> But I think, you know, the housing opportunities may be here, but the economic conditions and the services [aren't]. And because of the other social problems, it hasn't been comfortable for people to really come to Harlem in the droves that were anticipated. In the height of the eighties, when studio apartments were going for $300,000 down on Ninety-sixth Street and you could get a place up in Harlem, you could buy a whole building for that. That means people said, "We'll think about it." But because these other things weren't cleared up, it's not comfortable for the white gentry to come back.

Asked why she thought more whites should move to the community, Joan Sanders, an executive in a prominent Manhattan advertising agency, responded:

> I think the retail businesses would change. You'd get a lot more little things like the Food Emporium. You know, small viable dress shops, things like that. We would have more drugstores. I mean, I gotta go down below Ninety-sixth Street to find a full-fledged drugstore on Sunday because they're closed [in Harlem] on Sunday. I think we could get a better grade of retail stores and a better grade of supermarkets. Or, if not a better grade, these would be upgraded to give you some of the same kind of products they give you in their

stores below Ninety-sixth Street. I mean, you could go in any of these grocery stores and be appalled at the meats they have and the things you can't get. I want a Porterhouse steak. Forget it.

Others argue that as whites cross that boundary, life in Harlem will improve because the city will show more respect for a community where whites reside. As a barometer of racial change, increasing racial integration in Harlem is perceived by the women in the following comments as a positive step toward remedying the ill effects of segregation.

Joan Sanders predicted that more white residents in Harlem would improve social services in the community:

I don't mind them [whites] coming in and joining them to clean it up. The safety will be much better when they come, because the cops will do the things that they should be doing to protect us. Oh, not as much as they will when the white people come in. I firmly believe that. Because they are their own people. People protect their own people, you know.

Barbara Ellis, like Sanders, cited the boost to Harlem's economy that she associated with whites moving into the community:

I think it's wonderful that it's happening, because it will bring people back. It would bring back the economy, like stores. Different stores would be willing to open up here, and you won't have to go all over the place to shop.

And Sanders talked about physical improvements in the community, greater safety, and the possibility of increased efforts to eliminate the drug problem:

I would like to see Harlem come back in the sense that I don't see a lot of vacant buildings, a lot of burned-out buildings, a lot of crumbling buildings. I want to feel safe in the neighborhood. And if whites coming is what it takes to get this place back on its feet, I am not going to complain about it. Like I said, as long as it means they are going to revitalize the buildings and streets. And if that means I'm not going to have to see the pushers, fine.

Pat Mason also envisions the positive role that whites would play in the redevelopment of the community:

We feel that there would be an advantage of some white people moving in. We certainly wouldn't want it to be a half. Quarter to a third maybe. This is the way I feel about it. Whites tend to have more money, they will keep the buildings up a little bit better. The trouble with black folks is that one-third of black people are poor. One out of three. That's high. So when people hear what happens in the black community, they don't understand why. They think that black folks are lazy and no good and don't care about education, don't care about taking care of themselves and all that. But when you're poor, much below the poverty level, living is a priority, just dealing with life day to day, trying to feed your children.

And yet even Mason, who advocates greater integration, sets a limit on the number of whites who should come to Harlem. The numerical limits offered by some long-term residents reflect the long-held fear that a white presence will inevitably mean a displacement of black culture and community life.

Spencer Thomas grew up in "the valley" and as an adult has moved to "the hill," where he now lives with his wife and ten-year-old son. When he was ten years younger, Thomas says, he and his wife were willing to be "urban pioneers." They purchased and rehabilitated a Harlem brownstone on Hamilton Terrace. Although his days as an urban pioneer are over, Thomas defines his real-estate purchases in Harlem as his contribution to the community:

I have a commitment to Harlem and to the people of Harlem. I'm here to stay. And so we buy the real estate and say, "OK, here I am," like Christopher Columbus. I discovered it. We're here. It's mine. Unlike Chris, I'll have a deed. I say to people who want to make a commitment, "Let's do it, then. That's why I'm here."

These long-term Harlem residents will not rebuild Harlem alone. But when these same images—urban pioneer, Christopher Columbus, homesteaders—are applied to whites, conflicts arise. Many blacks in Harlem see an inherent racism in hearing their community viewed as a place to be "discovered" by white pioneers. "I think it's racism. It's the kind of racism that makes people see this as empty land," argued Paula Kimball.

It's like Columbus discovering America. You know, it's like, somebody wants to start a project and they discovered there's some empty land in Harlem. They don't notice that there are people living down the street and children playing in front. And they don't see it.

Due to years of abandonment of the community's housing stock and earlier residential displacement, there is available space in Harlem. While competition for space is not the major source of conflict, many residents still express an ambivalence about living next to whites. Experiences with real and perceived racism at the hands of whites contribute to feelings that Harlem should remain black.

Many of the long-term residents interviewed cited positive feelings of identity and self-esteem as integral features of a supportive environment in Harlem. Day-to-day encounters that define life in the black community can offer comfort and a sense of belonging they believe they would not find living among whites:

> I would not feel comfortable living in a Darien, Connecticut. If you grew up in an all-black neighborhood, that's where you feel more comfortable. I think that's why we stay right here and not move to Westchester County or Darien.

> I actually felt more at peace with myself as a New York resident living in Harlem. I am just more relaxed. Why? The attitude downtown would drive me crazy. I mean you couldn't go in the stores, they think you're going to steal something, you know?

Thus, the boundaries that situate them inside a black world, in effect marginalizing the black middle class, are not viewed entirely negatively. By defining the black community in opposition to other places—below Ninety-sixth Street, downtown, the suburbs of New York and Connecticut, or simply "up here" versus "down there"—residents' awareness of the beginnings and endings of worlds defined by race is translated into an appreciation of Harlem as a home.

Feeling rejected, carrying burdens, and constantly having to prove oneself are experiences associated with being black in a white world:

> It's nice being around your own color. I think there's not that pressure of keeping up with the Joneses, or being the only one, or having to prove that you're something other than you're not. I think if I was one of three families in an all-white neighborhood, I would feel uncomfortable. When I come home, I don't want to be an example. I just want to be who I am, you know, without feeling that I've got to carry a burden of proving that black people aren't this way.

> I feel more comfortable living amongst my own. I don't have to worry about, oh, gosh is someone going to reject me, or something like that.

Rather than seeing the boundaries of racial community as a restrictive imposition, these longer-term residents perceive personal rewards.

To many Harlemites, the move toward racial integration here is met with mixed feelings. Even those who welcome whites would limit the percentage. Some who initially said they would be receptive to whites contradicted themselves or switched positions later in the interview. Joan Sanders, for example, who was quoted earlier as saying she hopes whites will move to Harlem, qualified her position later in our interview:

> But I have a problem if somebody comes and says to me you have to move out because, you know, all the rules have changed. You've got to go because now white people are moving in and brother, you should leave.

Some said that in the 1990s, it is (or ought to be) passé to think in terms of race. Dwight Fisher, who owns a restaurant on 127th Street, has been in business in Harlem since 1961. According to Fisher, his changing customer base mirrors the racial transition he has noticed in the community over the years:

> Harlem's gonna be black and white. There's more whites comin' in this area every day. I remember when I first opened up this restaurant next door here, if we saw a white person in that line in the cafeteria, we was just as surprised as if you saw a rabbit run 'cross Broadway. But now sometimes you go out there and maybe 20 percent or 30 percent of them are white people. So it's a change that's comin'.

Fisher's menu reflects these changes in the community too. In addition to "pig feet and stuff," Fisher tells me he serves "filet mignon and dishes with hollandaise sauce." "Why I gotta have collard greens all the time? We've got to change this thing around a bit. Time changes things, you know. And we can't just be all black," argued Fisher. Fisher's menu, which offers more traditional black cooking along with "American" (i.e., white) food, strikes a balance that is often lacking in talk about the racial changes accompanying redevelopment.

This vision is most noticeable for Harlemites who talk about moving toward a community in which blacks and whites live together:

> I feel as though this is the only way we gonna break away from these prejudices and things of that nature. If we begin to live together and go to school together, we'll get to understand each other. 'Cause this is all it is anyway. It's a lack of understandin'.

Whether Harlem is black or white, residents will continue to deal both inside and outside of the community with racism, prejudice, and what Fisher defines as a lack of understanding. The forces that shape social interactions between blacks and whites are not the creation of Harlemites, nor do they hold relevance for discussion of redevelopment only in this particular community. Answers to questions about how and why residential integration will or will not be successful in America depend on understanding the ways people feel about living in racially integrated communities. And these questions must be understood as part of the larger racial drama that historically has shaped American life.

Residents discussing day-to-day life in settings as large as New York to the more intimate spaces in Harlem and its streets offer numerous (and contradictory) opinions about integration. Although many of their comments may sound racist, paranoid, suspicious, and even, at times, simply inaccurate, they must be understood in terms of power:

> I don't know whether it's a question of keeping white people out, I think it's a question of keeping Harlem in control of the black folks. There's a difference between those two ideas. It's not a question of saying I don't want any white folks in Harlem—that's not what I'm saying. But we have to make sure who is going to have control. I don't give a damn where white people live. What I'm concerned about is whether or not I'm going to be dominated and controlled and exploited by them. And they can do that without living here.

Essentially, it is a disparity of power, accompanied by control and exploitation, that has made historically black and white neighborhoods. And by extension, this dynamic has made interlopers and outcasts of blacks and whites who would cross racial lines.

It is for this reason that some have encouraged a younger generation of African Americans to come to Harlem. Long-time residents Barbara Ellis and Pat Mason put it like this:

> Now, whites can't come unless you let them. What we try to do is get these young people to put in for these [brownstone] applications. We help them as much as we can. Don't tell me about how they're going to take Harlem over. The only way they're going to take Harlem over, [is if] you're going to let them. That's the gentrification. You're giving it away. If you don't want them, then you come. And that's it. Come back here. And that's the only way you're going to save Harlem. With most people, they get educated, they get good money, then they're gone. Then they say, "Oh yeah, Harlem is gone!" Yeah, Harlem is gone. You gave it away.

> We don't mind some integration. I think it should help. Now what we don't need of course, we don't want the whites to move in en masse, because we would like to still keep Harlem essentially a black area for many reasons. First

> of all, it's the black capital of the world. And second, because it gives us a good strong voting bloc, at least potentially a good strong voting bloc. With a black middle-class mix, we will have stronger voting power.

Mason claims not to mind whites' entry into the community. But as she continues, citing politics as a concern that goes beyond simply repopulating the neighborhood, she makes a distinction between black and white middle-class residents. She equates the return of middle-class blacks with political power in the community and, perhaps incorrectly, assumes a bloc politics based on race.

Because much of the community opposition to gentrification has been framed around black and white racial lines, black gentry are seen as different from their white counterparts and as a necessary part of the redevelopment process. While some residents distinguish middle-class blacks from white gentry, others are less sympathetic to this strategy. Disagreements about the return of a black middle class to Harlem, alongside debate about black versus white gentrification, provide compelling evidence that simple lines of race and class cannot alone determine insider and outsider positions.

A range of cultural symbols stand at the center of Harlem's redevelopment conflicts. Representations of Harlem are curiously suspended between the glory and tragedy of the past. These representations clearly shape attitudes about what and who should be the future of the cultural capital of black America. But it is not an automatic, or easy, embrace of race that defines these symbols. Disputes about the names, buildings, monuments, and historic designation, for instance, also give rise to divided thinking.

Even among black insiders to the redevelopment process, history and culture do not provide a straightforward set of meanings that guide either advocates for redevelopment or those resistant to change. The arguments raised for and against economic redevelopment strategies in Harlem reveal various ways that race and community preservation are worked through a range of positions connected to economic, and not merely racial, interests. As the voices of community insiders make clear, there are multiple perspectives on Harlem as a black community, the role of middle-class blacks and whites in the community, and the value of Harlem's heritage.

When race and culture stand out as central concerns shaping the discourse on redevelopment in Harlem, advocates for the preservation of Harlem as a black community often hold positions in opposition to those who define development solely in economic terms. As a result, numerous ideologies of gentrification are evident. Those who have defined the issue in terms of maintaining Harlem as a black residential space may overlook the role that black gentry—as class actors—play as the vanguard for the very thing they oppose.

The contribution of the black gentry to the collective process of inverting Harlem, in its modern-day renaissance, from hell to heaven takes many forms. Through symbolic uses of the community, these middle-class blacks struggle to make the transition from community outsiders to insiders. But their struggle reveals a number of interesting dilemmas behind the insider/outsider and black/white dichotomies that have been used to frame resistance to or support of gentrification in Harlem.

BUY
BLACK
volume III
just right
soul
soul
soul
volu
just

chapter 3

The Dilemma of Racial Difference

At least you know here no one will burn a cross on your lawn.

Harlem newcomer Audrey Edwards

Home's just around
the corner
there—
but not really
anywhere.

Langston Hughes

"Come on in and don't mind the dust. I'm just here doing Kim's hair." June Wilson, a slight black woman dressed in a bright orange, yellow, and green African-print jumpsuit, welcomes me into the living room of her 145th Street brownstone. The room—a makeshift parlor with cardboard boxes for furniture, and paint-stained sheets draped about—reflects the chaos that entered Wilson's life when she purchased this house and moved to Harlem in the late 1980s.

The room is a wreck—exposed plaster, green paint peeling from the walls, dangling wires, tools everywhere. On one wall, a framed African print—a museum exhibit reproduction—explodes in black, red, and yellow zigzag lines. It hints at a more stylish life prior to this move. In 1988, Wilson moved to Harlem and four years later is still in the midst of the extensive rehabilitation of a nineteenth-century brownstone she hopes to "restore to its original glory." But progress is slow, she explains, "I've had to deal from the ground up, new heating, new heating system, new floors, new roof, new bathrooms, and I still deal with the plumbing."

Kim, a black woman in her early thirties, sits atop a high stool, a towel around her shoulders, a jar of hair cream in one hand, combs in the other. Today is Sunday—hair day, they tell me. Wilson alternately dips her fingers into the jar of hair cream and tugs at strands of Kim's hair. Neatly lined rows of braids take shape around Kim's head as we sip coffee and talk about Wilson's decision to move to Harlem.

Wilson gestures excitedly as she talks about her first years of brownstone living in Harlem. Despite her enthusiasm, it is not immediately apparent why this woman, a magazine editor, would choose to live here. She recites a litany of problems. Banks are not forthcoming with loans. There is no end in sight to living in a shell of a house. Plus there is the crime, the noise of the streets, and the overall negative reputation of the community.

A successful, middle-class professional, Wilson certainly had choices about where to make her home. When her work moved her from the Midwest to New York, why had she not heeded the advice of friends or the prodding by realtors who tried to steer her clear of Harlem when she arrived? For Wilson, living in a black community and working toward its improvement represent a respite from her work in a predominantly white environment:

> I know this is not such a positive thing to say, but I worked in an environment where I didn't see many people that looked like me. So it was important for me to set up house in an area where I would be the most comfortable. That meant being around black people who were race-minded.

Seeking "race-minded" people is not new to Wilson. Wilson's racial consciousness and her worldview were shaped by a keen awareness of the color line. This line was solidified in the segregated schools and neighborhoods of her youth. A firm commitment to race was reinforced through black pride at home. Her activist spirit was forged by direct political involvement in the protests and marches of the turbulent 1960s:

> If I see the storm, I usually try to make my way right through the middle of it. My family was very active in the civil rights movement, and we marched with Martin Luther King. So I had, like, several marches under my belt by the time I was eight. And, you know, we had the stuff down. My family was about building little revolutionaries to go out there. So this [the move to Harlem] in my head is easy.

Wilson shrugs off the disarray as a temporary state. Besides, with the racial socialization she gained from family and black institutions, Wilson considers her move to Harlem as putting her racial politics into practice. In fact, Wilson's renovation of the brownstone is meant to convey a larger symbolism, which I detect when she describes her own "revolutionary" role in Harlem:

> It's an easy community to become visible in because there are so many things to be done. And it's an easy community to win over if you have the right words. It's easy because its been hurt so many times. It's like a baby waiting to be nurtured.

Using a language and tone of mothering, Wilson depicts her arrival in terms of race and gender. Her words fall in line with a long tradition of birth and awakening metaphors associated with Harlem. But this is a description much at odds with the images of invasion and conquest that frequently accompany angry rhetoric over gentrification.

Throughout our conversation, Wilson talks about the purchase of her home not as an individual act but as part of a collective restoration and preservation effort. And in a twist, she places herself squarely on the side of those being invaded, though she is among the newcomers:

> I see it as a war, and there are a lot of soldiers here who are ready to do battle. They really are ready to do battle, whether it's working with the community groups, working with the churches, actively purchasing properties here and trying to turn them from diamonds in the rough into something that shines. You know, there are a lot of people who are getting caught up.

A commitment to race and community-building comes through in Wilson's comments. To the extent that she belongs to a broader movement, however, Wilson's account defies conventional wisdom. At a time when political and economic changes seem to obviate such a move,[1] a "return to the city" movement by blacks as gentry in a black community presents a fascinating vantage for examining the nuanced realities of race and class in post–civil rights America.

But new arrivals have at times been greeted with a mix of trepidation, suspicion, and distrust. Vocal opposition to redevelopment depicts a threat to the history and identity of the community. This explains, in part, why some long-term residents, community activists, realtors, and redevelopment officials, heard from in preceding pages, would voice a preference for a *black* middle-class role in revitalizing Harlem.

The arrival of middle-class blacks gives way to other contradictions. Community indecision and a lack of consensus over the years have combined to sustain a long-standing collective worry that "the whites are coming, the whites are coming." Over time, this cry has become one "official reality" defining, in racial terms, a crisis confronting Harlem. Where anti-development rhetoric moves race to a central location, the invasion by gentry is understood as a white-versus-black issue. The community is energized as a collective body when new life is breathed into old enemies—"whites," "outsiders," "the city." Caught in a familiar tangle of "us" and "them," Harlem girds itself against vaguely defined villains.

This community discourse circulates and ends up supporting a view of newly arriving middle-class blacks as Harlem "insiders." Newcomers like Wilson claim a place for themselves in Harlem's redevelopment story through an assumed, and automatic, "insider" status. But while it makes for romantic headlines,[2] the storybook tale of a black "renaissance and revival" is incomplete. By downplaying conflicts embedded in the economic forces that foster neighborhood revitalization, these accounts sidestep the possibility of a not-so-happy ending.

Academic studies of gentrification cast a critical eye at the class inequalities found in such neighborhood changes. From an economic perspective,[3] gentrification is a social process signaled by historical shifts in capital and real-estate markets. Cycles of investment and reinvestment occur in "blighted" and undervalued urban landscapes, pushing aside decades of neglect and decline due to disinvestment. Newly arriving gentry are viewed as class actors whose role in the process prompts questions such as "renaissance and revival for whom?"

In a community, on a block, or at a particular street, real people are actors thrown together to negotiate sometimes shared and often differing views of communities in transition. For an unknown amount of time the process of gentrification throws everything up in the air. The neighborhood, along with its housing stock, its residents, its market value, its reputation, its cherished traditions and shared memories, is pushed onto a stage of history that becomes a maelstrom of markets and money, design and displacement, capital and class struggle. The bottom line, in the end, is that rents tend to rise. Money matters—rising rents, a higher tax base, less desire for affordable or mixed-income housing—make it plain that all do not benefit equally from the urban "renaissance" and "revival" of gentrified communities.

Unfortunately, both of these scenarios—the white takeover and the yuppie makeover—make it difficult to account for Wilson and others like her who claim they are drawn to Harlem as a symbol of racial identity and community. Middle-class blacks are not a neat fit with the 1980s yuppie persona. On the whole, while the 1980s did give us Bill Cosby, in the mainstream of popular culture, middle-class blacks were marginal. But behind the noise produced by yuppie and baby-boomer trends, fads, and accomplishments, middle-class blacks were crying out to be heard. Accounts of (black) middle-class angst in a new cultural landscape by "post–civil rights" and "affirmative action" (black) baby boomers marked a not entirely problem-free coming of age.[4]

By looking at race as a multifaceted reality, we will be attuned to the shifting, fluid, and multiple identities found in the stories of Harlem's black gentry. They reveal identities that fit, and do not fit, within the historical straitjacket of black and white categories. Along with June Wilson, this chapter introduces eleven other black middle-class newcomers who purchased and settled in brownstones, co-op apartments, or condominiums in Harlem during the late 1970s, 1980s, and early 1990s. Race and racism bind these individuals to a shared narrative of black economic success and a desire to become homeowners in the black community.

Work as a Foreign Environment

What do you want to be when you grow up? It is a question that offers anything and everything. As Americans, we grow up believing that we are measured and judged as individuals. We embrace the idea that hard work and individual initiative translate childhood dreams, through aspiration and ambition, into accomplishment. Occupational attainment plays a vital role in the meaning of our national and personal identities. The Protestant work ethic is as American as apple pie. In hewing close to the values Americans cherish most, the mainstream civil rights movement successfully framed the race "problem" as an American dilemma. So that blacks could realize these achievement ideals, restrictions and exclusion in the polity and economy had to be challenged.

But once WHITE and COLORED designations are outwardly removed, how would we know whether and when we had dismantled the architecture of American apartheid? Would there be signposts to tell us how far we left the past behind? And since it was theoretically invisible, how could we be sure that the color line was gone? Out of the political economy and culture that shape U.S. society, Americans are socialized to embrace concepts such as justice, democracy, freedom, opportunity. Beyond tenth-grade civics, how do we reckon with such abstractions? What can we know and say about intangibles like equality and inequality? Action verbs make a more open society seem visible and attainable: level the playing field, open closed doors, knock down walls, and remove restrictive barriers. These words will be tangible pieces of "access" and "inclusion" that we carry as evidence that the 1960s happened, proof that we followed through with concrete gains.

A study by Richard L. Zweigenhaft and William Domhoff of blacks in white corporate America suggests, however, that black mobility into elite schools and occupations was limited, and by the mid-1980s had dwindled. They conclude that the blacks in their study had "gone more than halfway to meet the demands of white culture, changing in ways that the white power structure in effect demanded of them. But the power structure has changed little to meet them, and it continues to exclude them. It remains a structure that institutionalizes the values and practices of upper-class white males."[5]

Sociologist Charles Willie is among a number of social scientists who in the 1980s and 1990s pointed to more subtle forms of racism that middle-class blacks encounter in the spaces of integration. While opportunities for higher education, occupational mobility, and neighborhood integration are undisputed "fruits of integration," Willie, for one, argued that racial difference may have actually grown in significance, "especially for middle-class blacks who, because of school desegregation and affirmative action and other integration programs, are coming into direct contact with whites for the first time for extended interaction." Regardless of greater structural opportunities, middle-class blacks continue to face a boundary that is both restrictive and racially defined.

In interviews with Harlem's black gentry, it was not uncommon for me to hear stories about negative experiences on the job and with white neighbors that in part prompted the move to Harlem. Some had endured slights as subtle as whispered comments. Others had weathered more severe attacks in the form of racial slurs and, for one family, the firebombing of their new home in a white neighborhood.

A commonly expressed feeling is that in their own lives they continue to confront a color line that is perhaps more subtle than in pre–civil rights America, yet still defines a pattern of distinct relations between blacks and whites. Evidence of symbols and rituals of America's culture of racism, marginalizing blacks in the white world, is prevalent in both work and residential settings.

During America's Jim Crow era, the middle-class jobs held by a black bourgeoisie evolved within the strictures of a highly segregated occupational structure. This group of middle-class blacks counted among its members Negro doctors, Negro lawyers, Negro undertakers, and Negro teachers. Within the confines of a castelike structure, class and status positions were created due to the need for a professional and service class. This group would provide services within segregated communities and cater to the separate institutions that developed under an American form of apartheid.

Today, the jobs that Harlem's black gentry hold—as writers, publishers, musicians, filmmakers, engineers, corporate executives, administrators, teachers—signal their entry into America's occupational mainstream. Their credentials—graduate and postgraduate degrees from traditionally black institutions, as well as from state university systems and the Ivy League—plus effort and intelligence, account for high levels of success and accomplishments.

The interviews reveal a shared feeling that race is, if not an exclusionary barrier, always a factor in their job experiences. Race matters, they say, in terms of how performances are evaluated and in interactions with coworkers. Meritocracy and mobility from their perspective are not yet colorblind. Still, the discourse of "reverse discrimination" nibbled away at support for affirmative action. The 1980s was a decade when some declared victory in the civil rights struggle and the battle shifted.

George Carver, a corporate executive, recalled years of political struggles that were waged, in part, for occupational and educational inclusion:

> I was picketing. I was picketing. When CORE was integrating houses, I was picketing. In '65, I was in Selma and Vicksburg and Natchez and Jackson. Because in those days, you couldn't go to Harvard. In those days, you couldn't go stay at any hotel you wanted to anywhere in this country. For you and me. That's what I was fighting for. And the issues were pretty clean-cut. They weren't subtle, they were drawn sharply giving us a very clear focus.

Despite a remarkably successful career, Carver holds lingering frustrations that continue to shape his political attitudes about race. He is frustrated not only by shifts in the form racism has taken but also by its remarkably stable exclusionary attitude:

> So I've been fighting these battles for a long time. I'm over fifty. I'm fifty-one years old, and I remember being the first black at Northrop or Hughes, and I've dealt with a lot of discrimination there. Just being black. "Why are you here?" They weren't ready for us. They're not ready for us, you know. Now I fight for raising the glass ceiling.

With its subtleties, the existence of the glass ceiling is denied by many. Others cannot comprehend the mechanics by which such a barrier could continue to operate, given the rules of an American meritocracy in which a vocabulary of talent, skill, and accomplishment prevails.

But it is an invisible barrier that many black executives feel keeps them out of high positions in the corporate world. Social networks operate to identify and maintain social differences and point to the durability of this ceiling, according to the gentrifiers:

> Is there a glass ceiling? You bet there is. A gender ceiling and a racial ceiling. Do I find it in my work? See, I'm still an executive [in print media]. I'm the first black executive that [the magazine] has ever had. I'm used to being the first black, so I can handle that. But am I treated differently by the old boy network? You bet I am. I'm different. I didn't go to Harvard or Yale or Princeton, you know.

But even with the right credentials, race can still prevent access to such networks. Etta Harrison, a high school music teacher who has lived in Harlem since 1980, said that even an Ivy League education may not mitigate the effects of racism:

> So you put on all your good clothes and send your children to Harvard, Princeton, Yale. And then you go out there knowing that you understand and speak all the jargon and everything else that they say, and they still look at you and you're still a nigger. So now what?

Harrison's comment suggests that for blacks, visible physical differences mean that even when playing by the rules, they are still seen as inferior.

Carver shared a similar observation about how the visible fact of race is translated into a stigma:

> No matter what levels I strive to achieve and no matter what success, I'm subject to being mistaken for the elevator operator if I live, you know, on the East Side of Manhattan. And that happens. I check into hotels—the best hotels—wherever I go around the country, and somebody might mistake me for the elevator operator. It doesn't matter that I've got a briefcase in my hand and I'm wearing a $700 suit. I'm black. They don't see details. They just see color when they look at us. So that's happened. It doesn't happen here in Harlem, though.

For Carver, an executive, the symbols of success, defined in terms of an expensive suit and a briefcase, do not provide the status that he feels should distinguish the elevator operator from the executive. This status, Carver explains, is denied him by virtue of race. Color imposes an identity that class does not diminish:

> Being black and always living in black communities and having access to non-black communities, I've always known there's been a double standard, you know. I know people see me different. I don't have any illusions of that. And it doesn't matter how educated I am or how successful I am, all right. They'll always call me by the wrong name.

Very much aware of the fact that these racial constraints pose limitations for himself and other blacks, Carver is not satisfied to rest on his personal successes. "I know from painful experience," he said, pointing his finger at himself, "you've got to keep the focus."

> It only takes a couple of years of a conservative do-nothing administration in Washington which sets the rhetorical tone of this country where things can move back very quickly to the status quo.
>
> You can't turn your back on it. The minute you do, it just comes right back to where it is. I mean, there's racism on college campuses today unlike we've seen in years. Everybody walks away from it and everything's fine. And all of a sudden, everybody says, "Whoops! Damn! Have we slipped?"

Framed by the extremes of a more liberal era and the Reagan Revolution, Carver's personal success spans the arc of a national political transformation—from 1960s activism to what he defines as a do-nothing conservatism. Carver's rise to the top of the corporate hierarchy seems to provide proof that removing racial obstacles to opportunities and upward mobility succeeded. Between the time when Carver was picketing and when everybody walked away, the nation trumpeted its racial triumphs. But Carver did not lose sight of how racism endured.

Scholars of American ethnicity provide ample historical evidence on how the twin processes of mobility and assimilation meant "Americanization" for European ethnic immigrants. Within two to three generations, the decline of external constraints that would sustain ethnic boundaries gave way to the "ethnic miracle"—that is, the transformation of white ethnics into unmarked, plain American identities.[6] The inclusivity suggested by the gains of the civil rights movement—equal access and opportunities in housing, education, and public accommodations—gave rise to hopes that black Americans would embark on a similar course.

Since the early 1980s, sociologists have vigorously debated the meaning and significance of race and class for black America beyond the civil rights era. In fact, "the declining significance of race" became a landmark thesis, spawning a veritable industry of studies as critics and supporters alike lined up to agree or do battle with its author, William Julius Wilson. Without producing a consensus, the lively academic debate over the importance of racial difference and class in the end amounted to what theorist Thomas Kuhn would call a paradigm shift. Wilson's argument, with its emphasis on public policy, called for explanations of black poverty that could address the impact of economic dislocation brought on by deindustrialization.

While affirmative action might be one solution to America's race problem, he argued, it could not begin to address the growing gap between black "haves" and "have-nots." In essence, this gap called for acknowledging an important disjunction of race and class. Deconstructing "black" social groupings—as a middle class, a working class, and an underclass, for instance—complicated seeing race as an all-inclusive label. This disjunction now makes it necessary to look at the different forces—political, economic, cultural—that give rise to strategic and symbolic identities.

Kenyatta Davis works in a downtown high-rise, in publishing. She characterized the atmosphere of her work environment as inhospitable for blacks:

> I consider working with whites and working in the corporate environment as working in a foreign environment, and I treat it as such. You know, when I enter their milieu, I'm going to another country, and I behave accordingly. Meaning that I try to understand them as much as possible and speak in a language that they can understand as much as possible without giving up myself. And I try to teach them about who I am.

Drawing a distinction between two worlds—one black, one white—Davis defines herself as an outsider. Her work setting is experienced as an alien environment, and she likens entry into that world to foreign travel; she must tailor her language and behavior. The consequences, she explained, bear the psychological costs of integration:

> It's stressful, you know, what I have to deal with on a daily basis. They don't expect black people in that environment. It takes a lot out of me.

Davis argues that she, unlike her white colleagues, must employ strategies of survival and accommodation, in addition to plying the skills of her profession. But her efforts provide no guarantee that her coworkers accept her being there.

Greta Symes sees educational attainment and clothing and language as symbols of inclusion in the corporate world:

> You know we're educated in the finest schools. We work in corporate America. We can fall out of this house in our Armani clothes and our Ferragamo shoes, and we can speak correctly. You know, rounded vowels. As black, middle-class people, we have certain advantages, and we can function in the white world.

Like Davis, Symes suggests there is a line of difference between the white and black worlds. And armed with the proper tools, one can successfully "fall out" of one world and "function in" the other.

But Symes goes on to argue that the exclusion faced by middle-class black professionals is tied to a need for systems of meaning that accommodate the experience of living in two worlds:

> We are bicultural in this society. Many of my generation have always been in the minority. We have blazed the trail just like our parents did before us, and we are the token. We are sort of a transition generation. We have a special mission. We are very close to the civil rights struggle of the sixties, and we were raised by parents who went through the struggles of the forties, and so our mission is clear. We do race work every day and that is clear.

George Carver contends that as "tokens," middle-class blacks cannot afford to be lulled into believing that the struggle for race equality is a thing of the past:

> I'm rare. It's not like you run into George Carvers everywhere you go. George Carvers like me who happen to be black are, you know, one-tenth of one percent of the black population. So that's rare. Just because you can find me and five or six other blacks, my God! So affirmative action happened and change happened because you keep the pressure on.

Symes and Carver, by stressing that "race work" is a constant source of "keeping the pressure on," make clear that for middle-class blacks, entry to America's professional classes is but one step in a larger intergenerational struggle.

A feeling of exclusion on and off the job serves to strengthen racial identity. For Symes, this means seeking more inclusive cultural spaces away from her occupational setting:

> When we socialize and when we relax, we do that in a segregated setting where there are very few white folks. Essentially, we go out into the world, and we exercise our intellectual and political acumen in an integrated setting, and we come back and relax and let our hair down and complain and take refuge in the black community.

Home as a Refuge

Scholars of race and ethnicity explain patterns of migration by looking at push and pull factors, placing history and social structure as a context for movements of human populations. Push and pull are the twin forces that gentrification studies examine as well as they attempt to explain the makeup of gentry and why they end up in the neighborhoods they do. Politics, economy, and culture provide a starting point for narrowing factors that explain the actions of individuals as freely acting agents who are historically and socially situated.

In the case of Harlem, a critical social fact accounting for the presence of a black gentry at this historical moment is the significance of race. Further, the return by middle-class blacks to an inner-city, black community goes against the general trend of suburbanization and decreasing segregation for middle-class blacks on which sociologists have focused since the 1960s. The choice to come "home to Harlem" seems to defy one of the central gains of the civil rights era: the promise of residential integration. In fact, it is what makes Harlem's gentrification a unique case for exploring modern race meaning.

One of the consequences of middle-class black mobility in a post-segregation era is movement into "integrated" work and neighborhood settings that places middle-class blacks at the forefront of racial change in America. In interviews with Harlem's black gentry, I often heard expressed a feeling that they continue to confront a sometimes brutal color line as they integrate neighborhoods and workplaces.

When Reggie Smith, a television journalist, returned with his family from a long-term assignment in Kenya, he wanted to buy a home and to live in the city. He picked Harlem. Smith had a preference for a black neighborhood, he explained, like the one in Chicago where he had grown up. This preference was reinforced when he experienced what he called "a violent reaction from racism" in Chicago:

> In Chicago we bought a house in a white area that was firebombed before we moved into it. Because I travel so much, I was worried about leaving my

> wife and kids alone. I made a decision to live in a black community, no matter the ills.

For the Smith family, overt racism accompanied their entry into the white world. The firebombing of one's home, while an extreme case, is a harrowing expression of exclusion from white America. Although Smith's middle-class purchasing power enables him to afford to buy a home in a white neighborhood, his class position does not guarantee the family is welcome. Despite gains from civil rights legislation in the area of fair housing, choices about where to live are nonetheless influenced by racially defined constraints. In this instance, hostility and violent aggression informally replace codified restrictive covenants as a way to keep blacks from buying in white neighborhoods.

The migration of middle-class blacks into Harlem is not only pushed from the outside, though. Networks of people from within and outside of the community support this black in-migration:

> I started to meet people here in Harlem and just felt very much at home, started getting involved in a lot of community-based activities here, so whenever I had a chance, I was here anyway. And I started packing up, spending the night over here. You know, I just had clothes in New Jersey, it got to that point. So finally, a woman that adopted me as a godmother of sorts, she said, well, I think that we just need to have you here. And people started looking out for apartments. And within a year after meeting her, I wound up moving into her building. So that's how I wound up on Hamilton Terrace and in Harlem.

> I do see young professionals like myself moving in here, because I didn't move to Harlem alone, so to speak. I came by way of a network of friends, actually, that I knew from school, from my black-college experience. And then my next-door neighbors I knew from school from Atlanta—they both are professional actors. So I kind of came into a community of people. So I see individuals—musicians like Sherif Ani, people like Barbara Johnson—owning houses here, young professionals wanting to move in because they want to be with their own people, and they want a sense of community that they don't get in other parts of New York.

Malcolm Balderidge, a writer, defines getting "back to the community" as a way to counter the racism he associated with living on Manhattan's Upper West Side:

> I wanted to live here because I got tired of living in a very middle-class white community, not because I'm against white folks or anything like that, because I'm not. But I got tired of always having to prove myself.

"I was not willing to change," Balderidge continues, "and become a more proper-looking African American, you know, cut my hair and not be so energetic." He clutches and shakes a strand of his dreadlocks before continuing:

> Since I wasn't willing to become a Negro like that, then I decided I would leave. You know, I thought it would be best for my own psychological and mental makeup to live in an African American community where they don't ask me those kinds of questions, where they don't feel threatened.

For Balderidge, the suspicious and often frightened looks of whites in the elevator late at night in his prior residence were part of what he termed "racial harassment" at the hands of his neighbors:

> I lived in a luxury building, and getting in the elevator and [having] some white, some little white, snotty-nosed kid coming up to me saying, "What are you doing in the building? Who are you going to see?" You know, the whole kind of trip that I had to go through every day although I lived in there longer than they had. I mean, these were graduate students at Columbia, you know, who were asking me questions like, "Why are you in this building?"
>
> So I got tired of going through that kind of ritual, that ridiculous kind of scenario that you have to go through with middle-class white people who are definitely afraid of their shadow, especially a black shadow. So you get in an elevator when they see you every day and they're afraid. If it's 12:00 at night, they just can't deal with it, you know. So I got tired of that. I got tired of going through that. It wasn't my problem, it was their problem. It was just they weren't willing to change, you know.

Portia Hamilton was born and raised in Scarsdale, a community she describes as "very white, upper, upper class." After her divorce and a brief period of residence in North Carolina, Hamilton and her two children, Jerry and Shawnee, moved to Harlem in 1986. Hamilton's memories of growing up as one of "a handful of blacks" in Scarsdale point to the more subtle effects that race can have on blacks living in mostly white communities. "As a black female," she told me, "there were very interesting dichotomies. There was the best of both worlds and the worst of both worlds, so to speak":

> The white families got to be sure [what black families were there], and they did not offend us in any way, shape, or form. So they made sure we were in-

> cluded. Until we got to high school. And then you can really tell the difference. And I couldn't understand it. What I didn't understand is—it doesn't matter about what goes on when you're in the elementary grades. What makes the difference is when you hit the age where you're sexually active and you think about reproduction. And that's when you can start seeing differences. The parties decrease, the invitations to parties decrease, and that kind of thing. So my friends became more my church friends than my school friends.

While Hamilton notes the acceptance she and her brother experienced in "genteel, old-money" upper-class, white Scarsdale, in her teen years, differences defined along racial lines increased:

> I was just frustrated, and I was sick and tired of being there. And I just wanted to be somewhere else. I think part of it was fear. Most of my friends at the time were white, and I was dating a young man who was white. And we went up and down in that relationship, our mamas and daddies fussing at us. I think it was the fear that motivated me. The fear that I would not have a social life more than anything else.

More and more, Hamilton's childhood friendships and activities with white schoolmates were replaced with a social life centered in the black church she and her family attended.

Hamilton and her brother each reacted in their own way to their social distance from the larger white community. Her brother, she said, became withdrawn and bickered at home more and more. Her strategy was to leave:

> I rebelled against it myself. My brother rebelled against it, too. And we rebelled in very different ways. When I got to eleventh grade, I said, "Listen, I've had it with this white world up here. I've got to do something different." So I did. I convinced my mother to let me go south to live with my aunt. And I thought I'd died and gone to heaven.

Having escaped the alienation of white Scarsdale, Hamilton completed high school living in an all-black community, at an all-black school. Hamilton described the transformation:

> It was the best thing that could have happened to me. I was absolutely petrified. I mean kids using profanity and fighting with teachers. I mean, I was not exposed to it. I would sit back like a scared kitten. But my grades improved. I shot up to all A's. And it helped build my self-confidence. What I have since learned as an adult is there were always those subtle messages when we were

> growing up in Scarsdale that we really weren't quite good enough. And it may not ever have been articulated that way, but you got the message. And so my self-esteem was nil.

Hamilton's move to the South, an experience she likens to having "died and gone to heaven," shaped her later decision as a parent to move with her two children to Harlem.

Hamilton was drawn to Harlem by the press accounts rather than by friends who lived there:

> The kids used to fuss—mommy you have to get married again. And I'm saying, "I'll never get married living in Scarsdale." So I said, let me come to Harlem and be part of this "renaissance" I'm hearing so much about. And I had dreams and visions, and I saw art parties and political conversations going on in homes. And I felt that's where I needed to be. So I came.

Hamilton reasons that her own children, first raised in Scarsdale, then with relatives in a black community in the South, "needed that exposure to a much larger black community."

For Ruth Baxter-Brown, a journalist, the attraction of having a home in Harlem was to provide a balance between two worlds, offering a haven from her job downtown:

> I have real strong feelings—I really wanted to live around black people. I really did. I really got tired of going downtown and having white folks act like I don't belong down there. I get that all day long. I don't want to hear that shit when I get home. When I get home, I want to have people wave at me when I come up the street. And that's what I get living in Harlem.

Baxter-Brown looks to Harlem as a community that allows her to recreate the world in which she grew up, a black community in the Midwest. In Harlem, she says, community rituals of her neighbors signal that she belongs:

> It feels like home. It's the kind of neighborhood I grew up in. I like being on the street where I know everybody. I like coming up the block and having people stop and say hi. I like knowing who is home from college and who is just out of the hospital.

George Carver also defines the move to Harlem as a way to resolve the tension of straddling two worlds: "I feel that way wherever I live because I'm a black American, African American. We live in two different worlds, different cultures." While he suggests that there may be other strategies that blacks employ to deal with their marginality, the move to Harlem is a statement of the appreciation for black culture among middle-class blacks:

> Well, I mean, we're talking about blacks being accepted, blacks being comfortable with who they are and what they are, blacks accepting their own culture and their own values. That's what it is. An expression of that may be coming to Harlem. Thinking that I made it is determined by the fact that I have left. That's no longer it.

Carver believes that middle-class blacks, despite having accrued material rewards from their success, are in search of deeper meaning in their lives:

> We used to think having a swimming pool or having that BMW was all that ever mattered, or sending our kids to Harvard was all that matters. Hey, there is a lot more.
>
> Part of the definition is intellectual. It's how you view yourself. And part of the issue about Harlem is, blacks still think making it is getting the hell out of here, moving to Scarsdale. You know how many people I know who are black who used to live in Harlem, but yet don't read black magazines, but got these nice corporate jobs? They ran away from their culture. Well, they're going to be running back. There's guilt that comes from the reawareness of people saying, "Hey, I ran off and did all of these things, but I'm still the last hired and first fired, I still have less of an economic cushion to fall back on in hard times. I still, after all of this, two cars and all of that, I really when it counts—where it counts—don't really have anything. So, what's been missing is, I've been chasing this dream that really doesn't protect me."

In this comment, Carver argues that the tenuous position of the black middle class, coupled with the lingering racism they experience, fuels this longing for a "return" to something of deeper significance.

But Etta Harrison said a lack of assimilation elsewhere was not a motivation for her own move:

> I don't really give a damn about that. I mean that's why you go home at night. Because this is home. You need to be in an environment where you feel comfortable. Where you don't always have to project a certain kind of image to people. We are here because we feel comfortable to a certain extent. I've chosen to live here in Harlem. That's it. I'm not interested in knowing the white folks who won't talk to me about who I am as a black person. I know who I am. I don't want to discuss it with you, you know. I don't want to be explaining

> myself. That's why you come home. That's why you're here. Because other people will look at you and know who you are, and they don't have to ask anything about you.

Yolanda Jackson, a city housing official, cited frustrations over racist encounters with her former neighbors as a primary reason for moving to Harlem. Jackson recounted throwing a party for a Senegalese filmmaker in the Upper East Side apartment where she formerly lived. As she and guests enjoyed cocktails on the balcony, neighbors on a balcony overhead began shouting racial slurs. To add to Jackson's embarrassment, another neighbor called the police to register a noise complaint.

Though she laughed as she retold the story, Jackson described that episode as one of a "handful" of unhappy encounters with white neighbors, including the time a neighbor mistook her for a maid when they met up in the building's laundry room. There and at her job, Jackson says, she was always aware of a boundary—made clear through the words of neighbors and coworkers, or simply indifference—that had defined her as an outsider: "It's like always this attitude that you feel and sometimes is articulated in the things people say or how they respond to you [that] you don't belong there." On the one hand, Jackson's job in an integrated setting and her residence on Manhattan's Upper East Side are evidence of the dissolution of a codified color line that once restricted black-white contact. But in those integrated environments, some whites, through words and actions, erect a boundary that to Jackson implies that "you don't belong."

Interviews with Harlem's black gentry revealed, again and again, an emotional tension arising as they crossed once restrictive boundaries:

> When you're out there getting your tail kicked by people who don't care who you are enough to even call you by the right name, or mistake who you are when you walk into a restaurant or a building, even the one you live in, that's important. That's very important, you know. Blacks have to manage a lot of rage. There's a lot of reasons why we suffer from hypertension and other diseases at a disproportionate rate. That happens to be one of them, in my opinion.

Sociologist Orlando Patterson characterized the resurgence of racism in the 1980s as a result of "homeostasis," that is, continuities that accompany change. In any historic era, this homeostatic principle—the maintenance of relatively stable conditions by internal processes that counteract any departure from the norm—is a means of gauging the persistence of certain features of race relations.

"It comes as no surprise," writes Patterson, "that just as the black working and middle classes began to make some headway under the impact of affirmative action laws, there was an upsurge of direct racism, reflected most crudely in the upsurge of KKK and other neofascist groups as well as the increased number of overt racist attacks (including one unambiguous old-style lynching of a randomly selected working-class black southern youth) but more subtly, and far more dangerously, in the powerful cultural signals given by the Reagan presidency that racist intolerance is once again acceptable."[7]

Increased contact with whites gives rise to encounters with racism and heightens, in a way that would seem to defy expectations, racial consciousness among middle-class blacks. As told in stories about work and home, the rituals of segregation that were once used to maintain social distance and establish positions of superiority and inferiority continue to shape contact between whites and blacks. Social scientists argue that "harsh discrimination against blacks . . . leads blacks to form an 'oppositional social identity' and an 'oppositional cultural frame of reference.'"[8] Fordham and Ogbu identify "beliefs and practices that protect black people's sense of personal identity against insults and humiliations of the dominant white group," such as through "unconventional ways of moving, gesturing, talking and thinking that are viewed as irrational and frightening by whites." The push and pull factors that draw middle-class blacks to Harlem indicate the roots of such oppositional practices and identities.[9]

That Was Then, This Is Now: Symbolism, Romanticism, and the Harlem Renaissance

As middle-class actors in gentrification, the black newcomers in Harlem resemble and differ from their white counterparts. As described by this black gentry, a modern culture of racism persists in occupational and residential settings that accommodate members of the middle class but still feel exclusionary. Maintaining ties to the black community thus provides upwardly mobile blacks with an avenue of identity construction. In that process, Harlem becomes an available symbol to be reappropriated.

The architects of the Harlem Renaissance created an artistic and political movement that would, at best, support the birth of a "New Negro" and a culture that would improve social conditions for blacks in America. But through their construction of Harlem, they also provided an enduring legacy of place. Against the background of the racism elsewhere that Harlem's black gentry describe, racial identity is shaped through tensions of race and class. As a resistance strategy, residents draw on the multiple meanings of Harlem as heaven in order to counter the discrimination that mars their entry into integrated settings.

While Harlem as symbol exerts a powerful pull, the history and meanings these newcomers are drawn to are idealized and revolve around Harlem's past promise. To Harlem's black gentry, the place continues to stand for racial pride. In part, though, the Harlem that they speak of is based on nostalgia:

> Harlem is the most famous African American community in the world, symbolically speaking. So people come here looking for certain things—the 1920s, which I still think is what this whole image rests upon, say from twenties to the fifties, the golden era of Harlem, you know, Sugar Ray Robinson, W. E. B. Du Bois, Langston Hughes, and all these people who were here, in a sense, you know, Uptown. And I think that that's what the whole thing was built from. Duke Ellington, the bands and 125th Street, the Apollo Theater.

As past home to luminary figures—W. E. B. Du Bois, Langston Hughes, and Thurgood Marshall, for example—Harlem is a historical site to be preserved. Drawing upon these memories makes it possible for newcomers to speak of their position in the community in terms of continuity with the past and a sense of responsibility and stewardship:

> So I think for that reason, we ought to be able to understand why we should invest in it our own energies and our own creative efforts. To the degree that we can do that, I think that we should work to help to better the image. I mean, the image has been sullied since the 1920s. It's been really just taking a beating, you know.

The symbolic connection to an artistic past is not lost on Malcolm Balderidge, who says there is a "certain thrill in walking down the streets that Langston Hughes and Malcolm X once walked":

> I used to go to a bar up on 125th Street in the daytime, try to get lost, you know. I met this guy, and he said Langston Hughes used to write here. They had a chair with a plaque on the back—Langston Hughes's chair! This is where Langston Hughes used to sit and write his poems. And I used to sit in that chair sometimes. I felt good sitting in that chair, you know, just sitting in that chair.

Living and writing in Harlem, Balderidge connects with the past even through an object as ordinary as a chair. In this way, he defines himself as part of a continuing artistic presence in the community.

Kenyatta Davis, another writer living in Harlem today, mused on the importance of Harlem to her work as a writer:

> You see such a concentration of black energy here in Harlem—I mean the good and the bad. You know, the very bottom to the very top of it. And artistically it was important for me to have this experience, and I know that's true. I mean, Harlem is a crossroads. So to do your work you have to come here at some point. But I think the main point is that we are here and we are alive and we are vital.

During the Harlem Renaissance, writers like Langston Hughes and Nella Larsen, for example, were intrigued by the "sheer dark size" of Harlem, "teeming with blacks." Like the earlier writers, Davis draws her inspiration, in part, from the concentration of black energy in the community. Asked to define that energy, Davis identified the explosions of color and sound experienced during a simple walk down streets filled with black people "doing their thing." That, she claimed, makes Harlem a unique community:

> And when I first moved here, I was in Brooklyn, and I liked Brooklyn, and it was very interesting living in that milieu—kind of Afro-Caribbean milieu. But still I wanted to come to Harlem and ultimately feel more comfortable here. Because I'm a southern black, and you see more vestiges and more influence from southern black American culture than you do the Caribbean. The churches, for one. I mean people here go to church. There's churches all over, so you get that spirit—in the way that they speak. You hear southern accents. You hear that carry over here. And just the values. But I think mainly the church and the language styles.

As Davis shared her fascination with the Harlem Renaissance writers, she said that "for half my life I knew I would end up here at some point." Davis sees Harlem as a crossroads for the contemporary black artist. Because the production of black culture is no longer restricted to Harlem, there is a shift from the role it played during the Harlem Renaissance. The black artist is still drawn to this Mecca—once a center, now a crossroads.

Seeking a connection to the Harlem Renaissance is not just the provenance of writers and artists. Harlem's cultural history shapes symbolic images connecting past and present for others as well. To George Carver, the symbolism of Harlem is rooted in its past role:

> It clearly has special significance, but only for one reason. To blacks it is the home of the renaissance. It is the cultural center of blacks throughout the

> world. In fact, it describes why I wanted to come back here. I've lived all over this country, and I am very much aware of my cultural heritage. Therefore, that was a draw. I wanted to be in a community where its roots have a black beginning.

Harlem's past clearly holds importance for those who are familiar with it. Carver's claim that the "roots" influenced his move to Harlem suggests the persistence of Harlem's function as a symbolic home:

> The history of the renaissance is something [that] as a black [person] I very much am aware of—who walked these streets and where some of them lived and who they were and what their contributions were.
>
> Harlem is the cultural capital. There's no other place that can claim it. Do we need symbolism? You bet we do. Because as a race we're grasping. That's why we all flocked to Mandela. We need that stability. We need that emotional anchor. That's what's been stripped away from us for four or five hundred years.

Carver sees in Harlem the stage for expressing changing black attitudes:

> What's happening in Harlem is symptomatic of a bigger statement. It's a metaphor. Harlem is a metaphor, and people listen to a lot of things that's happening around the world. Well, I mean, we're talking about blacks being accepted, blacks being comfortable with who they are and what they are, blacks accepting their own culture and their own values. That's what it is. An expression of that may be coming to Harlem.

The symbolic construction of contemporary Harlem is, for this group of middle-class blacks, rife with conceptions of Harlem as a place filled with romance, hope, and pride. Knowledge of the Harlem Renaissance, its writers, and artistic work from the period defines this group as a highly literate class. In part, their notions of Harlem's meaning are derived from this intellectual awareness:

> This is where I wanted to be. I, too, did a lot of reading about the renaissance, and I thought that's what I was coming back into. I think that Harlem still represents many of the things that are built around being black in the United States. And I think that it is a wonderful breeding ground for artists and people who not only want to know about themselves but want to lead lives they would like to lead. What I mean by that is that in Harlem you can be black without any shame. Whether you're wearing dreads or whether you're walking around with a crown, whatever, Harlem is willing to embrace what-

> ever your definition of black is, and all the different things that are a part of that. It's all of the culture, all of that mosaic that [Mayor David] Dinkins is talking about now.

June Wilson was drawn to Harlem by the lure of Harlem's history and African influences. For Wilson, people walking down the streets with their dreadlocks and African-themed clothing are a welcome sight. The ideal community is a Harlem of multiple meanings. "You know, Harlem does represent hope," Wilson points out. "It represents art. Harlem is very quick to embrace all of the things our culture represents. You know, it's kind of the way we keep the flame going when it comes to our culture." And in articulating a vision shared by many of the long-term residents heard in the previous chapter, Wilson and other new arrivals envision Harlem as a resource for maintaining continuity with the past.

The Harlem that exists in their minds is both romantic and real. The romanticism that underscores their shared feelings of promise, though, must be balanced against the realities of today's Harlem. Not an imaginary symbol, a "sullied" Harlem ruptures the idealizing with its hardship and poverty.

The conflict between image and reality in Harlem is apparent in Kenyatta Davis's remarks:

> Of course I had the media image of Harlem as, like, the armpit of the world in terms of crime and drugs and all that kind of thing. So it's not like I had this totally romantic notion of what was here. I understood the reality of what happens across the country with black communities being left to die. So that wasn't a shock.
>
> But then there were the positive things that I was expecting to be here that were here. There are black communities across the country where one might feel safer in terms of crime, but you don't have the positive stuff, like the Schomburg Center for Black Culture, like the Studio Museum, like Liberation Bookstore, Abyssinian Church, you know?

May Dixon also describes a Harlem that is situated between heaven and hell:

> I'm very aware that I'm black, you know, and that is one of the things that happens when you live in Harlem, that you can just sort of relax on that level a little bit more. You don't even have to think of it.
>
> But you think about the things that are negative, too. I mean, of course, I see all those things on the street. And I think about people who consider moving here and moving up here. I mean, you have to have a different kind of

> attitude about life, and you have to be able to sustain a whole lot of stuff. I mean, because it's not just walking by people, kids on the street cussing and carrying on. I mean, but it's just seeing life, you know, sometimes in its rawest form, lived that way, you know.
>
> But it's always seeing, like, the beauty of, you know, the old men sitting on the corner and talking up a storm. Whatever the comment is on the street about whatever is in the news, I mean, hey, you know, you just have to laugh, because you're going to get a different take on it than anybody who'd ever analyzed it that way, you know. And Sunday mornings, the church people, you know, and all that. So I mean, you just have a feeling of belonging somewhere. I mean, I think that probably is what I get most from belonging here.

Greta Symes is an executive with Partners for Choice, a reproductive rights organization. Symes has lived in a brownstone on Sugar Hill for over ten years. "I think Harlem is a cultural symbol," shared Symes:

> There is some romance about these streets that you feel, especially as a resident. When you read Rampersad's Langston Hughes biography and you know that Langston Hughes lived across the street at 66 St. Nicholas Place. And when people talk about how Willie Mays played stickball out here, you know? And 409 Edgecombe is right around the corner, and we know that Walter White lived there. I think Thurgood Marshall lived there, and God only knows who else. So there's that history of the past. I think it's a cultural symbol that transcends geography.

But the dualism of Harlem's meaning causes an ever present rift between longing for the past and confronting the present:

> I don't see Harlem as romantic. I mean this is not romantic out here. Not at all. So sentiment is not the feeling you need to resonate to. There's too much that is hard and poor and difficult for people. You know people are not walking around the streets reciting, "Life for me ain't been no crystal stair." I mean crazy people are walking around here cursing. There's one man who's walking around here saying the weather report all the time because he is totally out of his mind. It's not romantic.

Symes is happily reminiscent about the Harlem of Langston Hughes. But almost in the same breath, she cites Hughes's poem "Mother to Son" to make a contrasting point: that, at the level of the street, life in Harlem is not about poetry or the past.

But some of the meaning Harlem provides—as heaven, hell, or both—is tied to age and experience as well. Brittany Rogers, a young woman who was born and raised in Manhattan, has always lived in integrated neighborhoods and gone to integrated schools. For Rogers, uptown and downtown, in terms of a "hipness" she associates with, means the Upper West Side and Greenwich Village. These are the spaces she identifies when talking about the friends and activities of her high school and university years.

When she first moved uptown, she tells me, she definitely would not have described her family's homesteading experience as the romantic venture of urban pioneers. Nor did she find the appeal of Harlem as heaven. She confesses that what stands out most in her memory of the move is that Harlem was a huge source of embarrassment:

> Hmmmm, it's funny because sometimes people will say, "Where do you live?" and I say, "I live uptown." That's how I start, right. And that was probably more when we first were living here because, I must say, I had a little complex about it. Mainly for me because everyone I knew lived downtown, and I always wanted to live in the Village. Now I've come to see this as our own Village, like our own, like, really interesting cool area.

Besides dodging the question with a vague answer of "uptown," Rogers would also identify the historic Harlem with markers pointing away from its blackness:

> But then—oh, I live uptown. Oh, where? Well, on 144th Street, you know, near City College, that's how I'd start. Oh yeah, it's called, like, Hamilton Grange. Well, what is it? Is it like Harlem? And I'm like, well it's kind of Harlem, but you know Harlem, and I'd go through this whole thing about where the name comes from, from a reluctance to say I live in Harlem. Harlem? Harlem is a Dutch word. . . . And you know, some people went, "Oh. Well, I would rather live in Harlem than Hamilton Grange, it's much more interesting." Harlem encompasses Columbia (and Columbia at one point tried to get rid of the designation that they were in Harlem. They were in Morningside Heights, and Harlem started right after the physics building where the projects were, you know). And if New York is divided into Clinton and Chelsea and all of that, sure then, we live in Hamilton Grange.

As Rogers shares memories from her early days in Harlem, it becomes clear that Harlem, as hell, plays a central role in the definitions of other people by whom she feels wrongly defined:

> In the minds of the popular public we live in Harlem, yeah. And I don't imagine how someone could look at me or my family and think that we lived in a tenement just because I said I lived in Harlem, if that was my concern—what

> people thought of me. But it was an immaturity. It's not politically correct, but this is the conditioning you have. My mom says it's because I'm a snob and that I'm a racist even with my own people. People still get freaked out if I have a party here. Well, how do I get there, Harlem? Now I'm like, you hop the A-train from West Fourth Street, big deal.
>
> But we have been through a sort of transformative process I would say, um, of attitudes because I don't know about your upbringing or anything like that, but the schools that I went to, the way that I was brought up, the things that we did. . . . Um, yes, I am black, right, but my acculturation is, I think, different maybe from the acculturation of the kid out on the street here. And so I have a different set of reactions, and a different set of assumptions and a different set of givens . . . which may not be good, and I may have been, may be, deluded right now as to myself and everything. But all you can do is keep learning and try to control your assumptions or try not to make your assumptions and just try and open things up a little bit more.

Insofar as Harlem plays an important role in her self-definition, it is partially as a source of embarrassment, not pride.

In a highly imaginative form, black middle-class cultural identity comes through an attachment to a system of meaning that signifies a communal life of black America. Harlem's symbolic boundaries provide a racialized space as an alternative to the world of integration. As respondents make clear, there is a racial dilemma of difference experienced within "integrated" work and residential settings that remains largely white. Out of its symbolic meanings, Harlem gives forth an ideology of race consciousness, racial pride, and collective strength. Through history and memory, it offers a chance to invent community. The contradictions of heaven and hell, however, are ever present.

chapter 4

Class Conflict and Harlem's Black Gentry

Strange,
That in this nigger place
I should meet life face to face;
When, for years, I had been seeking
Life in places gentler-speaking,
Until I came to this vile street
And found life stepping on my feet!

Langston Hughes, "Esthete in Harlem"

Brahmin Court is an old apartment building that recalls the architectural grandeur of Harlem's past. A fortress-like building, Brahmin Court commands the corner of 113th Street and Malcolm X Boulevard. The pungent aroma of marijuana surrounds a small group of people lingering on a dusty patch in a litter-strewn park across the way. Tall and narrow abandoned buildings reach skyward, their windows boarded against the sunlight. Here and there, doorways of neighboring buildings have been filled in with concrete blocks to bar trespassers. Passage through Brahmin Court's gate leads into a courtyard that is planted with roses and small trees.

The elevator of Brahmin Court, a new resident tells me, was once filled, along with the building's stairwells, with the odor of urine and feces. But today, a clean, well-lighted elevator carries me up into a sunny ten-room apartment. The rooms' high ceilings add to a spacious feel. Large, boldly painted canvases splashed with thick strokes of oranges, greens, blues, and reds fill the room. Antique furniture and polished hardwood floors grace the warm and comfortable home that Malcolm Balderidge, a writer and professor, and his wife have created for themselves in Harlem. His apartment, within the confines of Brahmin Court, seems worlds away from the beleaguered-looking street.

Such are the contrasts in Harlem that can mark public and private spaces as one passes from neighborhood to home. These contrasts capture symbols of a class distinction that position Harlem's black gentry as different—as middle-class home owners—from many of their neighbors in a poor black community. But even in areas where they have established the pleasant and secure lifestyle that accompanies middle-class home ownership, their experiences are as varied as the diverse Harlem locations in which they have settled.

Indeed, there are at times startling contrasts that distinguish the residences of Harlem's black gentry, depending on the neighborhood. For those who have settled on high on the well-to-do streets of Hamilton Heights, for instance, or in the landmark historic areas of Strivers Row and Mount Morris Park, communities of intact brownstones and pleasant streets are the norm.

The Hamilton Heights area, which sits at the western edge of Central Harlem, is home to City College. The quiet, tree-lined streets of well-preserved brownstones remind one of a suburban aesthetic that usually draws people out of the city. Couples push babies in strollers. A youngster gives training wheels his first spin. Young residents walk dogs and enjoy peaceful evening strolls under the trees. Hamilton Heights, Strivers Row, and Mount Morris Park—Harlem's middle-class enclaves—stand in stark contrast to the image and reality of life in more impoverished areas elsewhere in Harlem.

Those who have moved closer to the "trenches," as one woman labeled her neighborhood, reside in Central Harlem. Here, pockets of pretty homes, streets, and neighborhoods are mixed in among burned-out shells and abandoned buildings, empty lots, and other signs of "inner-city" decay that contribute to the overall image of Harlem as an urban wasteland. In these neighborhoods, class differences between gentry and long-term residents who are not home owners give rise to myriad challenges for the middle-class blacks who have chosen life in the urban ghetto as a supposed chance for racial solidarity.

For successful black professionals, the values of middle-class America—the importance of education, the ideal of home ownership, the work ethic, self initiative, and self-reliance—shape their visions of what life in the community should be. For these actors in the economic restructuring brought on by gentrification, neighborhood and home improvement go hand in hand with the capital investment this group has made.

When cast as a racial drama between blacks and whites, gentrification's class antagonisms can be overlooked. But as agents of economic change, Harlem's black gentry confront an uneasy alliance between symbolism and reality in the community they have been drawn to, in part, for establishing a racial bond. Their conversion of rooming houses and single-room-occupancy buildings to single-family homes, condominiums, and cooperatives in a largely poor community contributes to class conflicts that undercut any depiction of Harlem as a shared heaven.

In striving to establish a middle-class aesthetic within the realm of private property,[1] Harlem's gentry most directly confront the contrasting realities of the place. In spite of desires for racial collectivity, considerations such as material comfort, financial security, and home ownership define the black gentry in Harlem as class actors. At times, it is precisely the motives underlying actions to protect their investment that place them at odds with other members of the community.

But for both groups of newcomers—hill and valley residents—divided opinion over whether to assume the label "gentry" underscores the tensions that accompany economic changes brought by a new middle class, whether black or white, in gentrifying communities. Throughout interviews with black gentry, the range of responses to the question, "Are you gentrifying Harlem?" reveals the complexities of race and class with which this group struggles.

Some black gentry maintain that they see Harlem as "our place," claiming that the move to Harlem strengthens their connections to the black community. Ironically, however, the pressures of the color line this group seeks to erase by moving to a black community are transformed into a class division they must confront once in Harlem. Private battles over gaining occupation of their own houses and establishing rules regarding the use of their properties' stoops eventually spill out into more public spaces of the street and its surrounding blocks. In their search for a haven where they will be accepted among their own race, Harlem's black gentry routinely do battle with residents over change.

The range of voices and experiences that make up this chapter illustrates the ways black gentry negotiate class differences and antagonisms through a racial discourse that downplays the class conflicts inherent in the struggles of gentrification. Instead they want to be seen as a needed "social buffer."

A racial strategy is employed to negotiate the division between who is legitimately a community insider and who does not belong in Harlem. With a discourse shaped by race, they define themselves as a positive force in reclaiming and rebuilding the black community. This is an attempt to reshape the vocabulary of gentrification and rework terminology that contributes to real and perceived class conflicts.

These discursive strategies take a number of forms and fall into the following categories:

1. Other groups are pointed to by way of contrast to underscore their own commitment: whites, blacks not committed to coming, blacks who come but are aloof, the city, and big developers.
2. An older model of diversity within the black community is used to clarify how they envision their role in Harlem today: Blacks have a responsibility to return to their community; in doing so, they are rejoining a black middle class still in Harlem; with their arrival they reestablish needed economic diversity that signals a healthy, as opposed to dysfunctional, black community.

Chapters 4, 5, and 6 explore some of the realities behind this rhetoric of return.

Are We Gentry?

Ruth and Joe Baxter-Brown appear to be "typical" gentrifiers. They are a young couple, both successful journalists for prominent New York publications, in the midst of renovating a Harlem brownstone they have recently purchased. Knowing that I want to talk about their recent brownstone purchase, they jokingly describe themselves as "buppies," offering a black twist on gentrification's prototypical yuppie (young urban professional). It is a move that early on signals that during my interview with them we will discuss race as well as their class position.

We decide to meet one Sunday at Wilson's, a family restaurant on 145th Street—one of the old institutions of Harlem, they tell me when we arrange our interview—so that I can get some of the "flavor" of the community. Over the din of clattering dishes, waitresses bustling, and the maître d' greeting young and old churchgoers dressed in Sunday best, we discuss gentrification in Harlem and how they define their position in the community.

A waitress arrives with menus, and I let the tape player roll. Though the Baxter-Browns do not agree on the definition of gentrification, it becomes clear as they quibble that in spite of a racial similarity, they recognize the highly visible ways in which they are different from many of their neighbors. "Oh, yes. It was a little weird," Ruth Baxter-Brown remembers, describing their early days in the community:

> We went out every day. We dressed up. I mean, we weren't working-class people. It's not that people on my block don't work. Most of the folks on my block work. But we were buppies, you know. He leaves the house in suits, and I leave the house in suits. We both carry briefcases. We're both journalists. We work bizarre hours.

The visible characteristics of the young urban professional make people like the Baxter-Browns a rare enough sight in their neighborhood to give residents pause.

"At first there was a fair amount of resentment about it," Ruth Baxter-Brown confided. "We're bopping out of the house one morning and we kissed each other goodbye and walked off in opposite directions. Our neighbors were, like, dumbfounded." With their suits and briefcases, they also follow a schedule that has its own patterns distinct from, say, blue-collar shift work.

As a young black professional new to Harlem, Kenyatta Davis raised similar issues as she pointed to her downtown publishing job and manner of speech as signals of difference that residents noted when she first moved to Harlem:

> When I start to talk to people on my block, they know that I am not your average resident, you know. They know that I have a quote-unquote gifted job and I work downtown. They ask me what I do. They have no clue of what I do—no understanding. But most blacks don't either.

Often the information gleaned from these early impressions is enough to add to nascent resentment. A woman in a neighboring building who was around Davis's age had studiously eyed her comings and goings. By the time she and Davis spoke, the woman had already decided that Davis would be snobbish:

> I had a kind of strange conversation with the super in the apartment building next to us once because she assumed that I never paid any attention to her and that I did not know her name. And she made some comment about "Well, I know you work downtown" and all that kind of stuff, "and you probably just never even paid attention to me." And I said, "Why do you say that? I know who you are, and your name's Roberta, and you're the resident

> manager. What are you talking about?" And it was like she had been itching to say something to me for a long time, and just found the opportunity.

When she was a high school student, Brittany Rogers moved to Harlem with her younger brother and their parents, who are both musicians. After two years, she entered college and moved downtown to an NYU dorm. There, her mother tells me, "she had only white punk people for friends." During the time she lived in Harlem and later during visits with her parents, Rogers noticed that she and her bohemian family attracted attention:

> As to being gentry, yeah, I feel different from the neighbors, and I don't know whether it's a matter of education or if it's a class thing. We're professionals. A lot of people around here are not professionals. I mean, I get funny looks when I'm walking the dog. So I know people notice us.

These reactions are an indication of how far Harlem has moved from its roots as a mixed-income black community. Class differences would be apparent although not necessarily remarkable in an earlier, segregated era. The new influx of blacks brings diversity lost to a patterned flight out. Attention paid to their language, schedules, pets, and other small details signals to gentry that they are not only visible but also scrutinized by neighbors.

Viewed in terms of money, jobs, and eccentric fashion sense, these black newcomers also bring with them habits of urban and suburban life that are seen as odd in the ghetto. Rogers and Portia Hamilton remember comments that could mean anything from insult to bemusement to shock over their manner of dress:

> I've been called bigfoot for wearing big boots or kind of downtown stuff. When I used to come back and visit and my hair was dyed purple, at times I got a lot more attention. But now the styles have crossed over so much.

> I go outside in the morning in my pajamas and my bathrobe and I'll move my car. Someone said, "Ms. Hamilton? You're the only one I know who would come out in your bathrobe." I'm just bringing the suburbs to the city, honey. I'm home. It's OK.

With their urban hip and suburban casual, a young college student and a former Scarsdale housewife attract notice and elicit comments as they import custom and fashion, revamping modes of style within Harlem's streets.

But the differences that make black gentry visible in the community are not noted simply because of what is seen as new or odd behavior. Hostile and suspicious responses to this group's differences are also reflected in the negative terms used to link gentrification with a feared white invasion, speculation, and residential displacement.

Malcolm Balderidge argues that the heightened visibility of middle-class consumption accounts for the hostility that greets the black gentry's arrival. As apartments begin to change hands, residents in a marginal community take note of competition for this newly coveted resource in their immediate surroundings:

> The other people are beginning to see that, but at the same time, it's a little anger. Because they've been lied to for so long and here's people like myself have come in. We're making some bread. We get the best apartments that they weren't even thinking about. They didn't even know what was up in here, you know. So then that makes them a little angry, which I can understand. You got this division, in a sense, in an area like this, between people who have some money and people who don't have some money. You know, that's what happened. You got that division and that friction although it's not as heavy as some of the papers make it out to be. But these people have money, those people don't have money, so there's this friction.

Claiming that media attention fuels class antagonism by playing up friction between haves and have-nots, Balderidge nonetheless draws sharp lines himself. He describes a changing building whose occupants, "these" and "those" people, coexist in a tense moment of transition. Apartments are won by those of "us" with knowledge and resources, and lost by "them," those without or who have been lied to.

Joe Baxter-Brown also sees this brewing conflict between haves and have-nots, a fact he says is rooted in the changing real-estate market. Baxter-Brown was born in Harlem and lived on 145th Street until the age of five, when he and his family moved to a Connecticut suburb. Because he left at such a young age, Baxter-Brown does not consider himself a Harlem insider. And over the loud protests of his wife, he tells me that he deems "gentrifier" to be an apt description of his new position in the community: "We have more money and better jobs than most of the people who live on our block. We moved in and they think we are very strange."

But Ruth Baxter-Brown, a native of Chicago, grew up in a community of blacks in the Sojourner Truth housing project. This fact, she argues, makes her no stranger to a black neighborhood. She feels strongly that gentrification is an incendiary issue and urges caution in applying the term.

While a community rhetoric years in the making has it that gentrification would amount to a white takeover, there is divided opinion on the issue of black participation in gentrification. Race does not guarantee that middle-class black newcomers will be regarded differently than whites.

Anthony Rogers, a musician who was raised in Harlem, returned to a brownstone with his wife and two children in 1984. Rogers thinks neither race nor class is the issue. An initial reserve toward any newcomers signals the customs and established habits of a close-knit community:

> They didn't talk to us when we moved on the block. Like the old black people that live here for years and years, you know, you're a new person so they wait to see who you are before you get involved. Before they get involved with you.

Once neighbors figure out who you are, what you're all about, why you live here, and how much interaction they want with you, Rogers reasons, they will signal their welcome, whether you happen to be black or white.

"Most of our neighbors," Joe Baxter-Brown confesses, "couldn't really, like, figure out that we were for real." He continues, "You know, I don't think you set yourself apart, but I think your circumstances set you apart. It's nothing that you consciously do."

As for the notion that he and his wife were not "for real," Baxter-Brown concedes that their move is viewed suspiciously because of perceptions that actors in the gentrifying real-estate market will pursue class interests that place them at odds with the community and its interests.[2]

In Harlem, what repeatedly has been articulated as a racial fear of a white takeover masks the more immediate changes in class composition. Housing speculation in Harlem, for instance, will mean that brownstones are bought and sold, stimulating market activity. But these houses will remain uninhabited as owners postpone occupation, awaiting further economic change to sweep the area. Another common practice called "flipping" leads to property investments that are rapidly turned over for profit.

George Carver, recounting the history of his house, notes that it was divided up as a rooming house in the 1940s. It had been abandoned and unoccupied, he estimates, for "roughly ten or fifteen" years. But as a sign of how quickly turnover can happen where there is faddish interest in brownstones, the house held two sets of occupants in the 1980s alone:

> So, that's the way it was up until a black, Harvard-trained, middle-class couple, MBAs both, bought this house, with the idea of gentrifying it. They bought it, and it had been empty for a while. And you couldn't live in it, but they lived in it. They chose to live in it. They cleared out a space—I don't know how anybody could live like that—on one of the floors, and that's the way they

> camped, and did that for two or three years. And then she got pregnant. At the same time, they made a lot of money in the commodities market. And so they said, hey, we don't need all this sawdust and we don't have to go through this, let's get the hell out of here. So they bought a house upstate, and they've become real middle class.

In the space of a decade, these two "Harvard MBAs" took the initial step in gentrifying the property. The Carvers purchased the brownstone and took over further restoration, becoming merely the fourth occupants, living among ghosts of those long since displaced.

Others participate in gentrification by investing in houses that they occupy but without making an investment in the community. These gentrifiers are barely seen as they come and go. They largely structure their lives outside of Harlem—or as an invisible presence within the community.

Conscious of criticisms that the absent home owner offers little for the community, June Wilson insists that her presence—and connection with people in her neighborhood—means she is not a gentrifier. Wilson contrasts herself to the "disconnected home owner" she describes as a nonpresence in the community:

> I'd like to see myself or at least describe myself as a part of a move to bring Harlem back to life. I think my intent is a little bit more than just buying property and living downtown and not knowing people.

In a community where close ties and familiarity with one's immediate environment are important, those who center their lives downtown and do not know people are viewed with hostility by others in the community.

Another fear accompanying newly visible class differences in this gentrifying community is that residential renovations and community improvements will inevitably refashion Harlem into a preserve of an upper-income elite. For long-term residents who imagine that the preferences of gentry will not include a desire for class diversity, newly visible class differences fuel fears that even black gentry are harbingers of class displacement:

> Yeah. I also know that some of my neighbors resented and feared my being here, feared me coming here and putting hundreds and thousands of dollars in this house. Because they're afraid that their tax base is going to go up.

George Carver points out that despite the fact that repopulating Harlem's abandoned buildings is a goal of many of his neighbors, there is fear over how far an elite class will go with its home and property improvements.

Having kept family homes, sometimes for forty or fifty years, elderly brownstone owners fear they will be priced out of the neighborhood.

Carver agrees that fears are justified, but he also holds limited sympathy:

> It's a valid concern, because that person who happens to live on this block owns that place, and it's been in their family for years and years. And when people come in and do what I've done and it's more than they have, they fear gentrification and focus on that. You'll find a lot of people here afraid for no reason other than their own economics, of people coming here changing the tax base. In conversation, you find out they really want to keep the status quo. But, three years later, their taxes didn't go up.

Carver's remarks suggest that in Harlem one of gentrification's class conflicts is a struggle for survival waged between different generations of black home owners.

Anthony and Mimi Rogers looked at housing listings in the *New York Times* when they searched for a Harlem brownstone. They also tapped into a network of elderly neighbors. The older generation of Harlem home owners provided access to an intergenerational turnover in the housing market:

> We started looking and looking. We started talking to elderly people who had these homes, saying like, "Gee, we're buying a house, and we could live downstairs, we wouldn't put you out." A lot of them were really frightened that the only thing that they really had would be gone . . . and some people had fallen back on paying their taxes so the city was getting ready to take their home. So therefore, they were selling dirt cheap so the city just wouldn't get it. And people were making arrangements so that they could still live there until . . . we're talking about seventy-, eighty-, ninety-year-olds, mostly women. You know, like really nice folks.

The network strategy used by the Rogers family shifts ownership from one generation of black middle-class home owners to a younger generation on their way up from the Upper West Side. Arrangements to avoid displacement of elderly residents by keeping them as tenants is a way to ease this intergenerational transition in Harlem. But for families that would use brownstone space for studios or work space or to generate rental income, this would not prove profitable.

Malcolm Balderidge disputes the notion that the middle-class gentry is laying the groundwork for class displacement. Instead, he argues that class diversity is an asset:

> I don't care how much money they make. So I disagree with the concept. I don't mind living in a neighborhood which is very varied in terms of incomes. I'm not interested in the fact that I have to live with a lot of people who have money, you know, I'm not really interested in that. I don't mind living next door to a guy who is a garbage collector or who don't have a job. You know, it doesn't bother me to live next door to a guy who drives a bus. In our co-op situation, we made sure that old people could stay here and that they could buy in at a low enough rate so people could retain their homes.

Balderidge sets a scenario in which occupational differences are a neighborhood fact of life. Then he points to what he considers an acceptable form of displacement:

> If there was people in here that was detrimental to the building, like junkies, like people dealing drugs, we tried to run them out. Just like anybody else. Just like many white people would do. . . . I don't want him to be a junkie. I don't want him to be a wino who breaks bottles in the hallway. I don't want him like the guy who used to be here, some mysterious idiot in this building who was shitting up on the eighth floor. And when you come out on a beautiful day like today, and you're going out and you just had a nice morning. And you walk out and there's a shit smell. I don't want that. I don't want the guy peeing in the elevator who we had here for a while until we tried to run him out. He hasn't been back for a while. I don't want that.

Other black gentry also are hesitant to associate themselves with the terminology of gentrification. Etta Harrison, who has lived in Harlem since 1980, argues that a problem with such terminology is that it does not distinguish between black and white gentrification. Talking about the recent arrival of a black middle-class family on her block, she identifies this difference:

> Because I consider him someone who has a family who is looking for good housing and finding an opportunity to do that. I mean, maybe it's just the term that I have problems with, and I think that that's primarily it. Because when I think of gentry, and I think of the people or the "class of people" who are supposed to represent gentry, I think of them being out in the suburbs, primarily—and maybe a very small number of them deciding that they were urban animals, and they're going to move into the city and, you know, live in beautiful brownstones. But what I see is that there is no sense of community. I don't see them participating in the community, going to the churches in the community, or even shopping in the community.

Community participation, then, largely defines the black and white difference that Harrison describes. And, Harrison argues, the arrival of a new black middle-class population simply reflects a continuing tradition of a black elite living in Harlem:

> And we see the neighborhood changing. I just think that you have the same people who've always lived here, being replaced by similar-type people, you know. People with families, only middle-class black folks who want to live in Harlem, you know.

Speculation, displacement, and class warfare are loaded terms in community rhetoric and media attention. Black gentry carry contradictory attitudes about the gentrification process in Harlem. But with answers that produce reworked definitions or outright denials, this group makes it difficult to test the claim that as gentry, blacks play a different role than do middle-class whites.

Well into my Sunday morning interview with Ruth and Joe Baxter-Brown, we pick from plates brought to the table loaded with generous portions of eggs, grits, sausage links, strips of bacon, and toast. We cover a lot of ground, but throughout our interview, the Baxter-Browns return again and again to my initial question: "Are you gentrifying Harlem?" At one point, Ruth Baxter-Brown agrees there is gentrification, but she distinguishes between what she calls black and white gentrification. Black gentrification is different, she claims, making an argument similar to Etta Harrison's:

> Harlem's going to be gentrified—it depends on people's motivation for living up here, I think. Some people moved up here because it was cheap. I always wanted to live up here. My father used to talk about Harlem when I was a kid. I grew up in Chicago, and my dad used to talk about Harlem, and I always wanted to live here. So I like Harlem, and I, you know, I'd want to live here. A lot of people live here because they figured it was a way to make a fast killing in real estate.

Citing her prior knowledge and desire, Ruth crafts an argument around these two defining traits of blacks and whites in the Harlem real-estate market. She claims that because she likes Harlem and would live here anyway, her presence signals something more than a cold, market calculation.

Her husband agrees, in part, but is not so dismissive about the role of economics and the market in his decision making:

> Was there any of that for me? My reason for living up here was that it was cheap. I mean, you know, frankly, if I could have afforded to live someplace else, I probably would have. I mean, you know, I was born in Harlem. I stayed here until I was five. My parents moved to the suburbs. Ruth and I came back because, you know, like my relatives were here, my father had his office here. So, it's not like I was any stranger to it, you know.

Joe expresses a preference to be elsewhere that is unmet because of financial constraints. But he also claims that a birthright, along with family connections, gives him an advantage over whites with similar economic resources or restraints:

> So I mean, if we could have enough money to go someplace else, we probably just would have gone, but we didn't. I mean, that's the fact. That's the advantage you have over white folks. But if you're looking for a place to live, you have an entire city to look at. White people don't, because they're not going to come here.

Joe argues that even with his limited resources, because he does not view the black community as off-limits, he holds an advantage that *broadens* his options. At this point, his wife is quick to object. She takes issue with what Joe describes as the couple's broader options in searching for a home: "Yeah, but we don't have an entire city to look at. I mean, we didn't go look in Canarsie. I mean, we could, but . . ."

Contrasting Canarsie,[3] a white ethnic enclave, with Harlem, she argues that as black shoppers in the real-estate market, she and Joe face more *limited* options. But she wavers and then hesitates as she acknowledges that, in fact, her options are as broad as the entire city (at least according to laws upholding equal opportunity housing).

Before she has a chance to finish her thought, Joe jumps in and takes up the position his wife used to begin her argument: desire: "Yeah, we could. Especially now, we could. We just wouldn't want to."

While they fail to agree on the terms of this debate, Ruth and Joe touch on family, history, and desire as they struggle to articulate their role in Harlem's unfolding social drama. With their contradictory opinions about what constitutes gentrification, the Baxter-Browns, a young "buppie" couple, capture an uncertainty and unease that are evident among other black gentrifiers in Harlem.

The spaces that make up the interiors and exteriors of their new lives provide possible clues to the sources of this unease. The nooks and crannies of an aging brownstone, along with the stoops and courtyards of houses and apartment buildings, are the more localized and immediate battleground of the move home to Harlem.

Displacement, Owner Occupation, and Territorial Struggles for Control

By 1963, when Chester Himes declared Harlem to be like a "cancer on the body of a nation," a spiral of deterioration and disinvestment had been years in the making. From the 1930s to the 1960s, Harlem's declining social conditions were mirrored in the fall of its image as a magnificent city within a city. Where it became increasingly difficult to find meaning in Harlem as a promised land, or heaven, a new symbolic vocabulary was crafted. The dualism of Harlem as heaven and hell was born. Yesterday and today, Harlem's promise exerts a magnetic pull, as we discussed in earlier chapters.

Curiously, upon arrival, Harlem's black gentry assert their rights of home ownership through the symbols of Harlem as a bastard child. Filled with a distinct sense of purpose, they gut structures, renovate, and announce a middle-class presence by reappropriating this other Harlem vocabulary of garbage, ill smells, madness, bowels, decay, and vermin.

In their narrative accounts about gentrification, black gentry suggest that restoring the community to its former glory requires repossession and domestication. When describing their preservation efforts, Harlem's gentry identify themselves, implicitly and explicitly, as gritty and determined settlers, or as homesteaders and urban pioneers. Through this vocabulary, they invoke a "frontier mythology" that Neil Smith identifies as one of the central symbols and myths of gentrification:

> The social meaning of gentrification is increasingly constructed through the vocabulary of the frontier myth. This appropriation of language and landscape—the city as new frontier—seems at first playfully innocent . . . [B]ut this frontier imagery is neither merely decorative nor innocent, it carries considerable ideological weight. [A] frontier ideology rationalizes social differentiation and exclusion as natural and inevitable. [It] justifies monstrous incivility in the heart of the city.[4]

Cloaked in a language of combating dirt and uncleanliness, along with pathology and deviance, the ideals of the new Harlem home owner are to restore community order, stability, and health through renewal, a fresh renaissance. Black gentry claim that as class and race actors, theirs is both an individual and a collective goal. Here their narratives are constructed around realities found at an uneasy meeting point between racial ideals and class aspirations.

Associating a mentally healthy future with the absence of blight, George Carver remarks that as a new home owner, his "only complaint, to be honest, [is] I don't like the blight in every direction. That's depressing over time. I'll be glad when the day comes when that's gone. That will be gone someday."

Carver uses the passive voice to describe changes he awaits. But by viewing his house, like the homes and stoops of other black gentry, we gain insight into the class motives behind actors who impose such changes. He, along with Malcolm Balderidge, Mimi Rogers and her family, Portia Hamilton, Kenyatta Davis, and Ruth and Joe Baxter-Brown, plays more than a passive role in removing "blight."

Establishing residence in a new brownstone is least disruptive when property directly changes hands from an owner-occupant to a new owner. There are no tenants to dislodge. Renovations, unless desired, can be minor. Yet, clues about the class differences between new gentry and those they replace are deeply rooted in these homes:

> Hey, go behind some of these beautiful facades and you see blight. OK? I wouldn't live in those houses like the one that I bought and that a family lived in. I mean, there's blight on the other side of these walls. So, what you see isn't all good. That facade has just appreciated in value because people like me came in and got it, you know, and developed it. And the word got out, "Oh, that's pretty good. What's going on up there?" But two-thirds of these houses here, you know, you may or may not want to live in.

Carver's mission is to break down the distance between a beautiful facade and the blight that lies on the other side. Carver uses the logic of capital to rationalize this restoration effort. He reasons that where blight interferes with residential space that, by his standards, is habitable, there is little value in these houses. His capital investment is directly responsible for a beauty that is incomplete, if it is a mask for blight.

In the following series of remarks, Malcolm Balderidge describes a similar middle-class sensibility that he and neighbors at Brahmin Court have imprinted on their immediate environment. Balderidge points out a locked gate that now provides security and privacy for residents of the cooperative. This and the rose-planted courtyard, he says, are signs of successful attempts to seize control of their space:

> People like myself who have moved into the neighborhood want to see things happen. First of all, for selfish reasons. They are just like any other property owner, you know. They want to see the value of their property go up. We're buying these apartments, and, on an economic level, you want to see it go up rather than go down. I mean, that's just basic stuff. People who had the good sense to invest want to see their stuff go up. They want to see some nice things around here. So they're willing to work for that, you see. And that makes a whole lot of difference.

Balderidge points to an economic logic of investment and common sense to describe actions by new owners as "rational." Identifying those neighbors who hold a shared interest in property values, Balderidge links himself to a collective set of actors whom he can depend on to work toward the goals he holds:

> You can live in this building, which is kind of getting to be an oasis. When we first moved here, it was winos and junkies and everything in that courtyard. The gate wasn't locked. It was dirty with bottles broken, shooting dope in the corners, and, you know, everything. You could find everything in here. And now you can see, it's calm, you know, the courtyard is clean. And so we've had something to do with that.

One result of their rational action—putting a lock on the gate—is to overturn the status quo. The building is described as an oasis, a victory that is measured in the new middle-class boundaries that have been imposed. The derelicts and junkies stand for an old order that is no longer rational.

While George Carver has crafted a more livable space behind his own building's facade, he cautions others who have caught wind of gentrification in Harlem not to be fooled by appearances. Carver disassociates his rehabilitation from larger, more sweeping change by pointing it out as an isolated example. Like Brahmin Court, his building serves as an oasis. While the exteriors of other homes in Harlem may appear to be the same as Carver's, another reality, he suggests, lies behind them:

> Somewhere around the thirties and forties, the rooming house thing happened. Ceilings were lowered, false ceilings were put there, all the fireplaces were plugged. And rooms were chopped up into little rooms. Like this floor, for example, had two bedrooms and a common bathroom and a kitchen. The basement, which was two feet lower than what you see—I dug two feet of dirt out of that—was one common bathroom, one basement, and one little bedroom. The next floor that I live on, I mean the master suite, was another com-

> mon kitchen, a living area, a common bathroom, and two little rooms. The top floor had these two little teeny rooms. There were I don't know how many people living there, but it was certainly more than what it was zoned for.

Through the history of his house, Carver provides clues about at least two different periods of prior occupation. With higher ceilings, larger undivided spaces, and heating provided by multiple fireplaces, his old brownstone was most likely a residence for the white gentry class that occupied Harlem before its ascension to queen of the black belts.

In the 1930s, when the black population was around two hundred thousand, the houses were refashioned for an entirely different population. Ceilings were lowered, walls were inserted, and fireplaces were plugged—the luxuries of the urban aristocracy were no longer available. Renters replaced owners. Spaces were smaller and more confined. The number of residents within the house increased. Kitchens and bathrooms were shared. A single-family home held communal spaces shared by families, friends, and strangers. The subdivided whole pulled in multiple sources of capital. Clusters of residents crowded themselves beyond capacity to afford the rent.[5]

The passage of years, along with scant regulation and lax maintenance, led to the deterioration that Carver wants to erase. Where zoning rules may have been overlooked, Carver reverses conditions of lawlessness with his private reinvestment of capital.

To restore order to their own building, Brahmin Court's residents removed garbage. They replaced bottles and trash with rosebushes and trees. Armed with shovels and brooms, they cleared debris from the courtyard. A cast of human characters that included winos, junkies, men who urinate and defecate in public is swept from view. The mission of the new residents was to reinstate cleanliness and calm. Described as a derelict urban environment, the courtyard was ridden with vice, in part, because a gate was left open.

With their injection of capital, gentry reversed the disinvestment. The gate is now locked. Security is in place, making for a new reign of law and order. The new middle-class owners signal that external spaces such as this need to be reclaimed as the next frontier between their luxury apartments and the world outside.

Behind the facade of George Carver's brownstone, evidence of prior class transition and displacement within Harlem is already in place. Poised to reach back through the decades, Carver will push aside the blighted present. Hammer blows to the interior of the rooming house felled walls and ceilings and dismantled floors. Wide-open space gives way to the past:

> I came in with the intent of gutting it. Now, I put in what I could save, I mean, I saved every piece of original detail that was salvageable. Everything else is new. So you see old and new mixed here. And I took out walls. I don't like the traditional brownstones, you know, which are very narrow spaces. So I used the whole width of the house, you know, and opened it up. That room had a wall to it. So it now is a nice-sized room. And what I had to, I restored, and I brought back things.

The fact that the brownstone was caught up in an earlier wave of urban abandonment and succession challenges the notion that there are rightful and natural inhabitants of this property. The building houses a number of histories. Carver's own efforts to salvage and restore are a way to dislocate blight and replace it with "original detail."

Where that is not possible, Carver has moved beyond the building's current status to a blend of old and new. By his own hand, stripping and sanding, he has chipped away until interior and exterior are more in line with his middle-class tastes and means:

> My mother was a housekeeper. You know what I'm saying? And I didn't come up with a silver spoon. I've washed dishes, and I know where I'm from. I operate under no illusion. I mean, look at this house. This is 3,800 square feet. You can't find that in Manhattan, you know. And I want to live here until I don't need it anymore. You know what I'm saying? In a society where everything's been fast track, I like the fact that I can come here and chip away the paint and strip it and find tile and oak like this. And Harlem makes it accessible to me as a black. Because I couldn't afford a house like this on the East Side. Economics would keep me away from it. I don't want to put two million dollars in a house, you know.

Through effort, sweat, and money, Carver realizes his dream. He refashions a home of widened rooms. When the corporate workday is done, this black executive takes up residence in the master suite with its raised ceilings.

Carver knows that his restoration is yet another rehabilitation story adding to concerns about gentrification in Harlem. Will the absence of one more multiunit structure pave the way for a faster grab for the remaining brownstones?

But Carver did not move into an *occupied* rooming house. When he is asked whether his efforts result in other blacks being pushed out of the community, he hesitates, then gives this response:

> Which blacks? The ones that are—excuse me—urinating on the stoops, you know, aren't here really anyway. They're here because there's less hassle. But

> they don't own homes. They're not being displaced from homes. The fact that there's forty, fifty, sixty thousand units here that are boarded up and owned by the city, you know. I mean, you're not displacing anybody. There was no black living here that I kicked out to do this.

Residential displacement is a concern predating his arrival, he reasons. Here, Carver relies on broad (and imprecise)[6] statistics about the number of empty properties in Harlem. Thus, Carver can locate his new occupancy in a Harlem that has plenty of space. This logic allows him to sidestep direct responsibility for contributing to displacement.

Carver also makes references to people who are "not really here," and shifts blame to "the city." The realities of displacement are rationalized through a dichotomy—those who belong and those who do not: "Half the empty brownstones are owned by the city here. So, we're talking about a theoretical thing that's only an emotional buzzword. It's not real."

Malcolm Balderidge similarly dismisses the notion of displacement:

> The concept of gentrification, I think I don't like the concept. It seems to mean that you throw out people, the people who were here before. And then you come and you do something and you throw the rest of them out. And you keep doing that and you keep throwing people out. I mean, that's what I get out of it. I'm not interested in throwing out people, I'm not interested in that.

Balderidge goes on to describe a "democratic" process in which an absentee landlord in his building was simply outvoted by new tenants after the building's conversion:

> This guy had a large apartment, had a roomer in every room, so he was making all this money on the apartment. I don't mind him making money if they was going to be cool. But when they start fighting and not caring about the place and tearing it all down. You go up and say, "Listen, we're going to tell the IRS. We're going to tell the IRS that you lied on your income tax. Either you control these people or we going to tell the IRS on you. Because we don't feel like you doing this building any good. It's not us personally, I'm talking about the collective whole, the collective good will of the building. You are not doing it any good. You're making some money but you ain't even staying here so you don't have to put up with these fools. So you either get rid of them—we'll give you a couple of months or so—or we telling the IRS. And I know you don't want to be audited." I mean, it was like that. People might say that's gestapo. Somebody said you're ruining that guy's livelihood. I said, well, I don't care. I don't care about me ruining his livelihood. I do not care. I told him to his face I don't care I'm ruining his livelihood. I don't think he's doing

> the collective whole of this building any good, the collective interest of this building any good. So it's the collective versus him. So we all feel that he should not do this. I don't care. So it's just democratic. He was outvoted. You see?

Using the threat of the IRS, the collective wields its own might to impose a new code of conduct.

Balderidge repeatedly notes that complaints were lodged by the group, or collective, not by any single resident. But it is important to remember that while his allies form a collective, it is one that is made up of individuals as apartment owners. And their conflict seems not to be so much with renters per se but rather with another owner in the building.

As individual owners of spacious new apartments, it does not suit their tastes to take their chances on who will live side by side with them. While they each have chosen to occupy ten rooms and more of the spacious apartments, another of these "luxury" apartments is converted to a rooming house. The new owners have personal and aesthetic demands for the space they now occupy, which an absentee landlord cannot share. As owners with a united voice, the new cooperative uses a collective class power that is unavailable to renters who could themselves be ousted for complaining against their landlord. The absentee landlord holds some responsibility for ousting people according to a shifting preference for types of rental neighbors:

> I want clean people who have an interest in the building, who are interesting people, who are nice people, who don't fight and scream all night long and beat up their wives or the wives beat their asses. Or, you know, beat up their kids and, you know, throw garbage in the hallways. I don't want that.

As both Balderidge and Carver have told it, displacement, when it occurs, happens to "nonpersons." Even then, it occurs at the hands of someone else. Or it is held up as an example of a collective will. The lines of difference used to define exclusion draw a distinction between themselves and undesirable blight. By employing such reasoning, it is easy to depict charges of displacement as irrational. Sometimes the concept is dismissed altogether.

But another more immediate reality exists. Displacement can be found where rooming house occupants still occupy newly attained private homes. New owners take possession of houses and buildings that are populated by tenants of subdivided spaces who pay little to no rent. Winos, young students, single mothers on public assistance, elderly singles, crack users, and prostitutes turning tricks in the subdivided rooms within the property do not suit the ideals of house and home imagined by many gentry.

A Tale of the Swiss Family Robinson—They're Black, but That's Not a Problem, Is It?

On my second visit to their house, Mimi Rogers and her daughter Brittany show me photos that document the early days of their family's Harlem adventure. Together, the entire Rogers family did the work of renovating a turn-of-the-century brownstone. The photos, neatly arranged in glossy sleeves, take me back eight years with them to their early days of "homesteading" in Harlem.

"And this is how we lived," Mimi begins her narration, pointing to the first several pictures. An eviscerated space, the first floor of the brownstone is gutted. The internal organs of the house dangle all around. "This is our bathroom," she continues. "Oh yeah, this is a picture of the little kitchen, the wee wee kitchen. We used to have a little kitchen on a cart that we would wheel around. But Brittany, we survived. We were princesses, OK? My God, this is like a lifetime ago."

Mimi and her family came to Harlem in 1984. Pushed by a burst of market activity in their former neighborhood, they moved uptown from Ninetieth Street. Rising downtown prices simply put an affordable home purchase out of their reach. Spurred on by the growing media hype about gentrification in Harlem, this family of urban pioneers explored possibilities in markets beyond Manhattan's Upper West Side:

> Well, at one point in time—the *New Yorker,* the *Times,* in magazines—all the articles were going that this was the up-and-coming area. People were buying. You could see on the front pages in the living section, white people buying, buying, buying. But this is where you can get a piece of the rock for a little bit of money. These houses were going for $50,000, $45,000. They weren't even up to $75,000 or $100,000 at that time. We started looking at other co-ops first, and they were outrageous, and they weren't even as much room as we had had. We had a great apartment on Ninetieth Street, I mean it was fabulous. We could not move out of the city so we had to look within the border of the city.

Although market activity had displaced them from the Upper West Side, Mimi and Anthony Rogers were not ready to leave the city altogether. The Rogerses wanted to keep their commuting time and distance to a minimum. And, Mimi explains, they also needed to stay close to the private schools where their children were already enrolled. So the Rogers family set their sights north and made the trek uptown:

> So Anthony, being, you know, he's very adventurous, said, let's look uptown. Also, my niece had gotten married at that point, and she was living on 122nd

> Street. She's not there now, OK? As soon as we moved, she left. But she said, you know, it's not that bad, we should come up and look at the houses, they're great. So we started to get the *New York Times,* and we started looking at properties. And I hated it. So much work needed to be done. I mean, the houses that we were looking at.

For Mimi, the idea that she would ever end up home in Harlem was beyond her comprehension. Her husband is from Harlem, she says, explaining that for him the move represents a "smart investment" and a way to return home. But not for her:

> I hated it. I hated it. I don't hate it as much as I did. I didn't want to live in a community of poor blacks. I hated it. For Anthony, he didn't hate it. He loved it. It was like coming back home for him. But it wasn't coming home for me. I never lived here. And there wasn't any way that I thought that I would ever live in Harlem, ever in my life.

Mimi is from an interracial family. She grew up in Queens. As a married adult she has grown accustomed to living with her husband and their two children in communities with only "a sprinkling of other blacks." In the following account, she relates an episode from childhood that reminds her when and how she began to establish differences between herself and other blacks in Harlem:

> My uncle used to take my girlfriend and I in patent-leather shoes and little white gloves to Harlem every Sunday morning, kicking and screaming, so that we could see how other—our people—this is terrible—just to see that these were our sisters and brothers and these were our people and this is how they lived. And we used to go kicking and screaming. It was like, this is not us, you know, these are not, this is not us. So then to actually say we're going to live here . . .

Mimi's feelings about her 1984 move to Harlem extend back to childhood, where they were partially shaped. This neat compartmentalization of racial space is at easy reach. Worked through a child's eye, this logic is simple and follows her later into life. This would be the basis of insecurity about how family and friends would view crossing that line:

> My father said, you're crazy. It's a giant step backwards. Here you're trying to step ahead and you've done great so far and now you're moving to an area that people are not going to want to come see you. You're not going to want to give people your address. It was devastating. And for my friends, it was like, what is she doing? And I didn't want to tell people I live in Harlem.

The upward mobility that defines Mimi has acquainted her with the mores of neighborhoods where she and Anthony, along with their children, take for granted they will be in the minority. Feeling displaced herself, Mimi has lost something in the rite of passage that redirects her away from "success." That loss will never be found in a community her father defines as a "step down."

Mimi retells this story with a grave look on her face. Her hands are shaking. It is clear that attitudes about skin color, money, status, and professional standing have helped lay the groundwork for a series of boundaries she will erect when she arrives in Harlem. These lines of distinction are based on values conveyed to her through the family and friends in her interracial life. But Mimi has moved to Harlem, so perhaps she does not see these values as absolute. In fact, on each of the three days I interview her, she talks about incremental changes she noticed in herself as she loosened up and got on speaking terms with people on her street. That retelling the story has her so shaken suggests, however, that she is not completely free from others' notions about race:

> I hated it, OK? We're not talking about a princess growing up, but someone that came up in a family that the men did all of the hard work—like mowing the lawn. I mean, the stuff that my husband has put us through has made us, yes, better people, and we could survive. My children are better people for what we've been through. I have never in my whole entire life done anything like this. My whole life with Anthony has been an adventure. And a lot of it has been great, and a lot of it has been devastating. Anyway, I don't know if you saw *The Mosquito Coast*? That was us but like ten times worse.

Mimi repeatedly describes her husband as an adventurous type. While she may not be as adventurous as Anthony, the film version of Paul Theroux's *Mosquito Coast* lets Mimi create a mental script she can place herself into. In the film, Harrison Ford plays Allie Fox, a man who relocates his family to a Central American jungle to escape civilization. Once there, he proceeds to build a survival machine and make a go at bringing civilization to the jungle.

How to bring order to the chaos of her own family's restoration project was a big worry for Mimi. The pioneering image is a handy response to a disrupted sense of self in her family role of wife and mother. The narrative frame provided by the daring film family provides Mimi with a way to rethink the whole experience. She goes along with her husband's "free-spirited" plan for the renovation project but on her own terms:

> You know what it was? It was an adventure. It was like he made it sound like it was going to be fun. I mean, we're going to have a piece of the rock, and it's

> going to be a stepping-stone. And if we don't do it now, we're not going to have a million dollars to do it later on. We didn't do it before because like, you know, twenty or thirty thousand dollars, you know, it was a lot of money. So now it's a little bit more, but at least it's within our reach.

At $50,000 the brownstone is an affordable option for the Rogers family. Brittany echoes the economic logic of her mother when she jumps into the conversation. She explains her family's experience through the eyes of a daughter, a student, an artist, and a global traveler:

> It's very expensive to live in New York. And we were lucky to get this house as a place to live and as a place that we can have and that my parents can give to me and that I hope that we'll have for a long time. My father sometimes thought of it as a way of getting back to his youth or to the old neighborhood. And I think with immigrants that's a different kind of thing—wanting to belong to that one place where you first came to. His mother came from Haiti, and his grandmother came from the Dominican Republic. They moved into this neighborhood which primarily was Irish at that time—Saint Theresa is the local Catholic church—and they lived here, and there was a Polish community, and it was very Jewish up in Washington Heights. So it wasn't a black neighborhood. [Now] he felt like it was available so [he could] get back to [his] youth or something that is recognizable to [him] and also a good investment. I can't say that.

The brownstone was an affordable investment, but a complete transformation of the Rogerses' house would take place. The entire family chipped in. The Rogerses moved in, reclaimed the space, and secured it against the outside world. At the outset, however, a number of obstacles stood in the way of their dreams for starting renovations on the house.

"There were three separate apartments. There were sealed doors. This staircase was painted green, like a prison green, and there was six layers of paint," Mimi says, pointing to three pictures she has spread out on the kitchen table. "So the first thing that we did was that we got an alarm system." Then they turned to the dirty and difficult task of removing the people and the past of this house:

> Before we could even move into this place, we needed to do major, major renovations. So therefore, we needed the people out of the house in order to do that, before we could even move in. The woman that was living in this apartment—see, there were three apartments on this floor—she was a working woman. There was a door here. There was a kitchen, a bathroom, and a

> rug. A chair in the bathroom and a rug, OK? It was horrifying. She was a working woman. She had clients coming in and out, OK. That's what this house was like. Next door to us, it was a family. Next door to her was another rooming house. And over here, a rooming house. Across the street, maybe one or two families that lived there. So basically, everything was a rental from month to month or however they arranged it. SROs, I think they called them.

The Rogerses' new home, like many brownstones being reclaimed in gentrification, had been converted to a rooming house. Their intention was to restore the house to a home that is in line with the Rogerses' own desires as a family. The conversion meant putting out the former tenants of the house. In the following remarks, Mimi describes what she sees as a polite and civil approach to going about this business of displacement:

> The point is that we needed a place. So in pushing them out, we gave them enough time. They knew that the owners had changed hands, and we were very kind because they were, for all practical purposes, our sisters and brothers. And they were human beings. I just couldn't tell them to get out of my house and they had no place to go.

As she tells it, at first Mimi was patient, kind even, because she considered the tenants to be like herself. Emphasizing kinship bonds and a shared humanity, Mimi appears not to want to distance herself from the building's occupants. But time passed, and the moving out process was not proceeding along as quickly as she would have liked. Now she changes her tone as she describes becoming more aggressive in her position:

> We gave them months and months and months. And we started off very nicely. But then it got to be, we need some place to go also. And we are paying for this. So what's the choice? Possession, it's ours. So now you really seriously have to look or goodbye. And most of the people I found apartments for that were even nicer than what they had.

A tone of helplessness characterizes Mimi's question, "What's the choice?" Here she seems to accept the inevitability of displacement as a natural fact. She rationalizes this in terms of her ownership of the property, which is now invoked as a line of difference between herself and the tenants.

Her polite tone has given way to anger and defiance, but she recovers her civility by shifting back to a kinder stance. By stressing that the apartments she found for the tenants were better, she turns the fact of displacement into a positive situation for the ousted boarders. By now she is on the defensive.

Trying to regain her own humanity at this point, she distinguishes the treatment between old and young tenants she displaced:

> I wasn't unkind to any elderly person. There were just two elderly men here in their late fifties, early sixties. One young person who was in his early thirties was being extremely lazy, so I had to get a little aggressive with him that I wanted him out. And eventually, he did get out. He did some mean things as he got out, but he eventually moved out.

Rogers points out the amount of time and effort she put into the search to relocate tenants. As if to contrast her own industry and resourcefulness with the tenants' lack of seriousness, she describes her voluntary efforts in the hunt for apartments:

> I got the *Amsterdam News.* I would look for all of these people, which I really didn't have to do. And eventually, we did get them out. And it wasn't really terrible. It wasn't terrible. There was one last person who—he was a man that had little boys coming into the house for whatever reasons. And I wanted him out. He was a real pig, and I wanted him out.

Mimi turned to a community resource—the *Amsterdam News,* not the *New York Times* she and her family had used—to find listings to place her tenants. She makes this out to be an act of generosity on her part. But where she wavers between civility and incivility, in the end she comes down on the side of practicality. Wouldn't anyone in her position, she reasons, act as she has?

> So it became, you know, like our needs and their needs, and you give a little. But when it becomes really necessary, you know, you fight for yourselves. And you know, that's what happened.

In recounting the story of residential displacement, Mimi ranges widely in her description of the tenants of her building. At first she sees them as human beings. As she becomes more and more exasperated with their behavior, these "brothers and sisters" are described as lazy, mean pigs.

Throughout her narrative, Mimi portrays herself as a kind person, pushed by the actions of others to act unkindly. The tensions that she describes are clearly a result of residential displacement brought about by a class transition in gentrifying Harlem. What is also an intraracial conflict between the Rogers family and the former tenants must be understood within this economic context. But Mimi does not describe the displacement in terms of race and class conflicts that characterize gentrification. Instead, she recounts this episode and gives priority to her own family's needs as unsettled home owners.

In part, this is because Mimi, having come to Harlem as an unlikely place to call home, is feeling displaced herself. Her talk reveals anxiety about restoring order and stability for her own family. And even though her comments refer to a father, an uncle, a cousin, brothers, and sisters, she is not thinking about the black community as family. This distinguishes her from those who describe their move home to Harlem as a way to reestablish real and fictive kinship links with the black community. Instead, Mimi is worried about putting dinner on the table for her husband and two kids.

For Mimi as a wife and mother, her husband's decision to make the "adventurous" move to Harlem disrupted her own role in the family. She defines her position with a traditional understanding that situates men and women with clear roles in the family. A key concern about their role in the process of gentrification was that this move not tear the Rogers family apart:

> We can sit here now, even though this looks shitty now, it's like a palace. It went by very quickly, a lot of good and bad things happened, but I made up my mind that if we were going to do this, I was going to keep the family together first. And I think I did. Because we could have been torn apart. The kids were suffering. We didn't even have a stove for, like, how long? A year? I used to cook on a hot plate and a Crock-Pot. We didn't have a refrigerator. For a while we lived, like, out of a cooler. And in the midst of it, the kids have to go out and do things. We used to go to the door. We used to be, like, OK, dust us off.

The finished business of dislodging the tenants from their new home cleared the way for Mimi's identity to reemerge. This meant settling her own family. She captures the disruptive effect this move had for the family by pointing to the lack of a kitchen and an adequate place to cook. To restore order where the instability of the move had been disruptive for the kids, Mimi concocted her own recipe for success:

> But do you know what I did, Monique, really? Not to pat myself on the back, but because I saw so many families really being torn apart, it scared me. So I would make at the end of our day, when they came home from school and Anthony was doing his thing, I would, like, cook something and make us all sit and have family time to talk about what happened during the day. In the dust and the filth.

Through recentering family life around an evening meal, even one cooked using makeshift and primitive conditions, Mimi overcame the dust and filth that surrounded her family. Today her hearth and home are intact again. I sit with her in her new kitchen, and she proudly shows off the buttery oak cabinets. She continues pointing at pictures of the old house. I have to agree, the snapshots do give me a more precise feeling for that fleeting moment between the past and when it moves on to being the present.

And in her head, Mimi now can even envision a future with more renovation as they continue to make this house their home: "We were going to build a thing out the back here like a bubble. That may happen still. We have to knock out the back and put a greenhouse, and then there would be a deck out there," she tells me.

"Look at Daddy!" exclaims Brittany, pointing to a picture of her father. He has a firm grip on a tool and is hard at work stripping layers of paint from a staircase. Brittany moved to Harlem when she was in tenth grade. After graduating from high school, she went to NYU. Asked to talk about her own role in gentrification, she is thoughtful and deliberate. She is well read on the history and literature of the place—as are many of Harlem's black gentry—the Harlem books, the Harlem heroes, the Harlem moment. With an air of authority she is firm, straightforward but trails off into defensiveness.

"My mother insisted that we find a place for all these people in other apartments," she tells me on the first day we talk. "Really?" I ask. "Yeah, I mean you feel very, it's a strange feeling. I mean your topic is gentrification. What's gentrification? Are we gentry? I mean we just want someplace to live. So we found a place, but people lived here already. What do we do with them? And other people are, like, later. So we thought that was not right. There is gentrification, and there is Trumpism . . . or whatever, you know? I mean, there's being a bully and not caring about the community. If you're not trying to come into a community to overthrow it but rather to add to it and enrich it."

Putting herself lower on the food chain than billionaire developer Donald Trump provides a broad cover. Her family may not be solely responsible for class transitions and displacement, but clearly Brittany reads lots of clues that portend change for Harlem:

> It's weird having a geographic thing. When you walk 144th Street on Convent Avenue, there are elderly black people, there are white yuppies, black yuppies, artists, all kinds of people. Go on Amsterdam [and] there are poor people who are unemployed. People who hang on the street, and people who deal drugs . . . like, 144th between Amsterdam and Broadway is harsh. I was shot at, walking from Broadway from the number 1 train. I had a bag. I was walking, and all the sudden I hear guns, and I'm like, oh shit, into a gutter. Then you walk here, and it's all BMWs and Volvos and stuff like that. So for someone who has a political consciousness, you're in a bind because you don't

> know how to feel. You feel like, do I belong here? Well, I need to live somewhere, and I need to pursue my life as an individual and as a creative person, OK? Should I try to work with the community or something to make it better too? [But] I get pissed off a lot because people are selling crack on the corner. There are vials on the street, and I'm like, I see it, the cops have gotta see.

Brittany is observant, and she can dissect every detail about the neighborhood characters and goings-on around her. When she labels herself with politics, she is already negotiating a stance about race in a way that defines her as a political person in contrast to what she imagines to be gentry as a status-seeking group, perhaps.

Brittany's comments are linked to a generational voice that has moved race and identity into the terms and struggle of a new generation. In one sense, Harlem could be her home place. Her father is from Harlem. But as a family heirloom, this is an inheritance that is at odds with how she sees herself as a Manhattan teenager. This positions the "eyes of others" on the Upper West Side. Her anxiety about Harlem centered on how she wanted others, especially her classmates at private school, to see her—especially once she moved uptown during her teenage years.

Today, Brittany is a "twenty-something" fresh out of college with a degree in film studies. I ask her to talk about race and high school. She shrugs, raising a conspiratorial eyebrow when she explains that she just got used to being in the minority. At the time of the move, the teenager she was, outside of Harlem, clashed with how she imagined her family's relocation inside Harlem. Hers is an attitude markedly different from the views of others voiced in the previous chapter, of those who claimed to be pushed to Harlem by frustration over the snail-like pace of dismantling racism in "integrated" settings.

In fact, Brittany even disavows her own link, as an insider, to a Harlem lineage. She cuts ties of race that would bind her to a grandmother's Harlem and a Harlem that is her father's old neighborhood. A different vision shapes her black experience. The storied history of the neighborhood, the chance to restore its stunning architecture, and an appreciation for the intricate delicacies of design have won Brittany over with the passage of time. Each time we talk, she takes an authoritative, get-the-facts, know-the-history approach, and always shares detailed stories about the buildings and players in the community:

> This is a bastion of white history really. Alexander Hamilton's house was his country home, and then all of these houses were white people's country homes, and then no one wanted to live up here anymore, and certain things

happened to them. 125th Street, now that is a seat of black history. Things happened there, and that's more a story of people rather than buildings, you know. So we're creating a new history of people who live here now and of an understanding of the overall history of New York as a great melting pot for what it's worth, you know. Maybe not a melting pot so much as one of those military dishes with the compartments in it, you know? You can kind of like mush your peas and your mashed potatoes together if you want to. It's beautiful up here, and it can be really peaceful. I sit at the window sometimes, and I used to travel a lot because I was a photographer, and I'm like, it looks like Italy, it's got that kind of peace . . . which a lot of Harlem [doesn't have]. It's too bad that everyone can't have a feeling of peace where they live; that it's only people who can afford to buy a building and have a garden and to do these things.

Despite some of her discomfort about class and displacement, Brittany takes a matter-of-fact and proud tone when she talks about her family's role in the restoration of Harlem's architectural heritage:

[You] do all of this work [to restore] more original detail—like all of the wainscoting and stuff. Our stairway is probably the best piece of original work and the foyer. And that was all covered with eighteen layers of green paint, and you do it with a hot gun or chemicals that burn your hands. And you do it because you're like, this is where we have to live. You don't have anywhere else to live, you know? Ummm, you tend to resent people, like, wanting to steal it or breaking into it. I take it much more personally than even just having my shit ripped off because it's like this incredible investment—not only in time but emotionally and mentally, and you want people to understand that you just didn't come here and you're not ripping them off in a way, and it's hard you can't make that clear to anybody.

Her words collide. While she talks to me, Brittany is hesitant and then really talkative. At times she seems embarrassed. But she is thoughtful and forthright about the kinds of contradictions she sees in her family's arrival in her father's old neighborhood:

And after you've done so much work on a house, when you've taken what could be considered a piece of history—a history of New York—and tried to restore it from someone who has already commercially exploited it by dividing it into SROs to give housing to poorer people, yes, but they're being exploited in a certain way by having to live like that—I mean one room, one sink, dinky kitchen . . . the way that it was renovated was not well done, generally these aren't. So you think, I brought this back. We lived here. We had no water. There's humor to it, but I was really happy to go to school. We had no water. We bathed in buckets in the basement because they were rerouting all this plumbing. There was plaster dust for at least four years. We had plaster dust . . . and I wear black [laughs], it was just disastrous. It sounds really petty, "I had fashion problems." But I'm just saying we went through really a lot. The backyard was about four feet deep in old works and crap and you just wouldn't imagine. Mrs. Jenkins who lived in my parents' bedroom, umm, had about a foot of garbage, and I don't mean trash. I mean, like, banana skins and chicken bones and stuff where you had to put on boots and shovel it, and my father's really into this. It lets the family [work together]—the whole family will do this, and it'll be really great.

I used to live in Germany. They loved the fact that I was from Harlem because everything black is very exotic to many Europeans. But it depends. I've been through definite snobola modes you know, pompous ass modes personally, where I have not been embarrassed, but I have framed where my parents live in different ways, "oh, my parents bought a townhouse uptown." You know because you worry. It's very complicated, and it's immature sometimes, but you worry about what people think, you know, because you feel like in people's minds as articulate and well dressed and multilingual as I may be, they still think I'm like some kind of nigger, you know, and if I say that I live in Harlem, it's just going to contribute to that. And so all of the good stuff that the thousands of dollars have been spent to give this to me will be nothing in their eyes because they'll take some H-word and think, "Oh. Well, all black people live in Harlem," like that. And that's problematic. And that's something I definitely went through a couple of years ago.

As we see in this and in the previous chapter, for Brittany the reality of displacement and belonging are at the top of her mind. She is clearly uncomfortable when asked to comment on the contradictions and tensions of her position and that of her family as they create a new chapter of history in Harlem. With time and distance, however, she comes to conclude that living in Harlem is OK. And by claiming her place as an artist and preservationist, she grafts the narrative of her family's place in Harlem today.

Portia Hamilton purchased in 1986 a single-family home that had been subdivided into one-room apartments. The house is fronted by a porch and a small patch of grass. A walkway now planted with red and pink geraniums leads to the sidewalk and street:

> When I started looking for a house to buy, I mean, I was truly ignorant. And what I would do is, I would take different routes home in the evening, so that I would have the opportunity to see different parts of the community. I saw these little houses, and I said, that's it. Front porch, front yard, will give me a little bit of the country in the city, and that was the selling factor.

Hamilton's route to Harlem originates in suburban New York, where she grew up, and passes through North Carolina, where she has lived for extended periods. The Harlem house, with its porch and yard, represents a blend of Hamilton's rural and suburban past. With her flower-lined walkway, she plants this vision in the urban environment and roots herself to a future in Harlem. Here Hamilton will craft her own ideal as a home owner in Harlem:

> I got the name of every owner on the block, and I started randomly calling people to see if they would be willing to sell. And most people said, no. Originally the owner of this house, who also owned the house next door to me, which is now boarded up, had said, no. But he was the only one who I thought might think about it. So I asked him, "Could I at least see the interior?" And he said, yes.

Her successful search for a house was a matter of persistence and effort. Hamilton convinced one owner in the transitional housing market to allow her to view the interior that lay beyond an exterior she was drawn to. But her glimpse at the interior of this house provided only a partial view of what was in store:

> Well, he brought me in, and I didn't see the entire house. Not every room. But he allowed me to come in and get a sense of what the house would look like. And some rooms I couldn't enter. And that was it. And then I made him an offer. And the fact that I offered him cash probably helped his decision a lot. And he sold. I was the first person to buy on this block, on this side of the block at any rate, in probably over twenty to twenty-five years.

Hamilton's persistence and effort alone did not secure the house. With money as a resource, she was able to buy. Even in a market she considers affordable, this is not an option available to everyone who would like to hold onto a piece of Harlem.

Then, the former owner of the house, in a manner of speaking, took the money and ran. He realized his profit in the transitional real-estate market. Hamilton says she learned her lesson too late: she should have demanded he deliver the house empty. What she soon discovered within the rooms she never entered was that she was not alone. Once opened, the doors revealed a handful of tenants abandoned by a landlord who left the work of displacement to Hamilton.

Hamilton describes the reaction to her arrival on her block and in her new home as "horrible." Not sure whether resistance to her presence was initiated from people on the block or from inside her home, she waged nearly four years of legal battles, paid close to one hundred thousand dollars in fines and legal fees, and spent three nights in jail at Riker's Island for contempt of court.

Asked to discuss the exhaustive battle over her property, Hamilton points to a number of factors. She planned to "let people stay, then relocate them" while she renovated one room at a time. But her first mistake, she claims, "was I put a lock on the front door and said only people who live here can have a key. And anyone else, they have to be admitted by whomever they are going to see." That move did not sit well with the community.

Hamilton tried to avoid the "monstrous incivility" the urban pioneer ushers in, in Neil Smith's words. But placing a lock on the door signaled an incivility that canceled out plans for relocation that she had considered a sign of generosity:

> I found apartments for everybody that was here. Every single person except for one person, the woman who died. Not only did I relocate them, I saw to it they had their rent paid. I also furnished anyone's apartment who wanted it furnished. Since I bought the house furnished, it enabled me to say any furniture that you have in this room that you are currently renting that you want is yours. And then I physically provided the moving capabilities for them. I had a station wagon at the time, and we moved them.

With her station wagon she cleared the way for a middle-class reinvention of the rooming house into a family home. Hers was not a move of circling the wagons. Her concern for civility and decorum remained intact:

> That was something I said I was going to do when I bought the place. Because, I mean, to me that's just the way things should be done and that's why I did it. To me, it was a moral obligation, not a legal obligation.

Hamilton saw no reason why her capital investment should mean the sacrifice of a moral ideal. The gap between the cost of this property—paid for with cash—and the price of entry into another world of middle-class home ownership was partially shared as a one-time resource to finance the displacement of tenants.

But Hamilton's move to reclaim this space represented more than simply a residential shift for the tenants. While their previous landlord did not interfere, Hamilton's arrival disrupted an ongoing source of income. Residents reacted to displacement of a way of life and a prevailing code of conduct:

> What I didn't realize, this house was being used for drugs. The bathrooms on this floor and the second floor were being used to turn tricks by the prostitutes. Folks were renting their rooms out for the prostitutes. So that was cutting into everybody's money. And the decision was that I shouldn't be here.

The fractured space of the rooming house provided multiple sources of profit for a landlord whose absence postponed dealing with drug use and prostitution. The divided rooming house was also a source of capital for tenants who were able to make use of hallways, bathrooms, and their own rental rooms as a marketplace. Gentrification brought Hamilton into this market space, and because she recombined ownership and possession of the building, her desires for a single-family home were at odds with tenants she had unwittingly assumed.

It would be fair to say that, together, Hamilton and the building's former owner contributed to the twin displacement of occupants and a prevailing way of life. But the landlord no longer had a presence in the gentrification. Thus he shared no part in the construction of a villain.

As a result, resistance was aimed against Portia Hamilton. The home owner was a direct embodiment of a change experienced directly by her tenants. Word spread, and soon others in the community shared this fear, rationally, albeit indirectly.

Apparently acting on the idea that Hamilton did not belong in the house, someone—she is still not sure who—escalated a campaign of harassment against her at her home and office, she said. The hostility took the following forms: "Knives pulled on my son. Things broken into, things stolen. They attempted to poison the dog. I have letters from people who threatened to kill me."

The ultimate humiliation came when a group calling itself "PRIDE FOR HARLEM" held a rally outside Hamilton's office. Using a sound truck and waving placards, the group declared that Hamilton was "a slut, and she uses drugs, and she's putting women and children in the streets, and she's prostituting."

When protesters showed up at her residence on another day, police were called in. It was then Hamilton learned about contradictory allegations being made against her that fueled these protests. An initial allegation, that she was a "white woman from Scarsdale," gave way to claims that she was "fronting for a white group."

A turning point for Hamilton came after her return from jail, following her contempt of court conviction. Simply trying to maintain a sense of civility, she confided, she dressed up, held her head high, and walked the streets of her block:

> When I got back here on the block that Saturday, the woman who had been instrumental in my going to jail in this court case was on the block bragging to people that she had me incarcerated and I had six months and all this stuff about what was going to happen to me.
>
> And here's Saturday morning, I come in like this, I'm exhausted. But I came in, I showered, I bathed myself, I got myself cleaned up and put on fresh clothes. And I started walking up and down the block and people were saying, "It's so good to see you home, Ms. Hamilton. I was so sorry to hear about it. I hope nothing happened."
>
> In some respects the woman then lost all her credibility. But you get a different sense of feelings on the block because people said if I could stand up under that maybe I wasn't as bad as people were alleging I was.

Middle-class resettlement of house and home, in the case of Hamilton, was not immediate and gave rise to a particular form of resistance. On the surface, conflicts of gentrification appear as a struggle between two sets of actors. Where displacement as a consequence of gentrification is lived as a struggle between new home owners and former residents, the actions, interests, and profits for previous owners go unnoticed.

When no landlord is identified to step in and take the place of providing an alternative, displaced residents react. This leaves persons like Hamilton to bear sole responsibility for disruptions brought on by middle-class resettlement in a low-income rental market. But with the absent landlord as a third actor in the process, the struggle between Hamilton and her tenants is more fairly seen as the result of a shift in owner preference as the property changed hands.

For the former owner, the property was a source of income. Hamilton held a vision of creating a family residential space. She imposed a plan to craft an interior more in line with the exterior. The front porch and patch of yard that appealed to her rural and suburban middle-class experience were a model for the future. Taking possession of her home, Hamilton stepped in as the architect of a new system of meaning for herself, the house, and its lodgers.

Hamilton's fight with former tenants carried her to jail and back. While her story represents an extreme case, other gentry share common experiences in asking or forcing former tenants to move. For the displaced tenant of a rooming house, power is limited to various forms of resistance to slow the reoccupation of these brownstones. They signal their departure through property destruction, theft, verbal abuse, or dragging their feet. The occupants of a rooming house are dislodged, but not without a struggle.

Chicken Bones and the Stoop: Public Space as a Personal Place

Yolanda Jackson, who moved into a Central Harlem brownstone in 1987, is annoyed by the crack problem on her block. And once, she says, she was confronted by a man armed with a machine gun as she climbed the steps of her brownstone. In addition, she adds, there is sometimes a disregard for projects, such as planting trees, that she sees as needed improvements for the neighborhood.

Inside their properties, new home owners exercise a level of control that they relinquish in the more public spaces of the street. The street is where the private world of house and home meets the broader terrain of an outdoor arena. The absolute authority they exercise as private home owners gives way to a series of negotiations with others in the public spaces they share. In the outdoors, different battles and new forms of resistance emerge.

The stoop, as a transitional space, is a passageway from the homes of black gentry to the public world of the street. Redefining a code of conduct for the public and private space of the stoop is another manner in which black gentry assert tastes and aesthetic values that reflect their middle-class identities. Through middle-class eyes, the street and the stoop provide a vantage point for incidents that violate decorum:

> My mother and I are sitting on the steps, and a girl in a white outfit comes running down the street looking this way, looking that way. And she goes across the street, gets behind a car, pulls down her pants, and starts to urinate, and we're like [she gasps] sitting there watching, and then she looks and she sees that we're there so she scoots more on the middle of the sidewalk so she's behind the car. But there are these guys who are sitting on the steps over there. I mean I was just blown away. One side of our steps goes to the downstairs entrance, and one side is just, like, a trench. People used to use that as a latrine seat, and they would like, um, take a crap off the edge of our steps. And you'd come out of the house, and you'd be like, oh man what is going on? And then you'd look. We couldn't believe it because it's a place to sit. There are people who don't have any place else to go, but you don't want that in your home.

As Brittany Rogers retells this episode, her tone ranges from shock to disgust to anger. She wavers as she tempers these reactions with sympathy for the fact that people have no place else to go. Her view that "you don't want that in your home" extends to behavior that does not belong in the trench—a gulf between one's home and the street.

In addition to the fact that Ruth and Joe Baxter-Brown stand out as young professionals, they found that their approach to their home heightened tensions with neighbors. When they moved in, they acted in a proprietary way about the space in front of their house. This action initially met with hostility:

> Joe wouldn't let people sit on the stoop anymore, you know. They used to hang out on the stoop and eat dinner and throw chicken bones down in the stairwell. We'd make them leave, you know.

The Baxter-Browns want to establish cleanliness and order in their own space. While the street is a gathering place, the stoop of a brownstone is not necessarily clearly either a private or a public space. To keep their property clean means imposing rules for an environment that extends beyond their house and doorstep.

The Baxter-Browns found that, as home owners, their move to reclaim outdoor space met with countermoves signaling resistance. "People set our garbage can on fire and cursed us out a few times," says Ruth. Still, despite the grumbling against her, she asserts home ownership as a claim that allows her to impose her own rules of order:

> When I would see people on the stoop, I would go and say, "Excuse me." And they start mumbling, "You people come over here . . ." And I said, "Look, I pay the mortgage here. You go home and sit where you pay yours." Sometimes you just have to do that.

While Ruth is willing to stand up to people who violate her rules, other home owners are not as aggressive in imposing new rules guiding outdoor behavior.

Kenyatta Davis has noticed a difference between black and white home owners in guarding the sanctity of the stoop:

> One of the things I don't like about the white household that's on our block is that they let people abuse their stoop. And I don't know if it's [that] they're fearful. I don't know if it's a missionary attitude. I don't know what it is. But I think it sets a bad example, especially in light of the fact that we don't allow that, you know.

When it comes to imposing a new code of conduct, however, many middle-class blacks also are sensitive about taking actions that set them apart from other black residents:

> I know when we initially moved in, we had to go through a little thing with the block, just in terms of establishing space and making clear to people that you can't eat and smoke and drink on our stoops. You know, we like you, it's cool. But you cannot eat on our stoop.

Trying to avoid the appearance of incivility, home owners make the request with encouraging words to signal that this is not a hostile action. Reassurance that "it's cool" makes the demand not so much an admonishment of behavior as a request to move it elsewhere.

But intraracial conflict between residents and black gentry is also the result of a struggle to define legitimate uses of the neighborhood. When Davis returns home from her office job downtown, she is reminded that the turf of the home owner is also the workplace of a drug economy:

> I mean, I wish that they were not there. It's very upsetting to me that they're selling crack and I know that they're selling crack. Because I think that they know that because I respect them, I don't like what they're doing, but I understand why they're doing it. For money—they're trying to feed their family. I don't see them as evil forces, these demonic people who are out here. These are good people who had made, in my opinion, a terrible choice—chosen the totally wrong way to solve a problem that all of us have. But I understand why they do that. It's not that they're bad people. I watched one couple out there, the wife was pregnant and they have a baby, and how they deal with their kid on the street while they're working, and they're like any other couple trying to raise a kid.

Davis, conscious of the choices available to her in the work world, sees that a similar interest in survival pushes people to positions in legal and illegal economies. She does not impose her own strict code of conduct to solve a problem that annoys her:

> The only control I have is that I do say you cannot do it in front of our stoop, and they respect me for that. So if you respect them, they will respect you, and they know that when I fuss at them, it's not because I look down at them.

While she would prefer not to see any drug transactions, Davis does not attempt to control an area beyond the front of her own house. She negotiates from a position of understanding and respect. With her request she takes some, but not all, of the street. And where an aggressive stance might have escalated tensions, the end result is that potential enemies take her side:

And after that initial establishing of turf, we're fine. They watch out for us. We get a tremendous amount of respect from even the crack dealers on the block. Now I receive them grudgingly—I mean, it's like, you know—but they do respect us and they look out for us and they enforce our rules for us. Like if there are new guys that come on the block to sell or whatever, they'll say, "Don't do that in front of 'Yatta's stoop. Don't sit on 'Yatta's stoop, don't hang on 'Yatta's gate." So that's evidence of respect that we get. Our block, our resident wino regularly makes sure our garbage is neat and pulls it out on the sidewalk. If we don't get there—the trash guy watches the house, and if anything suspicious goes on, lets us know.

Because Davis negotiated her position, others on her street now join her in viewing the gate, stoop, and even space in front of her house as boundaries marking old and new territory. By policing these boundaries on her behalf, they take part in creating and enforcing new codes of conduct.

In *Streetwise,* Elijah Anderson points to similar attempts by new residents to "ingratiate themselves with potential criminals" as a strategy for managing the public environment and dealing with the prospect of crime. Anderson refers to this strategy as a "peculiar combination of neighborliness and self-defense." The right mix of neighborliness and personal desire, notes Anderson, redirects hostility and aggression such that some newcomers are accosted while others receive protection or consideration, or are simply not bothered.[7]

While they impose a carefully constructed version of their class, racial, and gender identities in houses, courtyards, and stoops, the black middle class as gentry cannot exercise absolute control over the shape of the community as a whole, nor for many is this a goal. But the limited presence of a middle-class culture and climate—the lack of the familiar rhythms of middle-class life, from bedtime and late-night quiet to the amount of free time one has on weekends—can be an annoyance over which newcomers lack control.

This lack extends to services and shopping as well. Another common complaint heard from gentry, similar to that raised by long-term middle-class residents, is that services in Harlem are markedly different from those provided for downtown residents. Quality and convenience are, according to new gentrifiers, inferior and inadequate:

If I live downtown, when I get out of work, I can still do my laundry, I can still do my food shopping. I can still find a drugstore that's open. I can still find a video store that's open. I mean, all of those things are done with the

> assumption that everybody's out working during the day. So you've got to have something open at night when people come home. I've organized my life so that I pick up stuff on my way home. It is very frustrating. I mean, there is service redlining in Harlem, not just economic redlining.
>
> I want the services here. I own a car because I've got to drive all over Manhattan to get access to the services that I want—like my cleaners. The stores I like to shop in are not here.
>
> It's kind of sad that I can buy a carton of milk next to Columbia University cheaper than I can buy it around the corner, too, you know.
>
> I don't do the bulk of my grocery shopping here. I don't like going in to the grocery stores where the meats are smelly, the place is smelly. And so that means, OK, I'll buy canned goods or rice. I'll buy meat if I'm really in a jam. But that's hamburger, and I look at the date and check their stock.

Because their worlds exist beyond the confines of the ghetto, reorganizing shopping around a work schedule or driving out of the neighborhood in search of lower prices and better quality does not impose an "inner-city" racial or class tax on these individuals. Members of the urban poor whose freedom of movement in and out of an underserved area can be constrained by class—no car, no money for the bus—bear more immediate financial costs of service redlining.

The trade-offs these middle-class individuals make to live in Harlem, however, suggest that for those in search of racial belonging, it is not costless, as seen in terms of their own demands and expectations:

> There's a newsstand right here by me up on the corner. The one thing I did notice when I first moved here, it was interesting, because I'd get the Sunday *New York Times,* and there'd be no advertisements. And I'd go home to my mom's, and there'd be Bloomies and Macy's, and I'm saying, "This is strange."
>
> The newsstand at 116th Street and Lenox Avenue has the *Daily News* and the *New York Post* and that was it. [The owner] said no one would want a paper that's hard to read in Harlem, right? I'm a business writer. I've got to look at the *Wall Street Journal* or the *New York Times* or both in the morning before I go to work.

In Harlem, the newsstand as a provider and conveyer of consumer goods is a location whose offerings reflect the larger isolation of a community perceived as home only to an urban underclass. Unafraid to complain, new middle-class residents confront managers and employees of these businesses. At times their demands are met:

> I think he's East Indian or Pakistani or something like that. And I said, well get it. And you know, it's been fine for about a year. Like a little pile of *New York Times* is sitting on the newsstand in the morning. And the weird thing about it, right, was that after he got them in, if you get there later than eleven o'clock, they're gone. He said no one would want a paper that's hard to read in Harlem, right? [But] if you get there after eleven o'clock, they're gone.
>
> Then it dawned on me. So I made a complaint. I said, "You know there are folks north of Ninety-sixth Street who shop at Saks and Macy's and Bloomies. Would you please put the circulars in our papers?" And they started putting the circulars in the papers. It just had to be pointed out, I suppose.

New Harlem residents help reshape commerce and consumption. Their complaints, however, are intended to meet personal needs. They are not collective social actions. The argument that middle-class gentrifiers benefit the broader community through their efforts to overturn the practices of service and product redlining is open to question. Rather, their complaints result in importing the consumer tastes and practices of an elite to a community in transition.

And when in fact residential choice is available—even if, as some have told, it means not really fitting in—many are unwilling to wait for changes. Then the reality of a permeable boundary between Harlem and Manhattan makes the option of a reverse migration out of the community a great lure.

Greg Conner, a computer programmer in his late twenties, grew up in a predominantly white suburb in Connecticut. After graduating from Harvard, he lived in lower Manhattan for a few years before moving up to Harlem. In exchange for rent, he would contribute to minor repair work on the brownstone his family had purchased.

But after two years living in Harlem, Conner found changes in his lifestyle to be both inconvenient and a nuisance. He eventually moved back downtown to SoHo, where, he says, he feels more "in sync" with his neighbors:

> There's a lot of people who are my age and kind of working in similar types of jobs. And we're all dealing on the same level. Whereas, when I was up there, I felt a little bit unusual. You know, I'd get on the subway at 135th Street, and there's not too many people wearing blue suits, white shirts, striped ties, and wingtips.

> The people that I found you're surrounded with when you're living up there were just not the same people who I would surround myself with in my professional life or in school. They weren't going places that I was going. So it was a little bit unusual. You had things happen which I don't find happen down here in SoHo where I'm living now. At night you could hear loud music blasting out of cars, a lot more shouting on the street.
>
> There's no place really easy to get your shirts laundered. There's not a lot of restaurants or grocery stores or any types of shops of any kind. And what was there was catering to a different type of clientele. In SoHo, within five blocks of where I live, there's twenty restaurants that I can go to. I can get my shirts done at ten different places. I can jump into cabs instantly.
>
> Also, I found I felt like I had to go into a hunter mode when I would go out on the street. Like I was very conscious of where I was and who was around me. When you're in a jungle, you're on your defensive. You keep everything keyed way, way up. And I found it to be just not an uplifting place to be at all. It wasn't inspiring in any way.

Like Conner, many of Harlem's newest middle class voice similar feelings of frustration. They cite Manhattan's conveniences to which they no longer have access and wish they did. And they describe a set of lifestyle symbols, such as particular cars, the search for the *New York Times,* white collars and blue suits, that set them apart from the community.

But for those who are new home owners, a financial investment that signals their commitment also holds a firm grip. Ruth and Joe Baxter-Brown talked about the love/hate relationship they have with Harlem. "Sometimes I like it, but there are days when I distinctly say, you know, 'Darling, I love you, but give me Park Avenue.' Some days, you work hard, you come home," Joe begins to explain. His wife cuts in, "you're tired," she adds, then lets him continue:

> and you have to kick niggers off your front doorstep because they're drinking beer. You go into your house, somebody is next door and blaring their radio so loud that you can hear it in Yankee Stadium, you know. Then you come outside, and folks look at you as if you're strange because you're home from work and you would like a little peace and quiet. It's a pain to live in Harlem when you lead a life different from the life of your neighbors. When people don't have to be at work in the morning, they can stay up all night. When you have to get up in the morning, you don't want to hear that shit. You really don't. There are days when I was like, "Why the hell am I here?"

Ruth confirms this feeling:

> And each of us had days like that. The time I got really bugged all the time was one period where these women would come every day and hang out on our stoop. They didn't live there. And every night I'd come home, and I'd kick them off the stoop. One day I came out of the house, and I said, "Look, I'm not going to come out here anymore."

Joe and Ruth Baxter-Brown say that they are here to stay. They plan to make a home in Harlem and shared with me their goal of raising Sierra Leone, the daughter they hope to have someday. Their talk suggests that they do not want their professional lives and raising children to be at odds with their decision to live in Harlem: "I've always said to Joe, you have to love black people to want to stay up here, because it's hard."

In earlier pages, we saw a number of push and pull factors associated with race and racism that partially account for a black gentry in Harlem. But, as this chapter has discussed, dilemmas of difference, now based on class and home ownership, complicate these residents' arrival in Harlem, where they ostensibly came for solidarity.

What practices can overcome an outsider status that leaves the group of middle-class blacks still suspended between two worlds? Given that Harlem's black gentry face racial and class dilemmas of difference in their lives—at work and home—does the need for collective racial bonds take priority? Can racial solidarity in Harlem for this group be attained? How? Next we will examine how participation in the politics, economics, and culture of contemporary Harlem becomes a strategy for moving past these dilemmas.

Hey DuDe.
LET'S STOP KiLLing EACHOTHER
Self Destruction
Babies Having Babies is not the Move!!
There's a thin Line Between LIFE AND DEATH!!!
Do the Government
FREE SOUTH AFRICA
AIDS

chapter 5

Racial Bonds and the Communion of Fellowship

> The elevated swung me up to Harlem. At first I felt a little fear and trembling, like a stray hound scenting out a new territory. But soon I was stirred by familiar voices and the shapes of houses and saloons, and I was inflated with confidence. A wave of thrills flooded the arteries of my being, and I felt as if I had undergone initiation as a member of my tribe. And I was happy. Yes, it was a rare sensation again to be just one black among many. It was good to be lost in the shadows of Harlem again.
>
> **Claude McKay, *A Long Way from Home***

While the "return" to Harlem presents the opportunity for black gentry to seek out racial solidarity, their newness in the community marks them as outsiders. This outsider status initially stands in the way of realizing the goal to be seen as insiders even in a community that is racially defined. In addition, many of the ideals and actions reflecting their position as middle-class home owners contribute to tensions that potentially undermine the pursuit of a racially harmonious community.

Years after an era in which class differences were often eclipsed by a larger system of racial caste, Harlem's current black gentry, as successful members of the middle class, occupy a structural position in American society that is increasingly defined by their class position.[1] Class status, however, is a structural position that is also shaped by racial identity. For individuals who find themselves as members of both ascribed and achieved groups, according to anthropologist Victor Turner, the antithesis of structure—*communitas* or social anti-structure—arises, especially during transitional stages of history.

In this instance, middle-class blacks, who feel alienated in the largely white worlds of home and work outside of Harlem, see themselves as outsiders in those spheres. While the experience of upward mobility accounts for changes in individual status, middle-class blacks point to race as a strong factor in their continued marginality in American society. Marginals, writes Turner, are those who are

> simultaneously members (by ascription, optation, self-definition or achievement) of two or more groups whose social definitions and cultural norms are distinct from, and often opposed to, one another. What is interesting about such marginals is that they often look to their group of origin, the so-called inferior group, for *communitas,* and to the more prestigious group in which they mainly live and in which they aspire to higher status as their structural reference group.[2]

For many middle-class blacks who feel caught between two worlds, crafting an identity defined in terms of both race and class becomes important. Thus Harlem's newest black middle class engages in a search for a meaningful identity its members believe can be found in the black community. Many come to Harlem and look to a "group of origin"—their racial group—for *communitas.* A marginal group's use of *communitas,* Turner argues, is most evident during periods in which societies are in liminal transition between different social structures. More clearly, *communitas* suggests a "communion of fellowship" that emerges to bond people during transitional stages in history.

The post–civil rights era—representative of America's transition to a new pattern of black and white relations—is an instance of a liminal transition. In chapter 3, through interviews with new middle-class Harlemites, racism was identified as a key factor in pushing middle-class blacks from a predominantly white arena. In these interviews, they claimed that Harlem satisfies a quest for belonging found in the black world, a haven.

But middle-class blacks coming to Harlem also express a siege mentality that comes across in the accounts in the preceding chapter about home ownership and the struggle for territorial control. Their experiences partially belie the notion that race alone can provide camaraderie for blacks in the face of income and occupational differences.

But we will see that this siege mentality gives way to attempts to join the institutional and social networks making up the Harlem community. These actions are framed by the argument that as a group, middle-class blacks have a responsibility not to turn their backs on the ghetto. This responsibility is shouldered in a way that casts them in the social buffer role identified by William Julius Wilson:

> I believe that the exodus of middle- and working-class families from many ghetto neighborhoods removes an important kind of "social buffer" that could deflect the full impact of the kind of prolonged and increased joblessness that plagued inner-city neighborhoods in the 1970s and early 1980s, joblessness created by uneven economic development and periodic recessions.[3]

From Wilson's perspective, what is missing is not only key support for economic and political institutions in black communities across America. Also lost to a decades-long black flight from the urban cores was a moral ethos. The absence of a strong middle- and working-class presence in the black community, argues Wilson, meant a spiraling tangle of urban pathology, the result of a system of values that disappeared. Long-term residents interviewed in chapter 2 embraced this logic, setting the stage, in part, for accepting black gentrifiers as different.

As a space that is both real and symbolic, Harlem becomes a handy setting for blacks to act in concrete ways as a "social buffer" in a troubled community, as well as a place for them to rationalize social action simply through their "return" and presence. Middle-class black gentry engage in cultural, economic, and political actions in Harlem in order to express a larger commitment and solidarity with the race as a whole. As such, Harlem meets the needs of blacks who would reason that they have a racial mission to help lift up the inner city.

Rather than be seen as outsiders or intruders, Ruth Baxter-Brown and Malcolm Balderidge point to the historical function of the black middle class in segregated communities that provides them a natural position in the community as a whole:

> There was always a mix. There were always poor people living next door to a doctor, a lawyer, a teacher. And these people were the role models. All the role models moved out in the late sixties and in the early seventies. More middle-class people have to make the commitment to move back into the community and live in a community. And it doesn't mean that you have to live in a community of all middle-class people. I just think that middle-class blacks, professional blacks, have abandoned their community.

> I think that some of us decided to come back and live. I'm not from Harlem. I'm from St. Louis. I decided to come back to a black community because I

> had not lived in a black community for so long. I just realized that, you know, it was a lot of African Americans, especially a lot of us who were writing, who had been involved in the sixties and who were talking at that time about bringing back whatever skills and image we have to the community. And most of us weren't doing that. I thought that I could help, or lend whatever abilities I had and provide whatever kind of role model I could for some of the males. African American males, who I thought were hopelessly gone in another direction.

Describing themselves as carrying on a tradition, Balderidge and Baxter-Brown depict themselves as necessary role models coming back to the community. This defines their move to Harlem as a larger commitment they are making to the idea of reinvigorating the black community.

But their comments also reveal a symbolic function that Harlem plays in their desires for reconstructing a racial community. The emphasis on their move as a "return" and a "reversal" of black flight ignores the fact that neither is from Harlem. Instead, Harlem is a stand-in for black hometowns like St. Louis or Chicago. Therefore, statements that blacks have "abandoned their community" and that they need to "come back into the community" are more generally critiques of black middle-class geographic mobility in America. Implicit in this critique is the argument that this group naturally belongs in Harlem.

The desire is to move from outsider to belonging in a black community writ large. But this reflects an individual more than a collective quest. Complete participation in the life of Harlem has its limits and is in no way a rejection of integration or assimilation. Instead, black Harlem, as an oppositional symbol, is used in the construction of a race and class identity that is rooted in both black and white worlds.

On a more immediate level, in trying to get to know people, intimate face-to-face connections help establish a primary integration into the community. Most often, it is on particular streets or blocks or within institutional sites such as stores, bars, libraries, restaurants, and churches that a communion of fellowship can be realized. Specific actions that signal a willingness to participate in neighborhood rituals are necessary to move talk about community commitment beyond empty rhetoric.

At a secondary level, involvement in the political and institutional life of Harlem also helps solidify an insider position that signals community solidarity. Through a shared interest as actors in the renovation and revitalization of black Harlem, middle-class blacks define theirs as a mission to help reclaim Harlem, fueled by racial responsibility. In this instance, the passage from outsider to insider involves using community institutions, organizations, and associations to work toward a collective goal of preserving Harlem as a racially defined space.

This chapter explores community participation as an avenue toward the construction of a middle-class black identity in Harlem. The types of behavior black gentry describe as evidence of their participation in the community's social life also expose some limitations to reaching a communion of racial fellowship that are due to class and gender differences.

Informal Networks: Coming into the Fold

In the hot and busy outdoor public life of a Harlem summer day, children, parents and grandparents, friends, and neighbors fill the streets with play and conversation. A cluster of young girls, their braids flying out behind them, take turns swinging a jump rope. The rhythmic flick of the rope punctuates the singsong of their double Dutch. Men gather around card tables set up on the sidewalks, passing time around games of cards and dominoes. Their talk and arguments are loud, often playful, but hold all the seriousness of a congressional session.

The life of the peopled streets of Harlem bears the intimacy of a small-town community. Here, friends can be distinguished from strangers. Events that stand out from usual routines are keenly noticed. Older women look out from a window perch or peel back their curtains, keeping a watchful eye on the comings and goings of the street.

Like sentries, older men and women provide an unofficial "protective service," eager to report any deviation from routine—there was a stranger on your step, they will tell you, along with the time he was there, whether he rang the bell or stood idly on the stoop.

Greta Symes, who has lived in her Sugar Hill brownstone since the early 1980s, talked about the communal spirit that is a way of life for residents of the black community:

> There is a certain level of cooperation and camaraderie, I guess, that people who are oppressed share. And for those of us who are in the middle class trying to make life in these houses and trying to improve the neighborhood as much as we can, we stick together. But we do that in concert with those people who have businesses here and with people who are also interested in the neighborhood who live in the apartment buildings.

Symes's observation of the collective spirit that binds residents is that it blurs boundaries. On her block, community means shopkeepers, home owners, and apartment dwellers who come together because of their common interest in the welfare of their immediate environment. Symes defines this communalism as a response by members of an oppressed group to a shared status that minimizes differences of residential status.

Life in Harlem can be difficult for everyone. At times the city is negligent in providing adequate services, unless pushed. The police can be slow in responding to citizen complaints. And many infrastructural problems that cause day-to-day inconveniences mean that functioning water mains, paved streets, and adequate lighting, taken for granted in other communities, can be a recurring source of frustration for Harlem residents. The problems confronting Harlemites unite them in common struggles as they work together to keep their streets clean and safe.

On an early-summer evening, Symes walks with me to the subway after we finish our interview at her brownstone. Along the way, she plays the role of neighborhood tour guide. I watch as neighbors are greeted and information is exchanged. She points to houses and apartment buildings, drawing on an intimate knowledge of her immediate environment, telling me names and brief histories of present and past occupants. Some were famous, such as Langston Hughes.

Two doors down from Symes's brownstone is a city-owned building whose doorway is sealed off with concrete. Heavy traffic in and out of the building at all hours of the day and night, says Symes, is enough to confirm residents' suspicions that this is a crack house. This particular abandoned property is a popular spot, Symes tells me, and is a continuing source of frustration for the block. Symes relates an episode about the crack house and a broken water main that is one occasion where the communal spirit of the neighborhood rose up against adversity:

> Yesterday we all woke up and there was a broken water main caused by the people in this local crack house. We all lost our water. Half the neighborhood was outside trying to talk to [city workers], find out what was going on, be supportive of each other, carrying buckets back and forth to the fire hydrant to get water with two-gallon jugs, getting their water and bringing it in. It was like being in a Jamaican village, I guess. Or someplace in the world. Being in Egypt where the women get up early in the morning before the sun is up, and they go down to the river, and they get water to carry it on their heads. I guess it went back to our primal roots or something. You know, you have that kind of thing that goes on up here and that's different from what goes on downtown.

Sharing the block with a suspected crack house means that apartment dwellers and home owners together experience temporary disaster as a shared crisis. Since a morning without water is inconvenient, neighbors rally together to set up an efficient system for coping with both their lack of information and water.

Yolanda Jackson acknowledges that this spirit of neighborliness sometimes "could get on my nerves." But she too recognizes the importance of communal action when confrontations over the negative impact of the drug culture become necessary. Jackson discusses the drug sales on her block. At first, this was a personal annoyance. But the individual action she took, reorganizing an existing but dormant neighborhood association, in the end mobilized the neighborhood. As a group, they confronted police:

> I got very active very early on the block. When I got on the block, there was a very serious angel dust problem, and it was really getting on my nerves. The block association had been kind of laying dormant, so I reorganized it and got people organized to go to the police precinct and demand that they clean the mess up off of our block. And it was very effective.

Jackson's action signaled to her neighbors that she cared about the quality of life on the block. Her solution also proved that she was willing to be involved with others. The result was that she was seen as someone who could make things happen. Then she became an important member of a neighborhood network:

> A number of people turned to me as someone they felt was knowledgeable and could get things done on the block. So I started filling out forms and reading for people who couldn't read. If they were having problems, I became sort of like a resource center.

Now neighbors come to Jackson with questions such as "Where should I go to get this and to get that?" She uses literacy and information as a resource in exchange for a mutual relationship of cooperation with other members of her block.

The anonymity often associated with life in a city as large and impersonal as New York is sometimes hard to detect in Harlem. Neighbors watch out for one another, and most people generally know the characters and routines in their immediate surroundings. From the elderly ladies who pay attention to comings and goings, to the men at the corner who maintain the order of a street or a block of territory, Harlem's gentry are drawn into the workings of community on a small scale. This provides a level of security as an additional benefit of community belonging for a new resident who is brought into this nexus of relationships.

Jackson, for instance, is aware that the unofficial and informal block watch is valuable for a single woman. When she returns to her unoccupied house at day's end or when she travels alone on the nighttime streets, she takes some comfort in knowing she does not navigate the terrain of her neighborhood alone:

> If they saw someone walking up on my stoop and they knew I wasn't home, they would tell them to get off the stoop, I wasn't home, leave. Then they would tell me that. They would describe who came up on the stoop or whatever. They watched out for me. I mean even down to the winos or the alcoholics. If I were walking home late at night and didn't drive my car, they would say, "We've told you about coming home late like this by yourself." One time a guy was behind me. I don't know if he was going to snatch my purse or whatever, but I turned around and I saw him, and when he saw me when I turned around quickly, he ran off. So I walked further up, and the alcoholics, you know, the drunks, said, "You didn't have to worry. We saw 'at motherfucker. He wadn't gun do nuthin to you. We had him scoped. You didn't have to worry about dat. But we keep telling you about walking in this neighborhood this late. We might not always be out here."

Their admonishment over her occasional but repeated practice of walking alone at night takes a friendly but firm, chiding tone. Aware of the dangers in their own territory, they caution Jackson like a parent might scold a child.

Other new brownstone owners come to appreciate this shared intimacy and the level of concern that lies behind it. June Wilson shares a story about a time when she was sick for several days. Two of her neighbors who had become used to her leaving the house and returning from work at regular hours noted an irregularity. They called her out of concern. "I was in shock," she says, laughing, "that on both sides of me they know my schedule."

For Wilson, this type of attentiveness reflects the familiarity that defines life in localized places within Harlem:

> They call me about things that go on in the area that they feel I should know about. And I certainly use the phone to call them quite often about different things. So, I feel comfortable. I mean, I probably feel more comfortable here than I did in New Jersey and that was [in] a doorman building with security. But I could have been in there dead for fifteen days and nobody would have even knocked to see if I was there. If there is no movement here for too long, I feel pretty comfortable that my neighbors will say, "What's going on?"

Wilson is not an unresponsive newcomer, indifferent to neighbors' information or concern. And she is not unwilling to share in this type of exchange. By her own account, Wilson will pick up the phone to call other neighbors, signaling that she places herself in a reciprocal relationship with them. For the new home owner to be accepted, actions that make up these relationships of familiarity must be a two-way process.

For Mimi Rogers, the level of watchfulness at first caught her off-guard, she says. But as a mother, eventually she welcomed the attention—especially the concern for her children's well-being:

> I had to sort of get accustomed to the fact that the elderly men that sit out here, that they were there kind of like to protect, and they knew everything that was going on. People that I knew that were in my neighborhood, that I met on the corner or that were part of the community, it was just "hi," you know, and go on. And it worked out very nicely, and they started to look out for the kids. They knew when my kids were coming home or who was going in my gate. They just watched, and you knew that by their saying, "There was a man out there knocking on your door. You weren't home, you know who he was?" They sort of watched out for you. An elderly man that lived next door, an old, I don't know whether he was Italian or what, but an old white man, one of the most racist, he hated blacks. He lived here for ages and ages. Can you imagine? But he just didn't like blacks. He was really nutty. But he used to watch out for us. The nastiest, most cantankerous man. He died, too, while we were here, and his house was sold to a black man, which he said never would happen. But he used to watch out for the kids.

For the concerned parent, a library, too, provides a place where children can find a safe harbor. Understanding the importance this institution holds for the community, Etta Harrison worked with a group of her neighbors to put on a library benefit, complete with jazz and poetry:

> Our library is beautiful. We gave a benefit for the library, and the libraries gave us an award because they said it was the first time in the history of the New York City Public Library that a branch library had a fund-raising for its library. We didn't know we were doing something special. It's just that our library is very important to us. And we hoped that we could raise funds to have it open one more day so the children could go every day. People can't afford day care, and the library is like a baby-sitting service. And there's not one of us around who has children that our child hasn't at some point sat in that library. You know, we'll be home late and don't want the kids to become latchkey kids. So we say, "I'll pick you up at five o'clock." Now that's our

> library. We all know the librarian. "Mr. Dwight, is my daughter there? Will you look out and see if Nicole is there?" You know, it's that kind of library. I mean you just feel happy because they're wonderful there. And all of us use that library.

For Greta Symes, another of the rewards of Harlem's intimacy is that there is someone to turn to in an emergency. As several residents in her neighborhood tell me, Mr. Washington, who owns a cleaning shop on the corner, is always willing to lend a helping hand:

> New York is a dangerous place for everybody. It doesn't matter who you are, how much money you have, what color you are, what class you are. This is a dangerous city. In this community there is a little more safe harbor because if I need something, I can call on a group of people who live nearby, and I know that they will help me. If I need something between 7 A.M. and 6 P.M. from Tuesday through Saturday, I know I can go around the corner to the cleaner's—Mr. Washington—and he will do whatever I need.

The security provided by residents' close watch of one another extends beyond concerns for individual well-being to a shared regard for property. For instance, owning a car that is parked on the street has built-in problems for any New York City resident. Parking spaces are hard to come by. Then there is the weekly chore of moving the car to comply with street-cleaning rules that dictate alternate side of the street parking. Purchasing an alarm system can provide a certain level of security for those who deal with the risk of car theft. But for each of these problems, a little neighborly concern also helps to relieve some of the headaches:

> They looked out for me. If they saw someone tinkering around my car, they ran them away. At six o'clock in the morning these little old ladies would call me up and say, "There's a parking space"—you know it's alternate side of the street parking—"you better get up and move your car to the other side of the street while you got a space."

> Some of our neighbors were nice right away. Like a couple of people in the rooming house next door, like when I had a different car than I have now, and I put it on the wrong side of the street. He'd ring our bell and say, "Ruth, you'd better move your car because they're giving out tickets." That kind of stuff. A couple of people were willing to do that right away.

> As a matter of fact, you know, I've got a car, and so if somebody comes and sits on my car, because I have a good relationship with people, somebody

said, "Man, don't sit on his car." I mean, those are people standing outside the building. "Hey, man, don't sit on his car, that's Malcolm Balderidge's car, that's Mr. Balderidge's. Don't sit on the car." I've seen it sometimes from up above. Just looking out the window, and I see somebody tell them, "Get off the car." They get them off the car. You know? Because they . . . like us, they like my family, they like my friends, you know.

Although tenure in Harlem for the newcomers I interviewed ranged from one year to ten, most could relate instances of friendly reminders, cautious warnings, or shared tips. The ways long-term neighbors reach out indicate how newcomers are taken into the protective fold of community watchfulness and cooperation.

But as Ruth Baxter-Brown points out, this is not automatic:

> It helps because we didn't set ourselves apart deliberately. Now, some people move up here, and they deliberately set themselves apart and don't speak to anybody, you know, they don't have anything to do with anything. And so as a consequence, they don't get to sort out those people who really are OK and the ones they really don't want to know. The people who kind of look weird but are basically all right. They've basically got good sense, and they're not going to bother you. And there's people who know everything that's going on in the neighborhood. That's someone you really need to know when you live in Harlem. I always thought it was dangerous to live in a neighborhood where as much stuff as can happen in Harlem happens and you don't know anybody. That's a bad idea.

What Baxter-Brown makes clear is that newcomers have to work at establishing a position for themselves in such informal networks of cooperation and concern:

> Well, a lot of these people are people who grew up there. You have to understand, these people live in Harlem who have never left it. There are people on my block whose children are older than I am. All right? I've got neighbors who have lived there fifty and sixty years. My neighbor just two doors down is eighty-two years old. Her children, all her kids, are older than we are. She and one of her sons are still in that house. But there are many people here like that. Harlem is not as empty as people believe it is. Many of these people spend their whole lives here. And they don't like to see people who are strangers. Just because we're strangers. White strangers get in double trouble, but we're all just strangers. And a lot of people who, when they start talking to us say, "Well you know, I've lived here all my life. And you haven't."

Yolanda Jackson sees upholding these long-established rules as one way for newcomers to fit themselves into neighborhood interactions:

> It's like they watched out for me, and I watched out for them. Those kinds of bonds were developed with the people who lived on the block, and some of these people had lived on the block for twenty or thirty years.

Long-term residence on Harlem's streets and blocks means that there are certain customs and habits that are unwritten along with strongly adhered-to rules regarding residence. These codes of behavior provide residents, whether home owners or renters, with a level of control over the streets and blocks they inhabit.

Such actions might seem snoopy or intrusive to high-rise dwellers accustomed to not knowing who lives in apartment 3B or 2C down the hall. It also reverses a code of suburban living where residents can live side by side for years and know little of neighbors on the other side of the fence.

But in an urban village like Harlem, children, personal property, schedules, and even personal well-being all can be a matter of public knowledge and concern. Neighbors will pick up the telephone or ring the doorbell, making an instant connection through an invisible barrier that surrounds individual private space. A more communal lifestyle shatters the zone that typically separates urban and suburban neighbors.

Friendship and Kinship through Community: Rituals and Spaces of Interaction and Exchange

On a day-to-day basis, Harlem functions for many as a world of communal spirit and kinship. There are specific emotional ties that the Harlem community offers when it functions on such a localized level. These ties pay off in collective belonging, something for which new black residents yearn.

Much like an extended family would, Yolanda Jackson's neighbors respond to death on their block through a collective experience of shared mourning. Jackson cites this as one of the kinship rituals she admires most about her new community. When someone on the block dies, Jackson explains, neighbors pool their resources:

> Depending on the financial stability of the person, we either buy them flowers or we just give them the money. We've even had to raise the money to bury somebody who didn't have an insurance policy. So people come together like that.

Jackson's mother died during the time she was living in Harlem. She recalls her neighbors' response:

> It was just really a wonderful feeling when my mother died. A thousand dollars came to me from the block. A thousand dollars. It came in two dollars, three dollars, one dollar, ten dollars. A man across the street gave two cases of sodas. Cakes came in, pies came in, chickens and hams. People watched our house for us. Now that's community. That's community and I wouldn't trade that.

The importance of this ritual in terms of the financial and emotional support it provides is taken seriously by members of Jackson's block. Jackson notes that one of the women on their block "doesn't believe in making financial contributions." Her unwillingness to participate in this ritual sets her apart, inviting scorn from neighbors:

> It's like culturally not with it for the neighborhood. You know like if you felt something for the person, you give a dollar or you give twenty dollars, thirty dollars, whatever. You give something. But she's opposed to that practice. What does she think? We're collecting that money 'cause most of the time people need that money to bury their people. You know what I mean? That's why the money's collected. They need it for something. And so the folks on the block say, "that weird white lady."

Sharing in the rituals of public life that define the bonds of community becomes an important way that neighborhood commitment is made public and interactive. These exchanges are important to move the private world of a home owner beyond narrowly defined personal spaces. The exchange of personal knowledge and information about family life is one way to make neighborhood connections more intimate. Circulating such knowledge gives the street the feeling of an extended family:

> I'm the president of the block association so I really do have to talk to people. But I felt like that anyway. I like my neighbors. I've come to know them. I know their kids. I know their grandchildren. I know who's in trouble. I know who doesn't have a job. I know who got laid off his job. I know who's in jail. To me that's just life, living in a neighborhood that's your own neighborhood.

Through an act as simple as sitting on one's stoop in the summertime with a cool drink and asking after so-and-so or nodding a friendly how-do to passersby, one participates in the shared interactions of the street. Public behavior provides security and signals communalism.

Ruth Baxter-Brown talks fondly about the stoop culture she remembers from childhood in Chicago. The stoop provides a stage not just for face-to-face interactions but also for gaining more intimate knowledge about important events, crises, and life changes in a neighbor's family:

> I like being on the street where I know everybody, you know. I like coming up the block and having people stop and say hi. I like knowing, you know, who is home from college and who is just out of the hospital. So, for all of Harlem's problems, it's still a neighborhood, unlike the rest of New York where nobody knows anybody, which I always hated. I feel safer when I know the people I live around, and in Harlem, I do. I have a real obsession for the way black folks live. We're loud, playing our radios and fixing our cars. We drink beer. We carry on. Man, I sort of like it. It's stupid, I know. It's not rational at all, but I have a real fondness for it.

For middle-class blacks, for whom the stoop also functions as a site of conflict, it can be the scene of connecting through neighborhood interactions. As a ritual space, the stoop defines belonging through participation in a community custom:

> See, every summer as it gets warm, I take the radio, I take a glass of iced tea, and I sit down on the stoop to keep other people off the stoop and remind them that we still live here, because they haven't seen us all winter. And it's also part of the neighborhood culture. People sit on stoops. That's part of black culture, anyway. So we come out and sit on the stoop. First of all, it says to them, well at least they sit on the stoop. We bring the radio out, we play BGO, the jazz station, because we like jazz. It also says, OK, so they're different from us, but they still sit on the stoop. It's part of the tradition of the community.

In this comment, Baxter-Brown reveals how initial perceptions of the young couple—two buppies who did not fit in and were not "for real"—shifted as they shared greetings and exchanged information within the rituals defining the stoop culture. For this couple, the stoop is a space where both similarity and difference are on public display. They broaden the meaning of this community tradition by using this public and private space to express an identity that is both black and middle class.

Private actions such as shopping and praying are also ritualized activities taking place in the public domain. The church and the market, for instance, provide spaces where interactions and cooperative networks cement bonds of familiarity across racial, ethnic, and class differences.

Attending church in Harlem enables Yolanda Jackson to reconnect to her spiritual roots. But the church also holds political significance. As a site where networks and interaction occur, the church facilitates the practice of coming into communion and service to the community. Beyond prayer and worship, as the following observations by Jackson, Kenyatta Davis, and June Wilson reveal, the church is an important place for political and social activism:

> Once I bought my house, I went back to church because I grew up in church. I have moved back to some of my spiritual roots. I'm really enjoying being part of Canaan Baptist Church. It's a socially responsible church in the community, and it's done so much in the Harlem community. So I got involved with the church, and I've gotten involved in projects at Harlem Hospital and other institutions in the community.

> I'm not a big churchgoer, but [in Harlem] I go to church periodically—just for the political energy that's there.

> If you go to the churches [in Harlem], you see congregations that are real heavy in terms of the influences where they are from—like the Caribbean. But you also see congregations with lots of southern black folks there, too, and they are finding ways to work together with each other. I go to the church on the corner. I've seen Koreans there. So there is an attempt at bringing in the people who are working here, the people who are living here. They are also worshiping here [together], and that's a good indication as to who's in the area and what their commitment is. Because when you start to worship together, that's another part of that bonding that takes place. That's very important to maintain a community. I mean, the church is the backbone, whether people want to deal with that or not. It has been for many, many years in our community, and it will be one of the parts that will help to bring us together, too.

The comments of each of these women highlight the importance of churches in the transition of the community and the need to integrate a newly diverse population. The Koreans that Wilson has seen attending her neighborhood church are a sign of an evolving multiethnic Harlem.

Even the local dry cleaner is the scene for heated discussion and political debate. When he has questions or is in search of something, the owner does not hesitate to ask customers with whom he is on familiar terms:

> He's really politically hepped up, wants to know more about everything. I mean, he asked me where could he get, you know, black history videocassettes and all that. And I told him, "You know, you should just tape a whole bunch of stuff that comes on Channel 13 in February, because that's as much as is going to be anywhere."

But the fact that a family has members from all walks of life still can place limits on the interactions among an *imagined* network of kin in a large and diverse community like Harlem. The criteria that shape rituals of play and dating are instances where class, race, and gender, and not race alone, shape networks of interaction.

Finding acceptable playmates for younger children is a middle-class practice that is accomplished through play dates organized by a limited network of selected parents. For children of these new residents, the street is not seen as an appropriate site of participation or interaction in the life of the community. Rather, it is a passageway between one's home and the world outside Harlem. In the following example, Etta Harrison describes why parents are anxious to find ways to keep their children off the streets:

> When I was the president of the block association, you still had kids playing on the street. Most of the owners don't like their kids playing in the street. They'll put them in back, or they'll go away. Lots of these people have weekend places. At one time, we were concerned about the safety of cars coming up and down looking for drug dealers. So you don't want your kids to play outside. And we fought very hard with the precinct to get rid of it and keep it off this block. But sometimes they'd chase them down. A car would be coming down here, and it was dangerous to the elderly—the seniors—and to the children. So we worked with them to get the street turned around. And I remember writing letters and encouraging that change in the street, which now goes one way.

With a literal reversal of the street, middle-class parents on Harrison's block hope to deter drug traffic that has plagued their immediate environment. And with economic resources that provide alternatives—backyard patios and gardens, summer and weekend homes—Harrison and others are able to keep their children from danger even as they shift the function and meaning of the street.

Harrison describes a network made up of other middle-class home owners and members of her church as a source of playmates for her fourteen-year-old daughter. She claims to choose these networks over neighborhood kids on the street because of shared values:

> Many of the kids go into families that there's violence, there's battery, there's a lack of values, there's promiscuity. The church is not important. You can't watch all these kids. So you select the kids that your kids can play with. You go to church and select a group of kids. There's a church group. They go on skating parties and dances at other churches.

By confining her daughter to the backyard and using the church as a networking arena for acceptable playmates, Harrison, as a mother, is able to shape the boundaries of her daughter's social world.

Dating poses problems for black women gentry in Harlem as well. In chapter 3, Portia Hamilton and Kenyatta Davis cited the promise of black marriage and dating partners as one draw of the community. In Hamilton's initial struggle with other residents on her street, she was labeled a "prostitute" and mistakenly identified as white and then as snobbish. These first encounters may not prevent her from pursuing a male partner, but they are not an auspicious start.

Davis describes dating difficulties she has experienced in and out of Harlem. As her comments make clear, interest and mutual attraction are not enough to sustain romance. Davis found that whether inside or outside Harlem, she was invariably meeting men whose attitudes and experiences differed in one way or another from her own. In either world, these men did not understand her:

> You catch a lot of heat socially in terms of romance. There was a guy on my block that I thought was just too gorgeous. And we obviously had a mutual attraction. But the more we got to know each other and the more he came to realize what kind of lifestyle I lead, the more he backed off. He was intimidated by the fact that I had a job where I read all the time, which makes me very vocal, very opinionated. I know men who don't want a woman, you know, walking around talking and analyzing and criticizing more than they do, or are an "intellectual" when they are not. So on one hand, my being a professional person was kind of intimidating to him. He was still struggling to find a profession. We were about the same age, and he had been to college. I don't think he got his degree. He just had enough hard times come his way professionally. So in that sense, I'm set apart socially. The more I learn, the more I'm exposed to, the fewer options I have for relationships. I just kind of have to live with it because you can't make people be comfortable with you. They'll respect a degree and wonder why the hell you want to live on 143rd Street, or you get those who understand why you live at 143rd Street but don't understand why you have to work all week to support the white man's world. It's

> difficult because it makes it lonely to be in either position. It means I just have fewer options in terms of relationships. And when I meet a man that is comfortable with who I am, then I'm just real happy about it. You know—grateful and all that stuff—and I mean probably one in fifty is [comfortable]. In six years of being in New York, I've befriended one man who works in the corporate world as I do, but who also lives in this community as I do and shares my same values on either side.

For Davis, education and experiences combine to clash with men's expectations. Davis takes on a resigned tone as she acknowledges that her professional status and race identification limit her dating possibilities across two worlds.

Talkin' the Talk: Interaction through Language and Conversational Styles

Shared life in Harlem has a conversational and linguistic basis as well. Newcomers point to conversations that take place on the street and in specific public arenas as an important element of a black cultural style.

For Kenyatta Davis, who is a poet, moving in and out of public spaces in the community provides a connection to black language that informs her artistic work. When black elders, all men, hold court at a well-known local restaurant, for instance, they become responsible for the oral transmission of community lore:

> It's so dramatic for me. Sitting in Pan Pan and overhearing serious political discussions. You know, people are talking issues, and you hear what they feel about it. There are many people in Harlem that have a great sense of history and will tell you at the drop of a hat their story about when Fidel was at the Theresa Hotel, their story about when Malcolm was on the corner, and who ain't shit and who is, and, you know, that kind of thing.

Carrying on a tradition established by Langston Hughes and other Harlem Renaissance writers, Davis has used Harlem as a subject in her own poetry and prose. And the role of a language one hears and uses in the black community, she says, is an important influence on artistic work:

> So much happens on the street for you to see. I mean, just walking through Harlem, just overhearing conversations and the things that are said and directed toward me. How men respond to you if they like what you have on. This is Africa here. I mean, through the names of the businesses, that kind of thing. Just being on the street and listening to people and watching the people, paying attention to their thoughts and feelings, seeing how this culture is

rooted in Africa. I don't have to make up or invent anything in the way of conflict or tension or drama.

Stressing the connection between language and community participation, Malcolm Balderidge shares a lesson passed on by James Baldwin, a Harlem native who exiled himself to France as an adult:

> I did the last interview with James Baldwin, you know. And I didn't have a tape recorder. But he was saying, "One of the things I'm sad about is I left New York like that. I should have had more courage." He said, "I got out of touch with the language. Didn't hear southern fried. Because it's beautiful, it is, it's beautiful. So I got out of touch with the nuances of the language, just the little bitty things. I just got out of touch with listening to it every day." That's why I used to go to my brother's bar, stayed three weeks at McHale's at the bar, listening to people. And just go from bar to bar to bar to bar. People used to think I was getting drunk all the time, but the reason I was going to the bar was so I could listen.

Life in Harlem provides a daily connection to black language, and this nourishment takes specific form in Balderidge's production of art:

> I think it's very important to stay in touch with the language, you know, because poets are the protectors of centuries of language. So for me to live here in Harlem and just walk out in the street and hear all this language coming at me is an everyday thing. I don't have to think about it. I walk out, and when I listen, I hear it. And poetry is the art of language so I have to be able to be in touch with that. It is totally different from when I lived in Santa Cruz on the beach. You know, I worry about that. Out there, there's another kind of language, you see. I'm going to hear something else. I mean, hear words used in another way. And I'm going to have to think about that. So I'm going to have to kind of make efforts to Scotch-Tape myself to certain places, you know what I mean? So I can hear some stuff, you know, so my ear won't get dead. The language is fabulous. I love listening to a language, I mean, as a writer, and as a poet. That is where it's at. That is the thing, you know what I mean? They make up all the new words. You say, Jesus, they make it up like this [snaps fingers]. And them rhymes. People are saying, "Where is the future of poetry?" I said, "You haven't seen it? I have." So those kinds of things will serve me well here, just living here.

Balderidge draws on the advice of James Baldwin to keep an attachment to people and public spaces in the community. Locations such as the subway, the street, or a bar all function as sites of black cultural identity and its transmission through language.

The style of language is one way to define a position in the community. Thus, for many newcomers, neighborhood and community interactions involve careful impression management. In particular, speech patterns and slang become important means of allaying anxieties about closing the social distance that, for upwardly mobile minorities, accompanies college education and acquired professional status.

In the following comment, Balderidge places a great deal of emphasis on the way behavior can be an obstacle or a bridge in dealing with Harlem diversity:

> I mean, they know somebody who's real and who's not. People know that. And I think that, you know, you live in a community like this which is varied and multitiered in terms of education and money and what people do and values and all of that. You have to be real, and if you're real, they deal with that. And they feel good about that.

In the previous chapter, Joe Baxter-Brown used a similar expression when he described why his neighbors' initial reactions to him and his wife were marked by suspicion. Neighbors were, according to Baxter-Brown, unsure if the couple—two buppies—were "for real or not."

Brittany Rogers moves beyond the conflicts over possible displacement associated with gentrification and approaches Harlem as a space where she fits in by constructing a "real" persona that she contrasts with that of an older generation of middle-class blacks:

> I have to say, I take the subway, and I walk around the neighborhood and stuff. I don't have any problem with, you know, the guys at the stores who say, "Hey baby, what's happenin'?" I'm down with most of the neighbors so I can't relate to it from the point of view of someone like my mother, or her cousin—they're from a different generation.

Through her slang, Rogers places herself as a natural player in the outdoor terrain of the neighborhood and the subterranean space of the subway. Moving back and forth from NYU to Harlem, she projects an anything-goes attitude that helps her survive as an urban villager moving between settings black and white. By claiming to be "down with the neighbors," she uses language that separates her—a young, black middle-class woman who has always pivoted between two worlds—from her mother and older middle-class Harlemites.

Where newness stands as an obstacle, how one acts can be crucial to acceptance. Wanting to "be real" signals a desire for belonging that gives rise to carefully designed strategies of action. This desire leads to behavior that takes into account the tensions produced by gentrification and fears of displacement:

> While there's this friction, if you go out of your way to let people know that you're OK, you don't let that stand in the way. You speak to them just like you would speak to anybody else. "What's happening? How you doing?" Yeah, I speak to everybody. I speak to everybody. I deal with them. We don't look down on them, we deal with them in a day-to-day manner. They do something silly, I'm going to tell them, "Hey, man, don't do that." They know I ain't no poot butt, you know what I mean? I might teach and might write and all that kind of stuff, but you do something silly, I'm going to tell you just like anybody else. And you gonna have to deal with it. Ain't going to be no stuff like, I like, want to say that to you. I mean, I'll smack you in your mouth. You know? You do this to me, you do it to me, I'm smacking you in your mouth. I'm not going to tell you, "Please, would you not do this?" I'm hitting you, man. You know I'm going to hit you, too. I haven't had to do that but once.

Balderidge moves back and forth between two speech codes to make the point that status differences do not stand in the way of his dealing with neighbors. His relaxed performance sprinkled with slang is of a street-savvy character, in contrast to the more uptight, proper-speaking character whose manner would seem out of place for street interactions.

For an unapologetic Balderidge, the language and culture of Harlem demands this shifting:

> I am what I am, and I know what that is. You know? I'm not ashamed of it. That doesn't mean that you don't carry information and intelligence and all that. Because you say "dese" instead of "these," "doah" instead of "door," "fo" instead of "for." You know what "for" means, but you also know what "fo" means. You know what I mean? I mean, all Americans, for the most part, are schizophrenic. So why not be schizophrenic? Jump back and forth, you know what I mean? In between both. If it's necessary. Don't get off on 116th Street and Lenox talking about, "Excuse me, do you know where Professor Balderidge lives?" I mean, if you're coming from Wall Street, realize that you're on 116th and Lenox. And that truly is an American thing to be schizophrenic. Not just black folks. Everybody. Double consciousness and the veil is everybody. It ain't just black people. Du Bois was wrong there when he said we were double conscious behind the veil. It's everybody in the United States. But you got to know how to deal with it and manipulate it to your advantage.

Additionally, through a "status leveling," Balderidge places himself in a position where he will not be seen as "looking down on anyone." He sprinkles a conversation with a slang that tumbles from the mouth of a tough character, unafraid to use violence if crossed. Balderidge also projects his version of a masculinity needed to adapt to the streets. Unlike the women in the previous chapter who negotiated uses of public space, Balderidge eschews a polite conversational tone, instead opting for a more direct and confrontational stance. As a male, this style may be more available to him in dealing with other men on the street.

June Wilson articulates a similar concern for erasing the boundary making her an outsider. She describes the types of actions that separate those who come to Harlem, sincere in their desire to be an integral part of the community, from those not interested in participating in the life and traditions of the community. A willingness to engage in conversation is an important bridge:

> [Because] my intent is a little bit more than just buying property and living downtown and not knowing people, I talk to the folks around here. I walk down the streets, I have conversations with the little folks in the bodegas. And at the block parties I talk to the ladies. I like that because it gives me a real sense of what kind of community I'm in, and it makes me feel like I'm back at home.

Making herself a part of the public space of the neighborhood enables Wilson to use walking and talking to "be real" in her position as a new type of Harlemite. The bodega is not only a site of commerce and trade, but equally a space where important face-to-face interactions take place. And like the bodega, block parties are a scene where intergenerational connections are made as well.

In part, knowing the value and importance of this type of participation comes from growing up in a black community. May Dixon, who grew up in a segregated community in the South, sees in Harlem a continuity with her own past. She finds evidence for this in a style of language and caring that defines the public spaces of her neighborhood:

> I like people speaking to me on the street. I like being in a community where, you know, somebody will say, "Good morning," or "Hi," or "How are you?" I mean, that was different, you know, from other parts of New York. And so I just feel comfortable. I mean, I feel more of a sense of community than I did living in another place in New York. So I mean, I really like it. It's about survival. The fact that every day I can walk out of here, and I don't have to believe

> all that crap on television and in the papers. I can see my Cotton Club cuties, you know. I can see people dressed up going to work, you know, working. I can see mothers with their babies in the playground. I can see what we as black people are and, I mean, really get a sense of community. And you say, hey, this is how we survive. I mean, that's just one part of it. Kids playing on the basketball court and block parties. Where else are you going to have that? Where else are you going to see that much celebration of self, despite everything that we've been through, and despite the junkies nodding out, or the winos laying out in the gutter? And you can also see us doing for each other here. "Hey, baby how you doing today? How you feeling?" How many black people ask each other how they're feeling, even hear somebody ask, "How you feeling?" Every day, I hear this. All the caring, you know.

Having grown up in a black community makes Dixon comfortable, for instance, with cross-generational arguments and discussions with her local dry cleaner, whom she identifies as a "race man." But even this relationship has its limits for Dixon, who gets annoyed at the lack of give-and-take in a discussion that heads inevitably toward a dead end:

> I feel comfortable having arguments with Mr. Washington, the cleaner, about politics and who's right and who's wrong. Well, Mr. Washington is really an interesting person, because he is very much a black, a race man. That's how we describe him, you know. But he has his own concept of what that is, I mean, and his own ideas. I mean, he's like some of these other brothers out in the street. I mean, you try to have a discussion, and if you're not on the same path, forget it. Because it just goes out the window. But you go in there, and I mean, you're going to have a discussion if he baits you into one, you know. Or if there's something that's topical that he wants to talk about, he'll say, "Ms. Dixon, what do you think about such and so." So you know, I mean, he's just an interesting person. I mean, you're always going to have a discussion or a conversation with him that goes up to this far, then that's it.

Black Gentry as Role Models

Reggie Smith speaks critically of his black peers who "refuse to accept the proposal that opening a shop on 125th Street is an honorable way to make a dollar." Smith looks negatively on black friends and colleagues who think "the only avenue is corporate America. As long as that value system exists, how can Harlem build itself up?" He explains:

> I meet blacks every day who don't want to come to Harlem. I propose holding conventions here—people laugh. I think it's a matter of coming back to the

community, investing in the community. The return of the middle class signals leadership. We're seeing pockets of the neighborhood turned around. People in these neighborhoods are retrained and reintroduced to the community spirit. People with ability have to come back—it's a brain drain for the community. There has to be a positive force.

May Dixon, talking about her decision to be in Harlem and participate in the life of the community, points to differences between black and white gentry. She imagines that in addition to a communion of fellowship with members of their race, middle-class blacks come to Harlem to serve as the type of positive force Smith sees as missing:

[Whites are] interested in the community but not as much as, say, a black family who is coming in with children, or a black woman or a black man who eventually will have a family here. Why do we come? Why do they come? They ain't coming for us. Let's face it. They're not coming because they want beautiful black people and they love them. We come because we want to be with black people, or we remember something from our own family, or about the black community, or because we can do things here. There are all kinds of reasons. Most of them are tied to our culture, our cultural ties, these are mostly cultural ties. So we can never forget where we came from. So we come here for that. In other words, we don't ever run around with our noses in the air and only talk to other gentry. We don't really. We don't forget what we're here for. We realize that commitment is to all of our people. You can't give your time but not your heart.

The collective ideal held by many of this group of new middle-class residents is largely shaped by an intersection of race and class that makes individualism unattractive. Kenyatta Davis argues that a middle-class connection to the black community is critical:

I care about black people all over the world. I won't necessarily be here for the rest of my life. But wherever I am, it will probably be a black community, and/or I will be involved in black communities. I might be in Lagos. And I would have the same concern and interest. I lived in Atlanta for eleven years, and I feel as attached to Atlanta as I do to New York. So it matters less that it's Harlem than that it's black. Because I know that if I don't care about my own people, then nobody else is going to care for them.

Malcolm Balderidge argues that as a successful writer and college professor, he would be remiss were he not to share his success:

And now people around here buy my books. You know, they go out and buy the books. "That's a strange guy, shit," they be saying to themselves. "He's weird. He's interesting," you know what I mean? "He says all kind of crazy shit. Did you hear what he said the other day to that lady down there? And that old man? Not to mention what he said to the drug dealer the other day. He said he'd hit him upside his head. Damn! And he's a professor, you know. I better go buy his book, see what's in his head, you know." So then they say, "I got your book, you want to sign it?" So I say, "oh, yes." So I sign the book, yeah. Then they go out and buy another one. And they like it, you know. And they bought the Ralph Ellison book. Some people bought the Richard Wright book, bought all my books, bought about five books. I think that's good. I mean, the best compliment I ever got, I think, as a writer. That's good, you know. You know, I like that impact.

George Carver also expresses a desire that his status have a positive impact on a younger generation of blacks. Carver understands that as a black professional he is a role model in worlds far beyond Harlem:

As far as role modeling, in spite of myself, I am. It turns out I like being one. I'm very sensitive to that. The fact that my name is in this magazine, the fact that I've made the pages of major publications and black media gives me outreach to communities, black communities, all over the country. I get letters from kids in Omaha, Nebraska, and Anchorage, Alaska. Black kids, OK?

In his neighborhood, Carver grounds his responsibility in a more immediate and intimate setting. As a highly visible model in the neighborhood and on his block, he does not distance himself from the younger generation. Instead he opts for direct contact with local children:

When I come here, they can see me on an everyday basis. I walk down the street delighted that kids come across, come off the stoop and walk me to my door. Not because I'm some hero, but I'm showing them that I'm accessible. Most blacks you'll find get too important for that, too snobby. So I don't have to brag about what I do or who I am. But kids on the block know that I'm the one that gave so-and-so the Hot Car racer set for his birthday, or whatever. Or you know, see them playing and give them ten cents to go buy Popsicles. It's little friendly things like that. They just see me as that guy who's friendly. But that's all part of the mentoring process, the role-modeling process.

Implicit is a critique of black professionals who abdicate their responsibility as role models.

In the following comments Malcolm Balderidge and Kenyatta Davis both argue that their professional standing is a resource for the community:

> You know, I feel in a collective sense, in a sociological sense, it's good for young people to know what a poet is. Or what a writer is. Because in most African American communities, they don't know what that is. I mean, they just don't know what you do. I mean, the thought never occurred to them how you did that. Or what you did or what that involved. You know, I remember walking down here one day after something I had written or they had written about me appeared in *Essence* or some magazine. And this woman comes up to me and says, "God, I saw your picture and I saw you in *Essence,* and I saw your piece. And you know, I used to think you was a pimp." I said, "You did?" I looked at her, I was stunned. My wife used to work, she was an accountant. So she used to go to work every day, you know what I mean? She would go to work every day and go downtown. She said, "I saw that woman coming out of there every day, and you weren't doing nothing, you was walking around all times of the day. I said what is that man? That woman working hard, and he don't be doin' shit. You must be a pimp, or a drug dealer or something." She had no idea what I did.

> I try not to magnify what I do because I don't think that as one person in the relative scheme of things I do a damn thing. But I think for each individual that tries to stay here and have some respect for the community, I think that that helps. So I help in that I just add one more person to a community of people that care about Harlem, that respect it, that don't want to see it die. Because I'm one more person who is house-proud in living here. One more person spending dollars here and just being a living example to other black people who are less fortunate that things can be better. Because I'm not rich, but I do OK. I do better than my mother ever did. I make more money than she's ever made. I'm the first out of a huge family of women to earn a college degree. So if I can be one more person walking around who survived academia, who survived the corporate world, that gives some kid out here an alternative, you know, to say, "If she could do that, and I'm smarter than she is, I can do that."

During the ten years Yolanda Jackson has lived in Harlem, her parents came to live with her in her brownstone. Until her mother's death in 1987, the older woman was involved in the life of the neighborhood. Her father continues to be a strong presence on the block, providing mentoring and support for a younger generation. Mr. Jackson, for example, shows movies and organizes parties and events for teenage boys "to keep them off the streets," Yolanda tells me.

Yolanda recognizes that because of her professional status, people on her block pay attention to her. Although this visibility is a source of some discomfort, she expresses a wish that her presence will provide a positive example:

> I would hope that I would be a role model. Whether I am or not I don't know. I know that people respect me. Almost to a distraction where people my age call me Miss Yolanda. And I'll say, "I'm Yolanda." But I have a certain amount of respect, and maybe somebody's daughter or son who sees me says, "I want to live like her or be like her," or something like that. They talk with me. They know me.

Portia Hamilton maintains that when she made the decision to move to Harlem, she did not intend to be a role model. She knew she would be active, she says. What she did not realize is that her activism would also be signaled through her personal comportment:

> One of the things I have come to realize since I have been here is that there is a great need for role models in this community. After work and on the block at community meetings, whatever. So I try very hard to present myself in a positive light whenever I can. Even in what I wear, the clothes I wear, I set a standard.
>
> I know profanity is not a sexist issue, but I said to myself, "What kind of example are we setting for the youth when you say to them the only way to express anger is by using profanity?" It's not necessary.

With attention to language and clothing, Hamilton is able to present a "front" of respectability for children on her street. She sees this as a necessary alternative to what she calls "demeaning examples and images" about blacks all over.

In *Black Metropolis*, the landmark 1945 study of Chicago's black belt, Horace Cayton and St. Clair Drake identified a function of the black middle class that they termed "advancing the race." According to Cayton and Drake, strategies for advancing the race refer to two things: individual achievement that reflects positively on the race, and organized social activities designed to raise the status of the group as a whole.[4] Cayton and Drake concluded that when upper-class and middle-class people talk about advancing the race, "what they really mean is creating conditions under which lower-class traits disappear and something approaching the middle-class way of life will prevail. Middle-class people want to remake the ghetto in their own image."[5]

Sometimes masked in a subtle language of superiority, habits, behavior, manner of dress, and speech are presented as positive and viable alternatives for all children coming up in Harlem today. These symbols are used to suggest that where the middle class has come from is where their neighborhood cohorts, given the opportunity, would desire to go. But the accomplishments of individuals cannot alone raise aspirations in the face of structural limits to opportunity and differing life chances among middle-class, working-class, and poor blacks in Harlem.

While the desire to serve up more positive images can be described in the noblest of terms, the collective persona that middle-class blacks project accompanies an anguish just beneath the veneer of their professional success. The extent to which they receive respect, esteem, and status from neighborhood cohorts provides psychic rewards for middle-class blacks upon arriving in Harlem. Stepping into highly visible positions within the black community helps replace an invisibility that makes them marginal in the alienating corporate and professional worlds they also inhabit.

CONDOMINIUMS
FOR SALE
212-870-4117

chapter 6

Home Ownership and Political Participation

Just as the newcomers seek to make bonds with the community through private behavior toward their neighbors, they join in the institutional and political life of the neighborhood for similar purposes. On a May evening in 1991, I attend a meeting of the Harlem Homeowners and Taxpayers Association. The meeting is held on 125th Street in the suite of offices that house Community Board 10. A housing commissioner from the office of Housing Preservation and Development, the city agency that controls Harlem's boarded-up brownstones and in rem properties, presides over a question-and-answer session.

Couples young and old, mothers with children in tow, and commuters just off buses and trains, briefcases in hand, newspapers tucked under their arms, intermittently file into the room and take seats in rows of folding chairs. A small crowd at the front of the room discusses last month's business with the association's president. Copies circulate of an *Amsterdam News* article about the relocation of a Harlem computer facility to downtown offices.

The meeting is a public forum where Joy Rappaport, a housing commissioner, fields questions and comments. Concerned and angry home owners stand up one by one to voice their complaints. As home owners and taxpayers, these Harlemites are disturbed by what they view as disrespect for their values of community and family. One man argues that there is a certain ethic that home owners in Harlem share. This ethic, he maintains, is destroyed when the city places "outsiders" into its properties:

> Most of Harlem's brownstones are in the middle of the block. On each end of the block, you have apartment houses. What is happening is you are fixing

> those houses up, but the type of people you are putting in there never lived in Harlem before, they don't know the values of how hard we worked for our houses. People that have been brought up in Harlem know when you bought a brownstone, you worked hard for it. Now these houses are being filled with homeless from all over the borough. I've never had graffiti on my brownstone, and all of a sudden it's everywhere. I think someone in city hall should look and see what type of person or who they're putting in. If they came from Harlem, they know what brownstones are about. But if they came from outside, they're going to destroy us. They're going to make us move.

Through their attendance at town meetings and their membership on neighborhood task forces, block associations, political committees, and planning panels, middle-class black newcomers join members of the existing community in a long-running and well-defined political battle. As college-educated professionals, Harlem's black gentry bring political savvy and familiarity with government systems and bureaucracy as resources they offer for the benefit of the larger community. Unafraid to pressure officials and confront government machinery, many of Harlem's gentry assume positions of authority and leadership in confronting the myriad problems that face the community.

Obviously, there is a high level of self-interest that prompts such political action and participation. But the larger goal, many argue, is to revitalize the community and preserve its traditions and institutions, the same struggle long-term residents have fought.

For some, this level of active involvement helps erase the line between insider and outsider for new residents. "I think you can learn not to be an outsider," Ruth Baxter-Brown explains as she shares how such a strategy works:

> If people really understand that you're committed, then you don't feel like an outsider. That's why I got involved in community politics. We have great police service, we have great sanitation service, in part because of our activism. I'm part of the traditional block association. We're in every Twentieth Precinct community council meeting. The police captain in the Twentieth Precinct knows me by name, by sight. He drives through our block to check on how things are. You have to work for that to happen.

In this way, individual acts of political activism contribute to the collective good. Others, too, have become actively and vocally involved in community politics. The demands and force with which many of these home owners voice their dissatisfaction to city officials and agencies make them highly visible personalities in the community—to their neighbors as well as to their local police precincts. Several people told me that since moving to Harlem, they had become known by name to local police officials who noted, often with amusement, the frequency of their calls.

June Wilson's community activism has been focused on maintaining Harlem as an attractive residential space:

> There's this group I've been involved in called Harlem Pride which has been put together within the last few months just for that reason, to let the city know that, wait a minute, we're not going to take this anymore, there are certain things we want you to consider when you look at the housing here. We're not allowing you to bring in the homeless from every other place in the city when people are walking the streets of Harlem without places to lay their heads. We're not letting you turn every place into a parole center, every place into a hospice for AIDS patients and not have the proper services in place to help these people through their transition. You know because if you don't have those things in place, it's a dumping ground, plain and simple.

Ruth Baxter-Brown recognizes a level of self-interest that is behind some of her political activism in the community:

> I'm on a task force on AIDS and homelessness. I sort of got in it by accident, because I got in a fight about them building an AIDS hospital—an AIDS nursing home—across the street from our house, which you know, sounds like self-interest, and in a lot of ways was self-interested.

But Baxter-Brown, like Wilson, maintains that her political activism is linked to an ongoing community resistance to city actions. This, she explains, positions her on the side of articulating a broader community interest:

> But we already had six other facilities in a two-block area, and I said, "Yo! This is enough." Marginal neighborhoods like this cannot take this kind of proliferation. We don't need a two-hundred-bed hospital and a shelter all in the same neighborhood. We need supermarkets and housing so middle-class people can come and stabilize.

Wilson and Baxter-Brown define their community involvement as a struggle against the city for better housing and living conditions. This helps to recast lines of insider and outsider by identifying a common enemy.

Echoing concerns of long-term Harlemites who express caution and, at times, disdain about the migration of middle-class blacks to Harlem, Wilson agrees that it does no good for middle-class blacks to move into Harlem and then distance themselves from the community. "I don't wear the middle-class banner like it's a badge that you get in the Girl Scouts," argues Wilson. Instead, she suggests, middle-class blacks should use available status or power to benefit the community:

> It can become important if I have an advantage when it comes to going in and trying to effect some change in the community. Whether it's getting a company to donate products to a welfare hotel, whether it's trying to get a meeting with someone in city hall, I think I owe that to the community. If you have juice anywhere, you should use it. You know, you should use your influence. You need to treat it like it's money and it's valuable. And so you should use your influence where it counts the most, spend it in the best way possible. Make it count.
>
> I'm involved in other things, like Copeland's Christmas Fund for Kids, which is a group that was started by Mr. Copeland of Copeland's Restaurant, which helps young folks. We devote the whole day of Christmas Day to kids in the area who are disadvantaged, whether it's welfare hotels or women in the battered women's shelters or homeless men. I work with a men's shelter. I have also been working with the Urban Shelter, which is a battered women's shelter. A lot of the things I work with, they find their way under the same banner. So I get involved in that way.

Wilson's argument that one's status cannot be worn "like a badge" underscores the line separating arrogance and neighborliness.

Portia Hamilton, after being targeted as an outsider by a group of activists during her struggles with former tenants, is sensitive about this line. She explains:

> The resentment is not so much because I'm a home owner. But it's because I have more information, and if I see something that needs to be done, I can call this one by the first name and get us a response in two or three days. I go to meetings, and I'll try to keep my mouth shut. Because I know people have feelings about me. When I reactivated the block association, they asked who the president would be. I said I thought it should be someone on the block who had been here for a while, not I as a newcomer. It looked like I was taking over and telling them what to do. So I said, now, I'll be here. I'll be in the background. I'll be on committees. I'll support them. Because I was sensitive to that. Here you are the newest person on the block, you're going to come in and take over?

But at times, these college-educated professionals bring their own ideas about the appropriate mechanisms for change. Ruth Baxter-Brown rejects the confrontational style that has defined past run-ins between Harlemites and the city to highlight the strategies of a new generation:

> White institutional power really does believe that people are going to roll over and play dead. We're not frightened by them. We're not intimidated by them. I was at Princeton. They don't know any more than I know. All right? Talking about what they can't do and on and on. Like, hey, you need to save that for that poor little old lady sitting over there who has always spoken to white people when she's trying to get paid, OK? Don't tell me what you can't do. You can do what you want. The question is this is a matter of will. Do you have the will to do this, or do I have to persuade you? So you say, hey, you can't do this, and we'll call the lawyer. We're prepared to raise hell in a sort of sophisticated manner. There are still lots of people up here who believe that the way to stop doing something is to get a human picket line and hold hands around a place. They call the police. The police will just lift you up while the building is torn down. That's what lawyers are for, girl. Out there holding hands. Later for holding hands. Hold up people's money. They understand that, right? You want to build a hospital? All right, you committed eight million dollars to this project. And every day that you don't get it built costs you money. I'm going to make you take a year. That's 365 days that your money is sitting there not making any money. So, you need to find another site for this place, because I'm going to make it economically impossible for you to do this. They understand that. Later for holding hands. Money talks, and everything else walks. White people really understand when you mess with their money. And that is a level of sophistication people have arrived at here now. This is why there's going to be a big mess in the coming years about just how many of those service agencies are put here. Just what I need, more customers and crack problems. More people which we know about, and God knows how many we don't know about. So problems with Harlem are the problems of any underserved community. We got some really angry people. And the question is whether or not Harlem will continually be underserved.

Baxter-Brown, who has taken an outspoken position in her neighborhood's battles with the city, defines her political activism as an individual style that is part of a larger collective resistance:

> I made a promise to myself one year that I wasn't going to let anything pass anymore, that New York was hard enough. Now I can't say that I never let anything pass, but I let a lot less pass than I used to, you know. And it's why when they said they were going to build this hospital over there, I said, "No, you all can't build that here." And I went to where we're having an alleged public

> hearing, and got up and gave this impassioned speech about the importance of stability in a community, and that I had as much right to fight for my neighborhood as anybody on Central Park or Park Slope or the Upper West Side or anybody else. And I had all the skills it would take to do that, and I was not playing.
>
> But I can't frighten anybody by myself that much. I need people to have a sense that there is a collective. When a block association shows up at a hearing, they all come. I've got a woman in my block who's ninety years old, got up out of her warm bed in the middle of January to come to that meeting. See, you can do stuff when you have that. So, I had a room full of cheering people when I'm speaking. That gives you the impetus that lets people in the opposition know that you're nobody to fuck with.

While the strategy to reclaim Harlem gives rise to broad-based community activism for Baxter-Brown and Wilson, Malcolm Balderidge favors thinking small. When he is accused of not participating in the big battles to save Harlem, Balderidge claims to imagine Harlem as a small and localized entity. To re-create Harlem one building at a time, or one block at a time, means acting more locally to revitalize the community:

> I think it has a great potential, if people who are educated, have money, and have some resources would come and give and lend individual kinds of efforts to make a collective effort which has impact. I don't think one person can make impact. I don't think my coming here made any difference. I think my coming here and then working with others, you know, and then us doing it together, made impact. Say on this building here and on this little area right here. Somebody said to me one time, "Well, why don't you get involved in Harlem?" This guy was from 155th Street. I said, "I am involved." He said, "Well I mean get involved in Harlem." I said, "Listen, man, I do a lot. But you have to do it in your own little neighborhood, your own little thing. That's the problem. Everybody thinks too big too quick. So let's get your own little building together. Get your building together first. We're going to get our building tight. You get your building tight. I ain't got time to help you get your building tight. I don't even know nobody in your building. I mean, I do know some people, but I don't know them. I'm surely not coming up there three, four days a week. I got too much to do. That's too much time. You know, I can come from my building, from my little apartment on the seventh floor and go down to the fourth floor for a meeting and be there an hour. I cannot spend an hour getting to your apartment, finding a parking space, you know, and then go upstairs, and then have to deal with that and then come

back. I mean, it's too much time. And plus I'm not really interested, you know. Harlem is an abstract. It's an abstract, you know, in the sense that it's Harlem. It's a myth. I mean, Harlem, one, you got Columbia, you know what I mean? You got Columbia University, you see. You got Morningside. You got all these different areas. Pockets and areas of Harlem. I mean, 116th Street is different from 125th Street. It is not some homogeneous whole. It's not that. You got a street over there, 123rd Street, right off Mount Morris. So what I'm saying, it's not homogeneous. And so it's a myth, this whole thing. It's a collection of different places. You got Sugar Hill. You got all these different kinds of neighborhoods. Jumel Terrace. You got real bourgeois people up around Jumel Terrace and 165th Street, all up in there. Then you have the whole thing up here at Lenox Terrace. So you know, you have all these different, disparate kind of communities thrown together. So get yours together. I get this little thing together, then if we get it tight, then we can say, OK, let's have a umbrella, OK? You have a representative on this board, a kind of board, you know, above politicians. Then we can put pressure on their asses, you know, but let's just get the step-by-step process. I'm a very patient person. You know, I'm a very patient person. It takes twenty years. It don't take one year. So we in too much of a rush sometimes to do things. Let's get it together. Let's get the thing together, let's get the money together. Then we can start doing it. Then we can say we got our apartment, we got our house, we got the complexes, we got the neighborhoods, you know, maybe two blocks."

Whether they act to bring change to their own houses, buildings, streets, or blocks, or whether they lead the charge for all of Harlem, black gentry as home owners face criticism about their political involvement. Newcomers can be tagged quickly as interlopers:

> I think in some respects I'm still considered an outsider. "You people" seems to mean anyone who's coming in and buying a house and working on it. They complain and fuss because Koreans and whites have all the businesses on 125th Street. Doesn't really matter what color you are, even though for many folks in this community "you people" always supposed to be white. But they lump us in as the "you people."

The logic that whites are naturally hostile outsiders who would reclaim Harlem today stumbles on a complicated ethnic and racial mix that has always been a fact of Harlem life. Old and new struggles for control in Harlem are peopled by Asian, African, and Jewish shopkeepers along with new home owners, black and white. Instead of being reworked through a multiracial vocabulary, categories are collapsed for simplicity, and *anyone* suspected of posing a threat to black Harlem is branded with a common label—you people—as an outsider.

Black gentry attempt to cope with this by taking part in an oppositional political struggle. Their accounts suggest that on behalf of the community, they do battle with the city that wants to turn Harlem into a "dumping ground." While the city has plans to use Harlem as a site for social-service facilities for a marginal population, new home owners concerned about the vitality of the community help to resist this use, and meaning, of Harlem.

An alternative model of residential land use fuels their political activism. Demands for shopping, economic services, park space, and other amenities are meant to reestablish Harlem as a desirable residential community where younger people, especially those with families, do not feel the need to escape. This means fighting for Harlem as a space for middle-class settlement. This vision of the community enables black gentry to see their localized and broad-based efforts as those of community insiders. This position also drives a self-interested, not-in-my-backyard politics against the city.

Shopping above 110th Street, using libraries and recreational facilities, attending Harlem churches, and frequenting restaurants and museums are ways to contribute to reviving the social, institutional, and commercial life of the community. Participation in these institutions cements bonds of familiarity, as well as connections that span generations, bringing old and young members of the community together.

Kenyatta Davis feels that her connection to Harlem is solidified through using community facilities and participating in community events, such as neighborhood festivals and block parties. She is also able to find peers with interests and outlooks similar to her own:

> I do feel connected in large part because I not only live here, I'm a member of the Y[WCA], so I use their services. I mean, rather than go to New York Health and Racquet Club, I'd go to the Y. There's a sauna there and there's a pool and there's Nautilus machines. I'd work out there, and it's a hip place to meet and network with people who are also in the community. I study dance at another community center, the Hansberry Recreation Center. I participate in neighborhood festivals. I'm involved in any rallies and that kind of thing that's come up, so I do feel very much part of the center. There's the Schomburg. I participate in a lot of activities there.

Yolanda Jackson argues that patronizing businesses in Harlem is a way to keep money in the community and provide jobs for residents:

> I try to do as much business in Harlem as possible. My dry cleaners is up here. I go to restaurants up here. There are African restaurants and Caribbean restaurants. There's a variety of things, so whatever your taste is you can just about find it in Harlem. There's the 125th Street Mart. It's really nice for ethnic clothes and ethnic jewelry. I shop there, especially at Christmastime. I patronize as many things as possible. In doing my house, most of the work that's been done has been done by black contractors, plasterers, electricians. I make it a point of trying to really keep the money in the community in that way. Every way I can, I do.

And while many old and new Harlemites maintain that it is important to keep their dollars circulating in the community, wider opportunities for shopping and dining compete. (Harlemites' strategies for dealing with scant shopping and dining opportunities were described in more detail in chapter 4.) Davis sees this as a paradox of integration:

> You have black businesses that were killed as a result of integration—cleaners, restaurants, newspapers folding up. We got so busy rushing down to go into somebody else's business where they didn't want us in the first place that we turned our back on our own. And that's not to say that I think that the black dollar should only go to black businesses. I don't even do that. I mean, if there's a dress I want at Saks, I go to Saks and get it. If there's one I want on 125th Street, I do that, too.

Through their own words, members of Harlem's new black middle class express a longing for racial community that bolsters their status and identity by grounding it in a shared ethnicity. By coming "home to Harlem," the new black middle class strives to construct an identity that will achieve a balance between race and class. While home ownership in Harlem satisfies a personal and psychological dimension of their identity, middle-class blacks establish themselves as members of a broader racial collective by also becoming actors in the public, social, and institutional life of the community.

Black gentry describe their participation in the political, economic, and institutional life of Harlem as one way to establish networks of alliances that unite them with the larger community. On a smaller scale, more intimate connections are established through informal networks of friendship and support. The rituals of neighborliness that define Harlem as an intimate community make this possible.

Attempts to foster community solidarity and empowerment show up in campaigns to reestablish the political and economic vitality of Harlem. While the activities can be seen as class-based individualistic actions driven by self-interest, they take on a racially defined meaning at the same time.

It is significant that this group's activities move them beyond the traditional individualism and self-interested action that defines middle-class behavior and is often a trademark of American culture. The ways in which black gentry talk about the values of home ownership and their position as role models and actors in the community point to a possible role for middle-class blacks as a "social buffer" in the black community.

Seeking out a communion of fellowship within Harlem is more likely, however, a strategy for resolving dilemmas that racism and racial difference present for middle-class blacks. This strategy is not without problems. Many of the same race and class conflicts that are the result of clashing values, rules, and behaviors in other gentrifying communities confront middle-class blacks upon their arrival in Harlem.

In a study of stalled gentrification in a Washington, D.C., neighborhood, Brett Williams finds one source of this tension to be the gap between ideals held by middle-class gentry and the realities of life in diverse communities. "Middle-class people," Williams concludes, "may have learned to work the metropolitan area, but many of them did not really know how to root their connections and resources in integrated life. Despite their rhetoric, they did not really know how to live in an integrated neighborhood."[1]

Shopping, praying, dining, acting as role models, owning homes, joining block associations, and trading talk and information with neighbors are some of the strategies used by middle-class blacks who "root their connections and resources" between a heaven and hell they find as newcomers to Harlem. But their ability to move in and out of Harlem to work, shop, and socialize means that their participation—the communion of fellowship they find in Harlem—is specific to time and place. It is part-time and voluntary.

Beneath all the community talk, it is clear that Harlem is a symbol that largely meets individual needs and therefore requires only a partial attachment. As Raymond Firth has noted:

> People use symbols to handle their problems of relationship with one another. For their actions to be effective, that is, for them to lead a viable social existence, the symbols they use must be individually meaningful as well as collectively recognized. But differences of interest lead to a lack of agreement on symbolic meanings as well as to manipulation of symbols in partisan fashion.[2]

With its duality as an emblem of heaven and hell, the realities behind Harlem's symbolisms hold limited promise for realizing a collective ideal. Intimacy and familiarity with other blacks are personal rewards for taking part in the ritual life of the community. But at the same time, these activities are motivated prominently by the desire to preserve the values of their properties by keeping streets clean, safe, and pretty. The civic participation of black gentrifiers in Harlem, heartfelt and commendable as it is, represents but a portion of lives that include jobs downtown and social and organizational connections far beyond the bounds of the neighborhood. These newcomers cannot be dismissed as opportunistic and self-aggrandizing. Nor as part-time community members can they be expected to shoulder the burdens of a long-neglected community. The idea that the black middle class, as a "social buffer," is the answer to the problems of the failing inner city is incomplete at best.

conclusion

The End of the Line?

> The problem of the twentieth century is the problem of the color line.
>
> **W. E. B. Du Bois**

> We Negroes are, because of historical circumstances, a migratory people, forever on the move, leaving one spot to seek for freedom in another. Precisely because of the fact that we are Americans—and indigenous Americans at that!—we are haunting the American landscape for our place, trying, as Americans, to feel at home in our native land.
>
> **Richard Wright**

Take Me Out to the Ball Game

I've ridden an A train to a baseball field close to the northernmost edge of Harlem. I have an appointment with Ruth Emerson, a wife and mother who grew up in Harlem and returned nearly twenty years ago to a Sugar Hill brownstone down the block from where she was raised. She settled here with her husband, Ralph Emerson, whom she met when they were undergraduates at Cornell University. The Emersons are black, which doesn't make it easy to pick them out among a sea of black faces—moms and dads whose screams and applause give away their booster status. Today is the season opener of the Harlem Little Sox, which had been dormant until Ruth Emerson revived the team.

Foster parents, friends, and siblings are here to root for the boys, a squad of scrawny figures whose brown faces—and, here and there, a white one—are lost under the bills of their Harlem Little Sox caps. The jerseys of the home team are emblazoned with the name of their sponsor, a neighborhood branch of a well-known bank. When we spoke on the phone earlier in the week, Ruth told me why she had started the team: "I just got tired of taking the kids to Jersey and Connecticut for stuff like piano, soccer, and a lot of their other activities, you know?" The Little League game is the picture of suburban-style bliss in an urban setting rife with history, vibrancy, hope, and tragedy.

With thoughts of Langston Hughes, I stand here, at the edge of heaven and hell in Harlem. My own trek—as a suburban teenager, a child of integration, Yale graduate, Harvard Ph.D.—has brought me to these parents and their children, two generations of middle-class blacks that stand as bookends to my generation. In my field notes from that Saturday at the baseball game, I scribbled over and over, next to entries about workplace, school, and home experiences of Harlem's black gentry, to write about the level playing field.

The interviews with middle-class blacks in this study revealed that even at the professional levels they have reached, many still feel blocked and frustrated by a glass ceiling. The move to Harlem is motivated by a desire that makes them similar to other American blacks who believe that in too many institutional arenas much is yet to be done to open up greater access and opportunity. The middle-class blacks whose stories I have told opened their homes to me to describe this state of being stigmatized and limited. The racism they speak of shows up most clearly in the architecture that structures their work lives and lived-in spaces.

Malcolm Balderidge told of being confronted by white neighbors in an elevator in his apartment building. We listened to George Carver, who revealed his irritation that professional peers fail to remember his name. These incidents, and others, add up—especially at moments when blacks, no matter their class position, have reason to believe they stand apart from mainstream America simply because they are black. As evidence of a continuing culture of racism, cobwebs of older racial hierarchies and systems of race meaning cling to integrated environments and provide a strong push toward strategies of reinvention, that is, the reinvention of race identities somewhere between the present and the past.

But positioning themselves in relation to other blacks, especially in a community where we are reminded that a disproportionate number of blacks are found at the bottom of the class structure, presents a tricky terrain of race and class that must be navigated. Kenyatta Davis, a young black professional woman, told of her dating frustrations as a consequence of being suspended between two worlds differently defined by race and class. Parents of young children worry about the perimeters of safety and belonging for the arenas of their children's play and playmates. But Balderidge and Carver, along with Davis and others, depict the return to Harlem as a necessary quest for personal connections, face-to-face contacts, and a psychic or symbolic association with other blacks. The talk of return is a framework that explores and expresses myths and truths behind an assumed position of racial belonging.

The middle-class gentry in this book exhibit an interesting liminality—a state betwixt and between—that arises from the interplay of race and class in their lives. Out of a reciprocal structure and agency dualism, black identity (or agency) for these actors is not entirely of their own making. As middle-class black professionals, they have arrived in Harlem during a sometimes tense moment of gentrification in the historically black community. Structural features of this gentrification appear in the real-estate market and include struggles over the history of Harlem. Integration into less segregated work and school settings, and unsettled facts about continuing institutional and cultural racism are also part of broader forces that all intertwine with psychological uncertainties, anxieties, and guilt over how they are viewed by others in both black and white worlds.

For this group, the double consciousness defined by W. E. B. Du Bois—that "sense of always looking at oneself through the eyes of others"—is doubled.[1] Middle-class black gentry in Harlem see themselves through the eyes of black *and* white others. They are insiders and outsiders in black and white worlds. Their clothing, cars, vowels and pronunciation, pets, habits, recreational activities, work schedules, and vacation times are under the surveillance of two sets of eyes. But different codes, rituals, responses, and knowledge are required for membership and belonging—here or there, uptown and downtown—necessitating switching and a "double double" consciousness.

A response to spatial isolation, discomfort, and, in some instances, fear has been to relocate and re-create real and idealized attachments to communities of racial identity and collectiveness. Precisely as once restricted avenues to political and economic racial justice and equality have opened up, many of the spaces of integration have become filled with new or rearticulated forms of race meaning and racism. Couched in a rhetoric of return, home buyers and renovators in Harlem become individuals whose actions encompass collective concerns.

But as social critic Michael Dyson argues, "the quest for racial unity has largely represented the desperate effort to replace a cultural uprooting that never should have occurred with a racial unanimity that actually never existed."[2] Indeed, movement, migration, and flight are forced and voluntary shifts resulting from oppression and freedom in the black experience. The historic moments of black history were always a stage upon which the individual seemed to be the collective. This flow of social forces seemingly produced blacks as a diasporic group of actors bound by a collective consciousness tied to time and place(s). Settlement and landing, too, are part of this migratory experience. Homesites and racially defined communal spaces accompany these migratory treks, separating, dividing, and rupturing but also and always potentially rejoining the experiences of blackness.

Beyond the slave ships of the Middle Passage, varying modes of transport push and pull blacks into shared spaces of Jim Crow segregation and beyond. These are spaces that can simultaneously be sources of restraint and resistance. The construction of a federal highway system, for example, allowed some blacks to embark on a path of "black suburbanization" at the same time as others were hemmed in and marginalized by "inner-city" urban space.[3] Today, MTV and Yo!MTV Raps give access (via television, radio, commercial space, marketplace) to a purportedly "real" or "authentic" geographic blackness.

Thus, for the black gentry in this study, a "return" to black Harlem as a location of the black collective past but also a collective present is possible. This would seem to differentiate today's black middle class from that described by E. Franklin Frazier in *Black Bourgeoisie* as a group who "because of their social isolation and lack of a cultural tradition . . . seem to be in the process of becoming NOBODY."[4] The rhetorical use of the social buffer concept when read in the context of return suggests that it is as much, if not more, about their own needs for identity and acceptance (becoming SOMEBODY) as it is about assisting the group in need of economic and social "uplift."

A more precise mapping of Harlem reveals specific class traits structured into housing stock taken over from a home-owning group that extends to the late nineteenth century. The houses and neighborhoods within Harlem that black gentry resettle reach back to many pasts. During the Harlem Renaissance, middle-class blacks lived in townhouses and brownstones vacated by a white elite. The salon space of the "Harlem literati" at Madame C. J. Walker's "black tower," for instance, was part of a moment of black arts and letters as high culture.

Home for working-class and poor blacks meant tenements, overcrowding, and brownstones divvied into spaces not meant to be inhabited. These home spaces were primarily located in Central Harlem, sometimes close to the tracks of the elevated train. The culture produced by this group took a form different from that of the "talented tenth." Despite the disdain of Harlem's elite for the music and gambling, drinking and card-playing activities that defined another type of Harlem culture, it is clear that the architecture and space of class had a role to play in the race meaning produced during the Renaissance years.

Today, as black gentry gut, empty, and remake brownstones, they brush up against an economic reality of Harlem history. Harlem's brownstones were first designed with a white elite in mind. Spacious layouts presumed families of a certain size and were for those with an ability to afford steep prices. As early as the turn of the nineteenth century, when Negro realtors began placing middle-class black professionals, whom they touted as respectable colored people, into Harlem brownstones, a bifurcation of the black experience in Harlem was already present. This black elite was pushed uptown, in part, by a desire to escape "slum conditions . . . and the influx of ignorant southern[ers]" in black neighborhoods downtown.

By the 1920s, however, when Harlem was solidly established as a black belt, its class diversity was broadened. With a wave of black migrants pouring into New York from the South, the demand for housing in segregated Harlem increased. The interiors of brownstones were divided, and they became boardinghouses. This was advantageous for landlords, who received multiple rents through commercializing the interior space of Harlem brownstones. The divided houses also offered a viable solution to housing those with low incomes. Boardinghouses rented space on a daily, weekly, nightly, or hourly rate—beds could even be rented. The rent parties of Harlem's heyday were intended to raise money for those short on rent.

When this practice of renting to lodgers was introduced, it produced what urban reformers called "lodger evil." People were jammed into every conceivable space—even the bathtub. In the "repeating or hot bed system," sleep was caught on the go. It was even reported that there were people living in coal bins and cellars.[5] In the long run, though, this practice hurt Harlem. Negligent and indifferent landlords provided little to no upkeep or maintenance. The stately brownstones, reinvented as boardinghouses, deteriorated. Social workers and urban reformers described slum conditions in Harlem as deplorable.

Most recently, the gentrifying market has become a stage where black actors engage over struggles of the community's modern incarnation. A clash within the community has developed so that there is now a mismatch between owners and occupants for the intended use of the brownstones. This fight for the use and meaning of Harlem unfolds in indoor and outdoor spaces as well as in the history of the black ghetto and around the symbolism attached to the community. In the parks, the libraries, the locked and unlocked gated courtyards, and elevators, and on the brownstone stoops, old meanings are rewritten and new meanings put in place.

Allison Carson remembers Mount Morris/Marcus Garvey Park as a landmark of the American Revolution, for instance. Malcolm Balderidge finds historic meaning in the ordinary—a chair used by Langston Hughes. At the same time Hughes is celebrated in a black-tie benefit whose tickets command hundreds of dollars. When the Cotton Club is celebrated as an iconic place, its history of segregation during the Harlem Renaissance is pushed aside.

Residential location and the terms of tenancy are tied to an ethos of home ownership that, even in the Harlem of the Renaissance, dispersed blacks in the community into different neighborhoods that were responsible for very different cultural productions. The space of a gentrifying community reveals a collision of economics, politics, and culture that signals multiple meanings of the types of blackness available in Harlem. Gentrification does not simply put blacks in opposition to whites or make them antagonistic actors in a differentiated black class structure.

Instead, gentrifying Harlem is a stage upon which we have viewed different productions of race. Analysis of the locations of production found in homes and streets must account for ways in which these blacknesses operate, but not as one authenticity to be chosen over others. Instead, Harlem holds numerous sites of potential race meanings. Becoming "SOMEBODY" for today's black bourgeoisie in Harlem is tied to the legal and economic underpinnings of property and home ownership as well as gender, age, and occupation, for instance.

In today's Harlem, formal and informal rules of home-owner associations provide a socially contracted and agreed upon set of behaviors and boundaries that shape actions and define goals for the "restoration" of the community. Houses and home ownership—not race, morality, or values alone—shape how Harlemites play different roles in the racial space of the black ghetto. For different black actors, Harlem's spaces empower and/or constrain to produce particular identities. At the level of personal freedom, autonomy, creativity, rebelliousness, and conformity, residents in Harlem already are situated within structural forces of polity and economy that come into play. So when Mimi Rogers is uptight and annoyed about people on her street who pick through the garbage, it is not necessarily a snobbishness she displays. Rather, as she tells me, she will be fined by the city if her garbage, an extension of the private property of her house, spills out into the space of the street.

Thus when actors like the Baxter-Browns, Reggie Smith, and Malcolm Balderidge speak of the return to the past as proof of their rightful place in the black community, theirs is a somewhat mythical or exaggerated remembrance of the past that automatically assumes the viability of reestablishing black community solidarity.[6] This tension was evident in the analysis of E. Franklin Frazier as well as that of Horace Cayton and St. Clair Drake in their studies of race and stratification in segregated communities. Earlier studies pointed to important differences in spatial positioning within the black community.

From Africa and into the diaspora, black community and culture are from the outset of a black experience in the modern world the workings of a differentiated territorial and geographic spatiality. Here is where the structure and agency of race meet to produce multiple kinds of blackness. As this book has shown, dichotomies like insider and outsider are not hard and fast. One does not have to be black nor does one have to own a brownstone to be concerned about Harlem's social conditions or to join with others in making use of neighborhood and city mechanisms to improve them. In fact, it would seem more broadly inclusive to think of the social buffer of urban improvement as a spatial location into which a variety of actors could step. This means that middle-class black gentry, black Harlemites who are not property owners, long-term middle-class black residents, and even white gentrifiers (who should be the focus of more Harlem research) can be actors engaged in a struggle to meet individual and community needs.

Black gentrifiers use their role as urban home owners to stake claims for belonging as being inherently tied to a dedication to race work. In part, community and media rhetoric make this possible. As a largely successful group of individuals, middle-class blacks in Harlem make it clear that they are responding to more fundamental problems in American culture.[7] And until our culture comes into line with the fact of constrained economic and political inclusion for minorities, the need for a return to blackness in many forms is likely to be felt. This return is as much about racial pride as it is a defense mechanism. This construction of race should not be viewed with puzzlement or alarm. But in the absence of broader American participation in "race work," overly simple positions like insider and outsider will continue to leave us with automatic or preconceived definitions about race and its boundaries. Middle-class black involvement in the gentrification of Harlem provides an ideal stage to rethink when and why and how we impose race identities, use them as strategic responses to racism, and employ them in antiracist work.

Acknowledgments

In the tradition of social science ethnographic methodology, interview subjects are all given disguised identities to protect their privacy and anonymity. Without the generosity of these Harlem residents and institutional community leaders, the bulk of this work would never have been done. I owe a huge thanks to all those who were generous with their time, information, contacts, and encouragement.

I recognize the following sources of institutional support: the Mark DeWolfe Howe Fund of the Harvard Law School, the sociology and Afro-American studies departments at Harvard University, Amherst College's sociology and Afro-American studies departments and Five College Fellowship Support, Occidental College Minority Dissertation Fellowship, UCLA's Institute of American Cultures and Center for Afro-American Studies, and the Occidental College Dean's Office.

I am grateful to a long list of persons in the various academic settings that have been my home. To colleagues and coworkers who over the years have provided support, advice, mentoring, and collegiality: Roderick Harrison, Werner Sollors, Steve Rytina, Annemette Sorensen, Aage Sorensen, Mary Waters, Steve Cornell, Skip Gates, Nathan Huggins, Deb Minkoff, Chris Smith, Jerrilyn Powers, Cynthia Marugg, Arthe Anthony, Elizabeth Chin, Martha Ronk, Jan Lin, Henry Gutierrez, Carolyn Adams, David Axeen, and Neil Smith. And to my students: Angela Chan, Carlos Hernandez, Kyle Kitson, Victoria Murray, Tucker Neel, Payton Phillips, Sarah Shanok, and Jeff Zimmerman.

To friends and family: Faye and Dalmas Taylor, Aunt Anne, Uncle Bud, Aunt Skeeter and Uncle Ty, Carla and Courty, the Ellingwood family, Demetra Giatas, Leora Romney, Steve Carroll, Jasper Reid, and Pony.

And to Ken, for bearing with me.

Notes

Introduction

1. See, for example, works by Charles V. Willie, and Elijah Anderson.

2. Pattillo-McCoy, *Black Picket Fences*, 2.

1. Harlem between Heaven and Hell

1. See Massey and Denton, *American Apartheid.*

2. David Sibley, "Outsiders in Society and Space," in *Inventing Places*, ed. Anderson and Gale, 107.

3. Ibid., 120.

4. Ibid., 112.

5. Soja, *Postmodern Geographies*, 6.

6. Soja, *Thirdspace*, 67–68.

7. Osofsky, *Harlem*, 90.

8. Ibid., 111.

9. See Osofsky, *Harlem.*

10. Ibid., 110.

11. Ibid., 17.

12. Ibid., 105.

13. See Frazier, "Negro Harlem," 72–78.

14. Ibid., 74.

15. Anderson, *This Was Harlem*, 341.

16. Allan Spear, "The Origins of the Urban Ghetto," in *Key Issues in the Afro-American Experience*, ed. Huggins, Kilson, and Fox, 154.

17. Osofsky, *Harlem*, 115.

18. See Charlayne Hunter-Gault, "Minister Hailed for Effort to Improve Life in Harlem," *New York Times*, May 10, 1977. Reverend M. Moran Weston of Saint Phillips Church in Harlem has initiated such projects as Senior House—a 200-unit apartment for the elderly; St. Phillips on the Park—a 260-unit low- and moderate-income complex; and a community center that provides hot meals, tutoring, and recreation. "Harlem's needs cannot be met," he said, "without help and resources from the wider community."

19. Adam Clayton Powell Sr. from his autobiography, *Against the Tide*, quoted in Osofsky, *Harlem*, 128.

20. See Van Vechten, *Nigger Heaven*. Carl Van Vechten's novel angered a number of blacks, who felt that white Van Vechten was exploiting Harlemites. Van Vechten was famous for "slumming" in Harlem nightspots and acting as an escort for more timid whites who wanted the black experience.

21. See Carl Van Vechten, *Nigger Heaven*.

22. Locke, *The New Negro*, 7.

23. Ibid., 15.

24. Du Bois, *The Souls of Black Folk*, 45.

25. Huggins, *Harlem Renaissance*, 5, 13.

26. Locke, *The New Negro*, 16.

27. Hughes, "My Early Days in Harlem," 312.

28. Davis, *From the Dark Tower*, 64.

29. Hughes, *The Best of Simple*, 20–23.

30. Larsen, *Quicksand and Passing*, 46.

31. Anderson, *This Was Harlem*, 222.

32. John Louis Clarke, "Mystery Novel Writer Is Interviewed over the Radio," *Pittsburgh Courier*, Jan. 21, 1933. Quoted in Deutsch, "'The Streets of Harlem,'" 159.

33. Deutsch, "'The Streets of Harlem,'" 159, 169.

34. Fisher, "The South Lingers On," 646.

35. Deutsch, "'The Streets of Harlem,'" 160.

36. Fisher, "The Promised Land," in *The City of Refuge*, 54.

37. Ibid.

38. Ibid., 59.

39. Duke Ellington, *Uptown*, Columbia compact disk CK 40836.

40. Stanley Dance, jacket notes to Ellington, *Uptown*.

41. Ibid.

42. Quoted in Osofsky, *Harlem*, 185.

43. Osofsky, *Harlem*, 128.

44. Lewis, *When Harlem Was in Vogue*, 221.

45. Anderson, *This Was Harlem*, 246.

46. Davis, *From the Dark Tower*, 10.

47. Hughes, "Harlem" (originally titled "Puzzled") can be found in *The Panther and the Lash* (1967).

48. McKay, *Harlem*, 15–16, 21, 198.

49. Ellison, "Harlem Is Nowhere," in *Shadow and Act*, 295–96.

50. Ibid., 296.

51. *Freedomways* 3, 3 (summer 1963), 261.

52. Ibid., 262.

53. Leaks, "Talking about Harlem," 263.

54. Murray, *The Omni-Americans*, 143.

55. Ibid.

56. Ibid., 114.

57. Clark, "HARYOU," 440.

58. Johnson, *Black Manhattan*, 281.

59. Clark, *Dark Ghetto*, xx.

60. Murray, *The Omni-Americans*, 24–26.

61. Himes, "Harlem, ou le cancer de l'Amerique," *Presence Africaine* 45, 1 Trimestre 1963: 78.

62. Hudson, *From LeRoi Jones to Amiri Baraka*, 21.

63. Sollors, *Amiri Baraka/LeRoi Jones*, 255.

64. Ibid., 29.

65. Baraka, quoted in Sollors, *Amiri Baraka/LeRoi Jones*.

66. Jones, *Blues People*, 134.

67. Ibid.

68. Jones, *Home*, 87.

69. Hudson, *From LeRoi Jones to Amiri Baraka*, 20.

70. *Harlem Nights*, by Eddie Murphy. While the film is a Hollywood shoot-'em-up, it does offer a wonderful portrait of Harlem during a certain era and provides a special sense of what it meant (and still means) to be part of the black city within a city.

71. Smith, "Postmodernism, Urban Ethnography, and the New Social Space of Ethnic Identity."

72. Quoted in ibid., 515.

2. Insiders and Outsiders

1. Long and Robinson, *How Much Power to the People?* 1.

2. Flyer distributed by the Harlem Committee for Self Defense, located in vertical file, "State Office Building," Schomburg Center for Research in Black Culture.

3. See vertical file, "State Office Building," Schomburg Center.

4. Long and Robinson, *How Much Power to the People?* 26.

5. AKRF, Inc., "Harlem Area Redevelopment Study: Gentrification in Harlem"; City of New York and Harlem Task Force, "Redevelopment Strategy for Central Harlem."

6. Robert A. Beauregard, "The Chaos and Complexity of Gentrification," in *Gentrification of the City,* ed. Smith and Williams, 36.

7. Ibid.

8. Ibid.

9. Daniels, "Town Houses in Harlem Attracting Buyers."

10. "Harlem: Black Tan and White Fantasy," *The Economist,* Dec. 1, 1984.

11. Vertical file, "Harlem Brownstones," Schomburg Center.

12. Louis Harris and Associates, "A Survey of Leadership Attitudes Towards the Quality of Life in Harlem," 23.

13. Ibid.

14. Ibid.

15. Wilson, *The Truly Disadvantaged,* 56.

16. Ibid.

17. Anderson makes a similar observation in *Streetwise.* Contrasting old heads, men of stable means who believed in hard work, family life, and the church, with an antithesis, the "new" old head, Anderson notes that "a new role model is emerging and competing with the traditional old head for the hearts and minds of young boys" (3). Anderson attributes the rise of the "new" old heads, who are "young, often members of street gangs and at best indifferent to law and traditional values," to the drug culture that has flourished in the context of spiraling unemployment, crime, drug use, family disorganization, and antisocial behavior (3).

3. The Dilemma of Racial Difference

1. As early as 1944, liberal social scientists embraced the idea that assimilation of the Negro—his community and institutions—would resolve the "American Dilemma" outlined in Gunnar Myrdal's landmark study. Myrdal identified a glaring contradiction between the American Creed and a pattern of race relations in the United States based on prejudice and institutionalized discrimination. Myrdal concluded that the tension in this moral dilemma would force white Americans to move beyond segregation and grant full citizenship rights to black Americans.

2. Magazine and news accounts during the 1980s made frequent use of terms such as *renaissance, revival, promise,* and *Mecca* in headlines, stories, and photo captions to describe the black "return to the city" aspect of Harlem's gentrification process.

3. See Smith and Williams, eds., *Gentrification of the City*; Abu-Lughod, *From Urban Village to East Village*; and Robert Beauregard, "The Chaos and Complexity of Gentrification," in *Gentrification of the City*, ed. Smith and Williams, for the structuralist argument on gentrification. Caulfield, *City Form and Everyday Life*, offers a critique of this position.

4. See, for example, Carter, *Reflections of an Affirmative Action Baby*; Cary, *Black Ice*; Cose, *The Rage of a Privileged Class*; Nelson, *Volunteer Slavery*; and Williams, *The Alchemy of Race and Rights*.

5. Zweigenhaft and Domhoff, *Blacks in the White Establishment?* 15.

6. See Waters, *Ethnic Options*. Waters argues that ethnic identity, no longer shaped by constraints of discrimination, prejudice, and hostility, largely functions in symbolic terms—as a matter of choice. Waters notes that because of visible signs of physical difference, blacks, Latinos, and Asian Americans may not experience this form of symbolic ethnicity in the same way.

7. Patterson, "Toward a Study of Black America," 484.

8. Zweigenhaft and Domhoff, *Blacks in the White Establishment?* 152.

9. Quoted in ibid.

4. Class Conflict and Harlem's Black Gentry

1. Michael Jager argues that as "slums become Victoriana the dynamics of social classes are revealed through the architectural and internal decorative forms of gentrified buildings and neighborhoods. An active process, urban conservation is the production of social differentiation"; "Class Definition and the Esthetics of Gentrification: Victoriana in Melbourne," in *Gentrification of the City*, ed. Smith and Williams, 78–91.

2. Although, as we saw in chapter 3, even among community insiders, there is a range of opinion about race, class, culture, and redevelopment that makes the notion that there is a shared community interest problematic.

3. See Reider, *Canarsie: The Jews and Italians of Brooklyn against Liberalism*.

4. Neil Smith, "New City, New Frontiers: The Lower East Side as Wild, Wild West," in *Variations on a Theme Park*, ed. Sorkin, 69.

5. Warren J. Halliburton and Ernest Kaiser offered a grim account of Harlem life during the Great Depression. As quoted in Anderson's *This Was Harlem*, the two describe soaring population growth in the period before the stock market crash, leading to overcrowding and want: "Two and three families were living in apartments meant for one family. Properties became badly run down from overuse and neglect, and the tenants grew sullen. Men, women, and children combed the streets and searched in garbage cans for food . . ." (242).

6. An update study by the Harlem Urban Development Corporation in

1987 counted 21,680 vacant units among the 211,403 total dwelling units in Harlem. Of the 189,654 occupied units, nearly all, or 180,149, were rented. Owner-occupied units totaled 7,299, and condominium units totaled 4,928. There were 58,087 publicly assisted units, and 10,336 units were owned by the city through repossession; "Survey of Harlem Residents Revisited."

7. Anderson, *Streetwise,* 78, 80.

5. Racial Bonds and the Communion of Fellowship

1. Anthropologist Victor Turner defines structure as the patterned arrangements of role-sets, status-sets, and status-sequences that are occupied by an individual. Turner, *Dramas, Fields, and Metaphors,* 237.

2. Ibid., 233.

3. Wilson, *The Truly Disadvantaged,* 56.

4. See Drake and Cayton, *Black Metropolis,* 390–95, 716. The two-volume study discusses ways of life and strategies for survival in the black ghetto. Their study deals with accommodation and conflict up and down the black class structure, one result of class differentiation within the segregated community.

5. Ibid., 710.

6. Home Ownership and Political Participation

1. Williams, *Upscaling Downtown,* 136.

2. Firth, *Symbols Public and Private,* 403.

Conclusion

1. Du Bois, *The Souls of Black Folk,* 45.

2. Dyson, *Reflecting Black,* xv.

3. I am thinking about Tricia Rose's discussion in *Black Noise* about the construction of the Cross Bronx Expressway and the roots of rap. This highway is responsible, in part, for the ghetto location for the production of a black agency that responds to the structural forces of deindustrialization.

4. Frazier, *Black Bourgeoisie,* 26.

5. Osofsky, *Harlem,* 139.

6. This is a point Mitchell Duneier makes in *Slim's Table.* In his discussion of the problems with William Julius Wilson's social buffer idea, he takes Elijah Anderson to task for his failure to more critically evaluate the notion that the black poor are bereft of values (124–30). Duneier also makes the point that harmonious images of the "old-time black ghettos are rooted less in empirical evidence than in anecdote and nostalgia" (129).

7. This is an analytic point William Julius Wilson made clear to his most strident detractors: the declining significance was found in the polity and the economy.

Bibliography

Abu-Lughod, Janet L. *From Urban Village to East Village.* Cambridge, Mass.: Blackwell Publishers, 1994.

AKRF, Inc. "Harlem Area Redevelopment Study: Gentrification in Harlem." Report prepared for Harlem Urban Redevelopment Corporation, New York, 1982.

Alpern, D. M. "A City Revival." *Newsweek,* January 15, 1979.

Anderson, Benedict. *Imagined Communities.* London: Verso, 1983.

Anderson, Elijah. *A Place in the Corner.* Chicago: University of Chicago Press, 1978.

———. *Streetwise: Race, Class, and Change in an Urban Community.* Chicago: University of Chicago Press, 1990.

———. *Code of the Street.* New York: W. W. Norton and Company, 1999.

Anderson, Jervis. *This Was Harlem: A Cultural Portrait. 1900–1950.* Reprint. New York: Farrar Strauss Giraux, 1982.

Anderson, Kay, and Fay Gale, eds. *Inventing Places: Studies in Cultural Geography.* Melbourne, Australia: Longman Cheshire, 1992.

Association of Black Sociologists. "Statement of the Association of Black Sociologists." In *The Caste and Class Controversy,* edited by Charles Willie, 177–78. Bayside, N.Y.: General Hall, 1979.

Back, Les, and John Solomon, eds. *Theories of Race and Racism.* London: Routledge, 2000.

Bailey, Bruce. "Gentrification Vultures Poised to Swoop on Harlem." *Heights and Valleys* 8, 1 (November 1984): 1.

Baker, Houston A., Jr. *Blues, Ideology, and Afro-American Literature: A Vernacular Theory.* Chicago: University of Chicago Press, 1984.

———. *Modernism and the Harlem Renaissance.* Chicago: University of Chicago Press, 1987.

Baldwin, James. "The Harlem Ghetto." In *Notes of a Native Son*. Boston: Beacon Press, 1995.

Banner-Haley, Charles T. *The Fruits of Integration: Black Middle-Class Ideology and Culture, 1960–1990*. Jackson: University Press of Mississippi, 1994.

Baraka, Amiri. *The Autobiography of LeRoi Jones*. New York: Freundlich Books, 1984.

Barth, Frederick. *Ethnic Groups and Boundaries: The Social Organization of Cultural Difference*. Boston: Little, Brown, 1969.

Bell, Daniel. *The Coming of Post-Industrial Society*. New York: Basic Books, 1976.

———. *The Cultural Contradictions of Capitalism*. New York: Basic Books, 1978.

Bell, Derrick. *And We Are Not Saved: The Exclusive Quest for Justice*. New York: Basic Books, 1987.

Benjamin, Lois. *The Black Elite: Facing the Color Line in the Twilight of the Twentieth Century*. Chicago: Nelson-Hall, 1991.

Benjamin, Playthell. "The State of Black America." *Emerge*, March 1992, 34.

Bercovici, Konrad. "The Black Blocks of Manhattan." *Harper's Monthly Magazine* 144 (October 1924): 613–23.

Billingsley, Andrew. *Black Families in White America*. New York: Prentice Hall Press, 1968.

Blauner, Robert. *Racial Oppression in America*. New York: Harper, 1972.

———. *Black Lives, White Lives*. Berkeley: University of California Press, 1989.

Blum, David. "The Evils of Gentrification." *Newsweek*, January 3, 1983.

Bourgois, Philippe. *In Search of Respect*. New York: Cambridge University Press, 1996.

Bray, Rosemary. "Taking Sides against Ourselves." *New York Times Magazine*, November 17, 1991.

Brown, Claude. *Manchild in the Promised Land*. New York: New American Library, 1965.

Caldwell, Earl. "Harlem's Problem: Y's and Wherefores." *New York Times*, July 27, 1981.

———. "The Irony of Central Park North." *Daily News*, May 30, 1984.

Campbell, Mary Schmidt. " Harlem's Promise." *New York Times*, March 10, 1989.

Carrington, Glenn. "The Harlem Renaissance: Personal Memoir." *Freedomways* 3, 3 (summer 1963): 307–11.

Carter, Stephen L. *Reflections of an Affirmative Action Baby*. New York: Basic Books, 1991.

Cary, Lorene. *Black Ice*. New York: Alfred A. Knopf, 1991.

Cashmore, E. Ellis. *Dictionary of Race and Ethnic Relations*. London: Routledge, 1988.

Castells, Manuel, and Karen Murphy. "Cultural Identity and Urban Structure: The Spatial Organization of San Francisco's Gay Community." *Urban Affairs Review* 22 (1982): 237–59.

Caulfield, Jon. *City Form and Everyday Life: Toronto's Gentrification and Critical Social Practice*. Toronto: University of Toronto Press, 1994.

Cayton, Horace, and St. Clair Drake. *Black Metropolis: A Study of Negro Life in a Northern City*. New York: Harcourt, Brace and World, 1945.

Chin, Elizabeth. *Purchasing Power: Black Kids and American Consumer Culture.* Minneapolis: University of Minnesota Press, 2001.

Chira, Susan. "New York's Poorest Neighborhoods Bear the Brunt of Social Programs." *New York Times,* July 16, 1989.

City of New York and Harlem Task Force. "Redevelopment Strategy for Central Harlem." Unpublished report prepared by City Task Force appointed by Mayor Edward Koch. August 1982.

Clark, Kenneth. "HARYOU: An Experiment." *Freedomways* 3, 3 (summer 1963): 440.

———. *Dark Ghetto: Dilemmas of Social Power.* New York: Harper and Row, Publishers, 1965.

Clarke, John Henrik, ed. *Harlem: A Community in Transition.* New York: Citadel Press, 1964.

Clifford, James, and George E. Marcus, eds. *Writing Culture.* Los Angeles: University of California Press, 1986.

Cohen, Anthony P. *The Symbolic Construction of Community.* London: Tavistock Publications, 1985.

Collins, Sharon. "The Making of the Black Middle Class." *Social Problems* 30, 4 (April 1983): 369–82.

Cordova, Teresa. "Community Intervention Efforts to Oppose Gentrification." In *Challenging Uneven Development,* edited by Philip W. Nyden and Wim Wiewel. New Brunswick, N.J.: Rutgers University Press, 1991.

Cose, Ellis. *The Rage of a Privileged Class.* New York: HarperCollins Publishers, 1993.

Coser, Lewis. "Presidential Address: Two Methods in Search of a Substance." *American Sociological Review* 40 (1975): 691–700.

Cottingham, Crement. "Gender Shift in Black Communities." *Dissent* 36, 4 (fall 1989): 521–25.

Cox, Oliver. *Caste, Class and Race.* Reprint. New York: Monthly Review Press, 1970.

Crain's New York Business (Crain Communications), vol. 5, no. 44 (October 30, 1989).

Cromwell, Adelaide M. *The Other Brahmins: Boston's Black Upper Class, 1750–1950.* Fayetteville: University of Arkansas Press, 1994.

Daniels, Lee. "Outlook for Revitalization of Harlem." *New York Times,* February 12, 1982.

———. "Koch Offers Housing and Economic Plan to Revivify Harlem." *New York Times,* August 26, 1982.

———. "Condos Planned for Harlem Brownstones." *New York Times,* January 26, 1983.

———. "Hope and Suspicion Mark Plan to Redevelop Harlem." *New York Times,* February 6, 1983.

———. "Town Houses in Harlem Attracting Buyers." *New York Times,* August 21, 1983.

Darden, Joe T. *Philadelphia: Neighborhoods, Division, and Conflict in a Postindustrial City.* Philadelphia: Temple University Press, 1991.

Davis, A., B. Gardener, and M. Gardener. *Deep South: A Social Anthropological Study of Caste and Class.* Chicago: University of Chicago Press, 1941.

Davis, Arthur. "The Harlem of Langston Hughes Poetry." *Phylon* 8 (1952): 276–83.

———. *From the Dark Tower: Afro-American Writer, 1900–1960.* Washington, D.C.: Howard University Press, 1981.

DePalma, Anthony. "Third World Center Stirs Again." *New York Times,* January 1, 1989.

Deutsch, Leonard. "'The Streets of Harlem': The Short Stories of Rudolph Fisher." *Phylon* 40 (1979): 159–71.

Deutsche, Rosalyn, and Cora Gendel Ryan. "The Fine Art of Gentrification." *October,* winter 1984.

Dickens, Inez E. Letter to author, June 19, 1989.

Dollard, John. *Caste and Class in a Southern Town.* New Haven, Conn.: Yale University Press, 1937.

Dorst, John D. *The Written Suburb.* Philadelphia: University of Pennsylvania Press, 1989.

Douglas, Carlyle C. "City Taking Bids for 149 Vacant Harlem Buildings." *New York Times,* May 11, 1985.

———. "For Some, City Auction of Houses Is Chance to Come Home to Harlem." *New York Times,* June 20, 1985.

———. "149 Win in Auction of Harlem Houses." *New York Times,* August 16, 1985.

———. "Harlem Warily Greets Plan for Development." *New York Times,* January 19, 1986.

———. "The Brownstone Project in Harlem Raises Hopes and Fears." *New York Times,* no date.

Douglas, Pamela. "Harlem on the Auction Block." *The Progressive,* March 1983.

Drake, St. Clair, and Horace R. Cayton. *Black Metropolis: A Study of Negro Life in a Northern City,* vol. 2. Rev. ed. New York: Harper and Row, 1945.

Du Bois, W. E. B. *The Philadelphia Negro: A Social Study.* Reprint. New York: Schocken Books, 1967.

———. *The Souls of Black Folk.* Reprint. New York: New American Library, 1969.

Duneier, Mitchell. *Slim's Table: Race, Respectability, and Masculinity.* Chicago: University of Chicago Press, 1992.

Dunlap, David. "2 Kinds of Housing for 2 Faces of Harlem." *New York Times,* April 9, 1986.

Dyson, Michael Eric. *Reflecting Black: African-American Cultural Criticism.* Minneapolis: University of Minnesota Press, 1993.

Edwards, Audrey. "You Can Go Home Again." *Sunday News Magazine,* February 3, 1980.

Edwards, G. Franklin, ed. *E. Franklin Frazier on Race Relations.* Chicago: University of Chicago Press, 1968.

Edwards, Harry. "Camouflaging the Color Lines: A Critique." In *The Caste and Class Controversy,* edited by Charles Willie, 98–103. Bayside, N.Y.: General Hall, 1979.

Ellington, Duke. *Uptown.* Columbia compact disk CK40836.
Ellison, Ralph. *Invisible Man.* New York: Vintage Books, 1972.
———. *Shadow and Act.* New York: Vintage Books, 1972.
Emerson, Robert M., Rachel I. Fretz, and Linda L. Shaw. *Writing Ethnographic Fieldnotes.* Chicago: University of Chicago Press, 1995.
Entrikin, J. Nicholas. *The Betweenness of Place: Toward a Geography of Modernity.* Baltimore: Johns Hopkins University Press, 1991.
Farley, Reynolds, and Albert Hermalin. "The 1960s: A Decade of Progress for Blacks?" *Demography* 9, 3 (August 1972): 353–70.
Firth, Raymond. *Symbols Public and Private.* Ithaca, N.Y.: Cornell University Press, 1973.
Fisher, Rudolph. "The South Lingers On." *Survey Graphic* 53 (March 1, 1925): 644–47.
———. "The Caucasian Storms Harlem." *American Mercury* 1927: 393–98.
———. *The City of Refuge: The Collected Stories of Rudolph Fisher.* Edited by John McCluskey Jr. Columbia: University of Missouri Press, 1987.
Fleming, Robert. "The Business Climate in Harlem Is Looking Bright." *New York Daily News,* August 7, 1986.
Foderaro, Lisa W. "Harlem's Hedge against Gentrification." *New York Times,* August 16, 1987.
Frazier, E. Franklin. "Negro Harlem: An Ecological Study." *American Journal of Sociology* 43 (July 1937): 72–88.
———. *Black Bourgeoisie: The Rise of a New Middle Class in the United States.* New York: The Free Press, 1957.
———. *Race and Culture Contracts in the Modern World.* Boston: Beacon Press, 1957.
———. *On Race Relations.* Chicago: University of Chicago Press, 1968.
Freedman, Samuel. "Harlem and the Speculators: Big Profits but Little Renewal." *New York Times,* December 19, 1986.
French, Howard W. "Harlem: Its Promise Is the Draw." *New York Times,* April 25, 1988, section 2, 1.
Fulman, Ricky. "Taking the Train and Bus: More Tourists Go to Harlem for Ermines, Pearls, Antiques, Jazz." *New York Daily News,* October 17, 1986.
———. "Of 149 City Brownstones Auctioned, All Are Still Empty." *New York Daily News,* October 17, 1986.
Gelburd, Gail, and Thelma Golden. *Romare Bearden in Black-and-White: Photomontage Projections 1964.* New York: Harry N. Abrams, 1997.
Gale, Dennis E. "Middle-Class Resettlement in Older Urban Neighborhoods." *Journal of the American Planning Association* 45 (July 1979): 293–304.
Gans, Herbert. "Symbolic Ethnicity: The Future of Ethnic Groups in America." In *On the Making of Americans: Essays in Honor of David Riesman.* Philadelphia: University of Pennsylvania Press, 1979.
Gates, Henry Louis, Jr. *Figures in Black: Words, Signs, and the "Racial" Self.* New York: Oxford University Press, 1987.
———. "What's in a Name?" *Dissent* 36 (fall 1989): 487.

Gault, Charlayne Hunter. "Minister Hailed for Effort to Improve Life in Harlem." *New York Times*, May 10, 1977.

Geertz, Clifford. *The Interpretation of Cultures.* New York: Basic Books, 1973.

Gennep, Arnold van. *The Rites of Passage.* Reprint. London: Routledge and Kegan Paul, 1960.

Gilman, Sander L. *Difference and Pathology.* Ithaca, N.Y.: Cornell University Press, 1985.

Glazer, Nathan, and Daniel Patrick Moynihan. *Beyond the Melting Pot; The Negroes, Puerto Ricans, Jews, Italians and Irish of New York City.* Cambridge, Mass.: M.I.T. Press, 1963.

Godfrey, Brian. *Neighborhood in Transition.* Berkeley: University of California Press, 1988.

Goodwin, Michael. "First of 198 New Apartments Open in Church Sponsored Renovation of Harlem Block." *New York Times*, January 20, 1979.

Graham, Shirley, ed. *Freedomways* 3, 3 (summer 1963).

Hacker, Andrew. *Two Nations: Black and White, Separate, Hostile, Unequal.* New York: Ballantine Books, 1995.

Haley, Alex. *The Autobiography of Malcolm X.* New York: Grove Press, 1965.

Hall, Stuart, and Tony Jefferson. *Resistance Through Rituals.* London: Hutchinson and Co., 1976.

Hampton, Rick. "Will Whites Buy the Future of Harlem?" *The Record*, July 1982.

Handler, Richard. "Who Owns the Past: History, Cultural Property, and the Logic of Possessive Individualism." Unpublished manuscript, no date.

Hannerz, Ulf. *Soulside.* New York: Columbia University Press, 1969.

Harlem Arts and Cultural Consortium 3, 4 (summer 1990).

"Harlem Entrepreneur Portfolio," summer 1985, vertical file, Schomburg Center for Research in Black Culture.

Harlem Magazine 8, 1 (1990).

"Harlem Rehab Plan Could Hurt Blacks." *Amsterdam News*, June 3, 1984.

Harlem Renaissance: Art of Black America. New York: Harry N. Abrams, 1987.

Harlem Urban Development Corporation (HUDC). "A Portfolio of the Harlem Area: Findings of the Harlem Task Force." New York: HUDC, 1973.

———. "The Global Economic Market from a Local Perspective: A View of Urban Problems." New York: HUDC, July 1990.

———. "Survey of Harlem Residents Revisited with Comparison to the 1973 Survey." Unpublished study prepared for HUDC by Kenneth Clark and Associates, December 1987, vertical file, Schomburg Center for Research in Black Culture.

Harlem Youth Opportunities Unlimited, Inc. *Youth in the Ghetto: A Study of the Consequences of Powerlessness and a Blueprint for Change.* New York: Orans Press, 1964.

Harris, Leonard, ed. *The Philosophy of Alain Locke: Harlem Renaissance and Beyond.* Philadelphia: Temple University Press, 1989.

Harris, Scott. "Battle Lines." *Los Angeles Times*, June 13, 1991.

Hayden, Dolores. *The Power of Place.* Cambridge, Mass.: MIT Press, 1995.

Henderson, David. *De Mayor of Harlem.* New York: E. P. Dutton and Co., 1970.

Herring, Cedric. "Convergence, Polarization or What? Racially Based Changes in Attitudes and Outlooks, 1964–1984." *Sociological Quarterly* 30, 2 (1989): 267–81.

Hill, Norman. "Blacks and the Unions." *Dissent* 36 (fall 1989): 496.

Himes, Chester. "Harlem, ou le cancer de l'Amerique." *Presence Africaine* 45, 1er Trimestre (1963): 46–81.

Hobsbawm, Eric, and Terence Ranger, eds. *The Invention of Tradition.* New York: Cambridge University Press, 1984.

Holmes, Eugene C. "The Legacy of Alain Locke." *Freedomways* 3, 3 (summer 1963): 293–306.

Honey, Maureen, ed. *Shadow Dreams: Women's Poetry of the Harlem Renaissance.* New Brunswick, N.J.: Rutgers University Press, 1989.

hooks, bell. *Yearning: Race, Gender, and Cultural Politics.* Boston: South End Press, 1990.

Hopkins, Ellen. "Harlem on Her Mind." *New York Magazine,* March 7, 1989, 51.

Hudson, Theodore R. *From LeRoi Jones to Amiri Baraka: The Literary Works.* Durham, N.C.: Duke University Press, 1973.

Huggins, Nathan. *Harlem Renaissance.* New York: Oxford University Press, 1971.

———. *Black Odyssey.* New York: Vintage, 1979.

———, ed. *Voices from the Harlem Renaissance.* New York: Oxford University Press, 1995.

Huggins, Nathan, M. Kilson, and D. Fox, eds. *Key Issues in the Afro-American Experience.* New York: Harcourt Brace Jovanovitch, 1971.

Hughes, Langston. *The Ways of White Folks.* New York: Vintage Books, 1934.

———. "Down Under in Harlem." *New Republic* 110 (March 27, 1944): 404–5.

———. *Shakespeare in Harlem.* New York: Knopf, 1945.

———. *Selected Poems of Langston Hughes.* New York: Vintage Books, 1959.

———. "My Early Days in Harlem." *Freedomways* 3, 3 (summer 1963): 312–14.

———. *Something in Common and Other Stories.* New York: Hill and Wang, 1963.

———. *The Panther and the Lash.* New York: Alfred A. Knopf, 1967.

———. *The Best of Simple.* New York: Hill and Wang, 1986.

———. *I Wonder as I Wander.* New York: Thunder's Mouth Press, 1986.

———. *The Big Sea.* Reprint. New York: Thunder's Mouth Press, 1988.

———. "Harlem Sweeties." *Flippin' the Script: Rap Meets Poetry.* Mercury Records, 1996. Sound Disk.

Hunter, Albert. *Symbolic Communities: The Persistence and Change of Chicago's Local Communities.* Chicago: University of Chicago Press, 1974.

Hurewitz, Daniel. *Stepping Out.* New York: Henry Holt and Company, 1997.

Jackson, Debra. "An Affair to Remember." *Savoy,* May 2001.

Jenks, Christopher. "Deadly Neighborhoods." *New Republic,* June 13, 1988.

Johnson, James Weldon. *Black Manhattan.* New York: Alfred A. Knopf, 1930.

———. *The Autobiography of an Ex-Coloured Man.* New York: Hill and Wang, 1960.

———. *Along This Way: The Autobiography of James Weldon Johnson.* New York: Penguin Books, 1990.

Johnson, Kirk. "Two Abandoned Blocks Are Renewed in Harlem." *New York Times,* August 16, 1985.

———. "Condo Plan Gives Harlem a Lift." *New York Times,* September 20, 1985.

Jones, James. *Prejudice and Racism.* Reading, Mass.: Addison-Wesley Publishing Co., 1972.

Jones, LeRoi. *Blues People: The Negro Experience in White America and the Music That Developed from It.* New York: Morrow Quill Paperbacks, 1963.

———. *Home: Social Essays.* New York: William Morrow and Co., 1966.

Kain, John F., and William C. Apgar Jr. *Housing and Neighborhood Dynamics.* Cambridge, Mass.: Harvard University Press, 1985.

Kaiser, Ernest. "The Literature of Harlem." *Freedomways* 3, 3 (summer 1963): 276–91.

Katz, Phyillis A., and Dalmas A. Taylor, eds. *Eliminating Racism.* New York: Plenum Press, 1988.

Keesing, Roger. "Theories of Culture." In *Annual Review of Anthropology* 3: 73–97. Palo Alto, Calif.: Annual Reviews, 1974.

Keil, Charles. *Urban Blues.* Chicago: University of Chicago Press, 1966.

Keith, Michael, and Steve Pile, eds. *Place and the Politics of Identity.* New York: Routledge, 1993.

Kellner, Bruce, ed. *The Harlem Renaissance: A Historical Dictionary of the Era.* New York: Methuen, 1984.

Kelly, Robin. "Harlem Disappears." *Metropolis,* April 2001.

Kilson, Martin. "Jesse Jackson and Black Politics." *Dissent* 34 (spring 1987): 512.

———. "Problems of Black Politics." *Dissent* 36 (fall 1989): 526.

———, ed. "Special Section: New Perspectives on Black Americans." *Dissent* 36 (fall 1989): 475–534.

King, Martin. "Harlemites Deserve First Crack at Brownstones for Sale: Rangel." *New York News,* July 27, 1981.

Kivelson, Adrienne. *What Makes New York City Run?* New York: League of Women Voters of the City of New York Education, 1979.

Koch, Edward I. *The Green Book 1985–1986: Official Directory of the City of New York.* Public Holidays in New York City, 1985.

Konner, Melvin. "Still Invisible, and Dying, in Harlem." *New York Times,* February 24, 1990.

Kramer, Bernard. "The Continuing Significance of a Racially Dual Society." In *The Caste and Class Controversy,* edited by Charles Willie, 140–44. Bayside, N.Y.: General Hall, 1979.

Kruger, Karl-Heinz. "Oh, Baby. Scheisse. Wie ist das Gekommen?" *Der Spiegel* 11, March 11, 1985.

Lacayo, Richard. "Between Two Worlds." *Time Magazine,* March 13, 1989.

Ladner, Joyce, ed. *The Death of White Sociology.* New York: Vintage Books, 1973.

Lamont, Michèle, ed. *The Cultural Territories of Race.* Chicago: University of Chicago Press, 1999.

Landry, Bart. *The New Black Middle Class.* Berkeley: University of California Press, 1987.

Lauria, Mickey, and Lawrence Knopp. "Toward an Analysis of the Role of Gay Communities in the Urban Renaissance." *Urban Geography* 6, 2 (1985): 152–69.

Larsen, Nella. *Quicksand and Passing.* New Brunswick, N.J.: Rutgers University Press, 1986.

"Leading Black Neighborhoods." *Black Enterprise,* December 1974.

Leaks, Sylvester. "Talking about Harlem." *Freedomways* 3, 3 (summer 1963): 263–65.

Lee, Andrea. *Sarah Phillips.* New York: Penguin Books, 1984.

Lee, Elliott D. "Will We Lose Harlem? The Symbolic Capital of Black America Is Threatened by Gentrification." *Black Enterprise,* June 1981.

Lenz, Gunther. "Urban Ghetto, Symbolic Space, and Communal Rituals: Zur Literarischen Verarbeitung Harlems in der Harlem Renaissance." In *Das Verstehenlernen einer Pardoxen Epoche in Schule und Hochschule: The American 1920s,* edited by Lothar Bredella, 78–113. Bochum, 1985.

———. "Symbolic Space, Communal Rituals, and the Surreality of the Urban Ghetto: Harlem in Black Literature from the 1920s to the 1960s." *Callalo* 11, 2, (spring 1988): 309–45.

———. "Getteorfahrung, Gettokultur, Gettoliteratur: Zur Afroamerikanischen Literatur zwischen den Wettkriegen (1914–1945)." In *Amerkanische Gettoliteratur,* edited by Berndt Ostendorf, 149–233. Darmstadt, Wissenschaftliche Buchgesellschaft, 1983.

Levine, Lawrence W. *Black Culture and Black Consciousness: Afro-American Folk Thought from Slavery to Freedom.* New York: Oxford University Press, 1977.

Lewis, David Levering. *When Harlem Was in Vogue.* New York: Random House, 1981.

———. "Harlem's First Shining." *Modern Maturity,* February–March 1989.

Liebow, Elliot. *Tally's Corner: A Study of Negro Streetcorner Men.* Boston: Little, Brown and Co., 1967.

Locke, Alain. *The New Negro.* Reprint. New York: Atheneum, 1981.

Long, Jacqueline, and Vernon Robinson. *How Much Power to the People? A Study of the New York State Urban Development Corporation's Involvement in Black Harlem.* New York: Urban Center at Columbia University, 1971.

Long, Larry, and Diana De Are. "The Suburbanization of Blacks." *American Demographics,* September 1981.

Louis Harris and Associates. *"A Survey of Leadership Attitudes toward the Quality of Life in Harlem."* November 1973.

Lynn, Mary, and Benjamin Berry, eds. *The Black Middle Class.* Saratoga Springs, N.Y.: Skidmore College Press, 1979.

Lyons, Richard. "A 10-Unit Harlem Condo without Subsidy." *New York Times,* June 26, 1988.

Maanen, John Van. *Tales of the Field.* Chicago: University of Chicago Press, 1988.

Mabry, Marcus. "The Ghetto Preppies." *Newsweek,* November 4, 1991.

Margolis, Richard. "If We Won, Why Aren't We Smiling?" In *The Caste and Class Controversy,* edited by Charles Willie, 104–10. Bayside, N.Y.: General Hall, 1979.

Marrett, Cora Bagley. "The Precariousness of Social Class in Black America." *Contemporary Sociology*, 9 (January 1980): 16–19.

Massey, Douglas M., and Nancy A. Denton. *American Apartheid: Segregation and the Making of the Underclass*. Cambridge, Mass.: Harvard University Press, 1994.

"Mayor Unveils Harlem Rehab Project." *New York Post*, August 26, 1982.

McCluskey, John, Jr., ed. *The City of Refuge: The Collected Stories of Rudolph Fisher*. Columbia: University of Missouri Press, 1987.

McKay, Claude. "Note of Harlem." *Modern Monthly* 8 (July 1934): 368.

———. *Harlem: Negro Metropolis*. New York: E. P. Dutton, 1940.

———. *A Long Way from Home*. New York: Harcourt Brace Jovanovich, 1970.

———. *Home to Harlem*. Reprint. Boston: Northeastern Press, 1987.

Mirabella, Alan. "There's a Party Going On." *New York Daily News*, August 7, 1986.

Moore, Keith. "Brownstone Auctions Start." *New York Daily News*, April 15, 1985.

Moore, Richard B. "Africa Conscious Harlem." *Freedomways* 3, 3 (summer 1963): 315–34.

Moore, Sally Falk, and Barbara Myerhoff, eds. *Symbol and Politics in Communal Ideology*. Ithaca, N.Y.: Cornell University Press, 1975.

Morris, A. B. "Harlem Building Bought by Determined Tenants." *New York Times*, February 17, 1985.

Murphy, William. "City Proposes Harlem Development." *Staten Island Advance*, August 26, 1982.

Murray, Albert. *The Omni-Americans: New Perspectives on Black Experience and American Culture*. New York: Avon, 1970.

Myrdal, Gunnar. *An American Dilemma: The Negro Problem and Modern Democracy*. New York: Harper and Row, 1944.

Nelson, Jill. *Volunteer Slavery: My Authentic Negro Experience*. Chicago: Noble Press, 1993.

New York City Partnership. Home page. http://www.nycp.org. May 14, 2001.

Newby, Robert. "Review of the Declining Significance of Race." *School Review* 87, 1 (November 1978): 100–106.

Newman, Dorothy. "Underclass: An Appraisal." In *The Caste and Class Controversy*, edited by Charles Willie, 92–97. Bayside, N.Y.: General Hall, 1979.

Newsletter of the Harlem School of Arts (HAS), 5, 2 (May 1990).

Norman, Gene A. "Homestead in Harlem." *Elle Decor*, June/July 1992.

Oliver, Melvin L. "The Enduring Significance of Race." *Journal of Ethnic Studies* 7, 4 (1982): 79–91.

Omi, Michael, and Howard Winant. *Racial Formation in the United States*. New York: Routledge and Kegan Paul, 1986.

Orfield, Gary, and Carole Ashkinaze. *The Closing Door*. Chicago: University of Chicago Press, 1991.

Oser, Alan. "Mixed-Income High Rise Takes Condo Form." *New York Times*, June 30, 1985.

Osofsky, Gilbert. *Harlem: The Making of a Ghetto*. 2d ed. New York: Harper and Row, 1971.

Overbea, Luix. "Harlem Faces Hopes and Concerns with New Renaissance." *Christian Science Monitor,* March 9, 1987.
———. "Arts Entertainment Help Harlem Revive." *Christian Science Monitor,* March 10, 1987.
———. "Luring Blacks Home to a Rehabbed Harlem." *Christian Science Monitor,* March 11, 1987.
Park, Robert Ezra. *Race and Culture.* New York: The Free Press, 1950.
Parkin, Frank. *Class Inequality and Political Order: Social Stratification in Capitalist and Communist Societies.* London: Praeger Publishers, 1971.
Paterson, David A. *Legislative Report from Senator David A. Paterson.* New York: July 1990.
Patterson, Orlando. *Slavery and Social Death.* Cambridge, Mass.: Harvard University Press, 1982.
———. "Toward a Study of Black America." *Dissent* 36 (fall 1989): 476–86.
Pattillo-McCoy, Mary. *Black Picket Fences: Privilege and Peril among the Black Middle Class.* Chicago: University of Chicago Press, 1999.
Payne, Charles. "On the Declining—and Increasing—Significance of Race." In *The Caste and Class Controversy,* edited by Charles Willie, 117–39. Bayside, N.Y.: General Hall, 1979.
Petry, Ann. *The Street.* Reprint. Boston: Beacon Press, 1985.
Pettigrew, Thomas. *Racial Separate or Together.* New York: McGraw-Hill, 1971.
———. *Racial Discrimination in the United States.* New York: Harper and Row, 1975.
———. "The Changing but Not Declining Significance of Race." *Michigan Law Review* 77, 3 (1979): 917–24.
———. "The Changing—Not Declining—Significance of Race." *Contemporary Sociology* 9 (January 1980): 19–21.
Purdum, Todd S. "New York to Fight Bunching of Unpopular Projects." *New York Times,* July 18, 1990.
Rabinowitz, Howard. *Race Relations in the Urban South, 1865–1890.* Urbana: University of Illinois Press, 1980.
Rainwater, Lee. *Behind Ghetto Walls.* Chicago: Aldine Publishing Company, 1970.
Rampersad, Arnold. *The Life of Langston Hughes.* 2 vol. New York: Oxford University Press, 1986–88.
Reed, Adolph, Jr. "Steele Trap." *The Nation,* March 4, 1991.
"Reviving Harlem: 54 Renovation." *New York Times,* February 17, 1985.
Rex, John. *Race Relations in Sociological Theory.* London: Routledge and Kegan Paul, 1970.
Rieder, Jonathan. *Canarsie: The Jews and Italians of Brooklyn against Liberalism.* Cambridge, Mass.: Harvard University Press, 1985.
Rose, Harold M. "The Future of Black Ghettos." In *Cities in the 21st Century,* edited by G. Gappert and R. Knight, 133–48. Urban Affairs Annual Reviews, vol. 23. Beverly Hills, Calif.: Sage, 1982.
Rose, Tricia. *Black Noise: Rap Music and Black Culture in Contemporary America.* Hanover, N.H.: Wesleyan University Press, 1994.

Rule, Sheila. "Business Panel Aims to Spur Harlem." *New York Times*, November 26, 1981.

Schaffer, Richard, and Neil Smith. "The Gentrification of Harlem?" *Annals of the Association of American Geographers* 76, 3 (1986): 347–65.

Scheiner, Seth. *Negro Mecca: A History of the Negro in New York City, 1965–1920*. New York: New York University Press, 1965.

Schnore, Leo F., Carolyn D. André, and Harry Sharp. "Black Suburbanization, 1930–1970." In *The Changing Faces of the Suburbs*, edited by Berry Schwartz, 69–94. Chicago: University of Chicago Press, 1976.

Schoener, Allon, ed. *Harlem on My Mind: Cultural Capital of Black America 1900–1978*. New York: Dell Publishing Company, 1979.

Severo, Richard. "Harlem Trying to Become a 'Must See' on Tour Itineraries." *New York Times*, August 15, 1984.

Sullivan, Janet. "North by Northwest." *Westside Spirit*, April 13, 1987.

Smith, Judith B. Letter to author, June 20, 1989.

Smith, Michael Peter. "Postmodernism, Urban Ethnography, and the New Social Space of Ethnic Identity." *Theory and Society* 21 (1992): 493–531.

Smith, Neil, and Peter Williams, eds. *Gentrification of the City*. London: Allen and Unwin, 1986.

Smitherman-Donaldson, Geneva, and Teun A. Van Dijk, eds. *Discourse and Discrimination*. Detroit: Wayne State University Press, 1988.

Soja, Edward W. *Postmodern Geographics*. London: Verso, 1989.

———. *Thirdspace: Journeys to Los Angeles and other Real-and-Imagined Places*. Cambridge, Mass.: Blackwell Publishers, 1996.

Sollors, Werner. *Amiri Baraka/LeRoi Jones: The Quest for a "Populist Modernism."* New York: Columbia University Press, 1978.

———. *Beyond Ethnicity: Consent and Descent in American Culture*. New York: Oxford University Press, 1986.

———. "Of Mules and Mares in a Land of Difference; or Quadrupeds All?" Unpublished paper, no date.

Sorensen, Aage B. "Theory and Methodology in Stratification Research." Unpublished paper, no date.

Sorkin, Michael, ed. *Variations on a Theme Park*. New York: Hill and Wang, 1992.

Stack, Carol B. *All Our Kin*. New York: Harper Torchbooks, 1974.

Suttles, Gerald D. *The Social Order of the Slum*. Chicago: University of Chicago Press, 1968.

Swidler, Ann. " Culture in Action: Symbols and Strategies." *American Sociological Review* 51 (April 1986): 273–86.

Taeuber, Karl E. "Racial Segregation: The Persisting Dilemma." *Annals of the American Academy*, November 1975.

Taylor, Monique M. "Home to Harlem: The Return of the Black Middle Class." *CAAS Report* 14, nos. 1 and 2 (1990–92): 18–23.

———. "Can You Go Home Again? Black Gentrification and the Dilemma of Difference." *Berkeley Journal of Sociology* 37 (summer 1992): 101–28.

———. "Gentrification in Harlem: Community, Culture and the Urban Redevelopment of the Black Ghetto." *Research in Race and Ethnic Relations* 7 (1994): 147–88.

Teaford, Jon C. *The Rough Road to Renaissance: Urban Realization in America, 1940–1985*. Baltimore: Johns Hopkins University Press, 1990.

Terry, Don. "In Harlem, Death in an Old and Busy Neighborhood." *New York Times*, May 6, 1990.

Thomas, M., and M. Hughes. "The Continuing Significance of Race: A Study of Race, Class, and the Quality of Life in America." *American Sociological Review* 51 (December 1986): 830–41.

Thurman, Wallace, ed. *Fire!! Devoted to Younger New Negro Artists*, vol. 1, no. 1. New York: The Fire!! Press, 1982.

Tobin, Gary A., ed. *Divided Neighborhoods: Changing Patterns of Racial Segregation*. Vol. 32. Newbury Park, Calif.: Sage Publications, 1987.

Toomer, Jean. *Cane*. New York: Liveright, 1975.

Trade Winds 8, 3 (March–April 1989).

Trade Winds 9, 1 (January–February 1990).

Tuan, Yi-Fu. *Space and Place: The Perspective of Experience*. Minneapolis: University of Minnesota Press, 1977.

Turner, Jonathan. *Societal Stratification*. New York: Columbia University Press, 1984.

Turner, Victor. *The Forest of Symbols: Aspects of Ndembu Ritual*. Ithaca, N.Y.: Cornell University Press, 1967.

———. "Liminal to Liminoid, in Play, Flow. And Ritual: An Essay in Comparative Symbology." *Rice University Studies* 60 (1974): 53–92.

———. 1967. *Dramas, Fields, and Metaphors: Symbolic Action in Human Society*. Ithaca, N.Y.: Cornell University Press, 1974.

———. *The Ritual Process: Structure and Anti-Structure*. Ithaca, N.Y.: Cornell University Press, 1977.

Valentine, Charles. *Culture and Poverty*. Chicago: University of Chicago Press, 1968.

Van Valey, Thomas L., Wade Clark Roof, and Jerome E. Wilcox. "Trends in Residential Segregation: 1960–1970." *American Journal of Sociology* 82, 4 (January 1977): 826–44.

Van Vechten, Carl. *Nigger Heaven*. New York: Knopf, 1926; Chicago: University of Illinois Press, 2000.

Wacquant, Loic J. D. "The Ghetto, the State, and the New Capitalist Economy." *Dissent* 36 (fall 1989): 508.

Washington, Joseph, ed. *The Declining Significance of Race: A Dialogue among Black and White Social Scientists*. Philadelphia: University of Pennsylvania Press, 1979.

Waters, Mary. *Ethnic Options: Choosing Identities in America*. Berkeley: University of California, 1990.

Wattenberg, Ben J., and Richard M. Scammon. "Black Progress and Liberal Rhetoric." *Commentary*, April 1973.

Watts, Jerry G. "Dilemmas of Black Intellectuals." *Dissent* 36 (fall 1989): 501.

Welch, Susan, and Lorn Foster. "Class and Conservatism in the Black Community." *American Politics Quarterly* 15, 4, (October 1987): 445–70.

West, Cornel. *Race Matters.* Boston: Beacon Press, 1993.
Wideman, John Edgar. *Philadelphia Fire.* New York: Vintage Books, 1990.
Williams, Brett. "Owning Places and Buying Time, Class, Culture, and Stalled Gentrification." *Urban Life: A Journal of Ethnographic Research* 14, 3 (October 1985): 251–73.
———. *Upscaling Downtown: Stalled Gentrification in Washington, D.C.* Ithaca, N.Y.: Cornell University Press, 1988.
Williams, Patricia J. *The Alchemy of Race and Rights.* Cambridge, Mass.: Harvard University Press, 1991.
Willie, Charles. "The Inclining Significance of Race." *Society* 15, 5 (1978): 10–15.
———. *The Caste and Class Controversy on Race and Poverty: Round Two of the Willie/Wilson Debate.* 2d ed. Dix Hills, N.Y: General Hall, 1989.
Wilson, William Julius. *The Declining Significance of Race.* 2d. ed. Chicago: University of Chicago Press, 1980.
———. 1980. "A Response to Marrett and Pettigrew." *Contemporary Sociology* 9 (January 1980): 21–24.
———. 1978. "The Declining Significance of Race." *Society* 15, 2 (January/February 1978): 56–62.
———. 1978. "The Declining Significance of Race: Revisited but Not Revised." *Society* 15, 5 (July/August 1978): 11, 16–21.
———. *The Truly Disadvantaged.* Chicago: University of Chicago Press, 1987.
Winch, Julie. *Philadelphia's Black Elite: Activism, Accommodation, and the Struggle for Autonomy, 1787–1848.* Philadelphia: Temple University Press, 1988.
Wintz, Cary D. *Black Culture and the Harlem Renaissance.* Texas: Rice University Press, 1988.
Wirth, Louis. *The Ghetto.* Chicago: University of Chicago Press, 1956.
Woodward, C. Vann. *The Strange Career of Jim Crow.* 2d ed. New York: Oxford University Press, 1957.
Wright, Richard. *The Color Curtain.* Jackson: University Press of Mississippi, 1956.
———. *12 Million Black Voices.* New York: Thunder's Mouth Press, 1988.
Zukin, Sharon. *Loft Living: Culture and Capital in Urban Change.* New Brunswick, N.J.: Rutgers University Press, 1989.
———. *The Cultures of Cities.* Cambridge, Mass.: Blackwell Publishers, 1995.
Zweighenhaft, Richard L., and G. William Domhoff. *Blacks in the White Establishment?* New Haven, Conn.: Yale University Press, 1991.

Index

Abyssinian Baptist Church, xv, 7, 79
Adam Clayton Powell Boulevard, xiv, xv, xvi, 31, 40, 42
Adam Clayton Powell Building, xx, 29
Adam Clayton Powell State Office Building, 29, 30, 31, 32, 34. *See also* SOB
Affirmative Action, 63, 66
African Methodist Episcopal Zion Church, 7
Amsterdam News, xiv, xv, 7, 110, 159
Anderson, Elijah, xvii, 123
Anderson, Jervis, 8
Apollo Theater, xiv, xv, xviii, 16, 45, 76
Architecture, xiv, 32, 34, 113, 114
Armstrong, Louis, 15
assimilation, xi, xxi, 65, 73, 132
Audubon Ballroom, 42

baby boomers, 61
Baldwin, James, 147
Baraka, Amiri 23–26. *See also* Jones, LeRoi
BART/S (Black Arts Repertory Theater/School), 23, 45
Basie, Count, 16
Beardon, Romare, 18
Beauregard, Robert, 33
Bethel African Methodist Episcopal Church, 7
Black Metropolis 155. *See also* Cayton, Horace; Drake, St. Clair
black middle class, x, xi, xvi, xvii, xviii, xxi, xxii, 37, 43, 45–48, 54, 59, 61–63, 67, 73, 82, 86, 88, 94–96, 119–25, 127, 130–33, 142, 144, 148, 152, 155–56, 160, 162, 166–69, 172–74
boosters, 33, 171
Brahmin Court, 99–101
Brown, Claude, 20
brownstones: auction of, 35, 36; boarding houses and SRO's, 103–4, 109, 114, 175; demolition of, 32, 34; free market sales, 33, 34, 36, 37, 92; home ownership, xx, 45, 53, 59, 86, 98–99, 116, 120–22, 127, 133, 135, 140, 144, 159, 162, 165, 167–68, 173, 176–77; house pride, 154, 160; renovation of, 34, 57, 36, 54, 99, 102, 114, 173
buppie, 88, 89, 97, 142, 148

Calloway, Cab, 16, 41
Canarsie, 97
caste and class, xvii, 63
Castro, Fidel, 31, 146
Cayton, Horace, x, xvii, 155, 166
Central Harlem, 174
civil rights movement, x, xviii, xxi, 58–59, 61, 63, 66
Clark, Kenneth, 21
class, x, xi, xvii, xxi, xxii, 59, 92, 110, 123, 126, 133, 143–44, 152, 167, 172–73
class differences, 59, 92, 93
class diversity, 93, 94
churches: migration to Harlem, 7; real estate in Harlem, 7; as source of community, 7, 77, 132, 143, 145
color line, 61, 74, 87, 171
Columbia University, 1, 11, 12, 70, 124, 165
Columbus, Christopher, 50
communion of fellowship, 168
communitas, 130
community: insiders versus outsiders, 3, 4, 60, 130, 133, 159, 161–62, 166, 177
control, 37; preservation, 39, 44
corporate America, 151
Cosby, Bill, 61
Cotton Club, 16, 42, 151, 176
Cox, Oliver, xvii

Daily News, 124
Davis, Arthur, 12
Department of Housing Preservation and Development, xii
Deutsch, Leonard, 14
Dinkins, David, 79
discourse, 87
discrimination, xxi, 63, 75
displacement, 50, 60, 91, 93, 96, 101, 103, 104, 109, 110, 115, 117–19, 148–49
Domhoff, G. William, 62
double consciousness, 149, 173
Drake, St. Clair, x, xvii, 155
drugs, 36, 47, 49, 95, 100, 112, 113, 118, 120, 122, 134–35, 144, 154
Du Bois, W. E. B., x, xvii, 10, 11, 13, 14, 24, 76, 149, 171, 173
Dunbar, Paul Lawrence, xv
Dyson, Michael, 173

Eastman, Max, 10
Economist, 35
Ellington, Duke, 15, 16, 19, 76
Ellison, Ralph, 18, 19, 153

Fisher, Rudolph, 11, 14, 15, 16
Fitzgerald, Ella, 16, 41
Frazier, E. Franklin, x, xvii, 6, 16
Frederick Douglass Boulevard, xv, 40
frontier mythology, 98

Garvey, Marcus, xv, 7, 11, 43
gender, xxi, 123, 133, 136, 144–45, 176
gentrification, ix, x, xi, xvii, xix, xx, 4, 30, 32–34, 47, 53–55, 59–60, 75, 87–88, 91–98, 100, 105, 109–12
gentry and gentrifiers, xx, xxi, 33, 47, 54–55, 60, 63, 75, 86–87, 90–91, 93, 95, 98, 104, 113, 119, 121–23, 125, 129, 131, 133, 135, 145, 152, 160, 165–69, 172–77
Great Depression, 16, 18
great migration, 161

Hamilton, Alexander, 113
Hamilton Heights, xv, 50, 81, 86
Harlem: as black capital, 17, 24–25, 54; in film, 15, 25, 26, 107; Harlem as heaven, 4, 19, 55, 82, 98, 168, 172; Harlem as hell, 2, 4, 55, 81, 82, 168, 172; Harlem Renaissance, xix, 4, 7, 10, 13–14, 18, 23, 41–42, 55, 60, 72, 75, 77, 146, 174, 176; history of, 22, 32; in literature, 15; as metaphor, 78; migration to, x, 5–7; in music,

15; as social laboratory, 21; symbolism and symbolic meaning(s), xx, 15, 20, 26, 38, 41, 131, 156, 168, 173, 176
"Harlem Is Nowhere," 18, 19. *See also* Ellison, Ralph
Harlem Nights, 25. *See also* Murphy, Eddie
HARYOU (Harlem Youth Opportunities Unlimited), 21, 22
Himes, Chester, 23, 98
"Home to Harlem," xii, xxii, 13, 14, 44, 68, 111, 167, 173–74
Hoover, J. Edgar, xvi
Hotel Theresa, 146
HUDC (Harlem Urban Development Corporation), xii, 38, 47
Hudson, Theodore, 23
Huggins, Nathan, 10
Hughes, Langston, 4, 5, 7, 10–12, 17, 57, 76–77, 80, 85, 134, 146, 172, 176
Hurston, Zora Neale, 10

Identity (racial), 22, 75, 146, 148
Integration, x, xi, xiii, xvii, xviii, xx, xxi, xxii, 6, 18, 22, 45, 47–51, 53, 62, 63, 66, 68, 74, 113, 132, 167–68, 172–73
Invisible Man, 18. *See also* Ellison, Ralph

Jackson, Mahalia, xv
jazz, 142
jazz age, 15
Jim Crow, 62, 174
Johnson, Bumpy, 39, 43
Johnson, James Weldon, 6, 21
Jones, LeRoy, 23–26
"Jungle Fever," 26. *See also* Lee, Spike

King, Martin Luther, Jr., xiii, 40, 41, 58
King, Rodney, xxi
kinship, 140, 144
Koch, Edward, 35
Kuhn, Thomas, 66

Larsen, Nella, 11–13, 77
Lawrence, Jacob, 18
Leaks, Sylvester, 20
Lee, Spike, 25–26
Lewis, David Levering, 16
Liberation Bookstore, 79
liminal, 130
liminality, 173
Locke, Alain, 9–10, 17, 20
Lumet, Sydney, 25. *See also Night Falls in Manhattan*

Malcolm X, 25–26, 41–43, 76, 146
Malcom X Boulevard, xii, 31, 42, 43, 85
Mandela, Nelson, 31, 78
Marley, Bob, xiv, 12
marginality, xiii, xxi, xxii, 2, 22, 48, 51, 62, 73, 91, 130, 161, 166, 174
Marshall, Thurgood, 76, 80
Martin Luther King Jr. Boulevard, xv, xvi, 31, 44
Mason, Charlotte, 10
Mays, Willie, 80
McKay, Claude, 11–14, 16–18, 129
mecca, 6, 14–15, 17, 30, 43, 77
Mosquito Coast, 107. *See also* Theroux, Paul
Murphy, Eddie, 25. *See also Harlem Nights*
Murray, Albert, 20, 21

NAACP (National Association for the Advancement of Colored People), 7
Nail, John E., 7
National Urban League (National League on Urban Condition among Negroes), 7, 11
"Negro Removal," 30
Negro Renaissance, 9, 20
New Negro, 4, 9, 75
New York Age, 7
New York Times, xvi, xvii, 35, 94, 105–6, 110

New Yorker, 105
nigger, 115, 126
Nigger Heaven, 8, 17, 44
Night Falls in Manhattan, 25. *See also* Lumet, Sydney
nostalgia, xx, 26, 38–40, 41

125th Street, ix, xii, xiii, xiv, xv, xvi, 1, 29–30, 43, 45, 76, 113–14, 165, 167. *See also* Martin Luther King Jr. Boulevard
Osofsky, Gilbert, 6, 16

Pan Pan, xv, xvi, 146
Parker, Henry, 7
Patillo-McCoy, Mary, xvii
Patterson, Orlando, 74–75
Payton, Philip, 7
Postmodern Geographies, 3
Powell, Adam Clayton, 29, 31, 39, 43
Pryor, Richard, 25

race, x, xi, xiii, xvii, xviii, xix, 14, 59, 60, 61, 63, 123, 127, 144, 155, 167, 172, 176–77
race work, 177
racial uplift, 13, 131
racism, xvii, xviii, xxii, 2, 3, 13, 50–52, 61–65, 68, 73–74, 82, 113, 127, 130, 168, 172–73
Red Rooster, 39
reverse discrimination, 63
rhetoric of return, xi, 88, 130–32
Robeson, Paul, 43
Robinson, Jackie, xv
Robinson, Sugar Ray, 76
Rockefeller, Nelson, 29
role models, 153, 155
Royall, John, 7

Savoy Ballroom, 16, 42
Sayles, John, 1, 2
Scheiner, Seth, 6
Schomburg Center, xv, xvii, 44, 79, 166
segregation, ix, x, xi, xiii, xxii, 2, 5, 6, 9, 39, 48–49, 58, 62, 68, 90, 173–74, 177
shopping, xiii, 48, 49, 95, 123–24, 142, 166–68
Sibley, David, 2
Simple, Jesse B., 12
Simpson, O. J., xxi
social buffer, 87, 131, 168–69, 177
Soja, Ed, 3
Sollors, Werner, 24
Smalls Paradise, 39, 42
Smith, Michael, 25
Smith, Neil, 98, 117
SOB (State Office Building), xx, 29–32, 34. *See also* Adam Clayton Powell State Office Building
Starbucks, ix, xii, xiii, xiv, xv, xvi, xxii
stoop, xii, 87, 99, 102, 120–23, 127, 133, 136, 141–42, 153
St. Philip's Protestant Episcopal Church, 7
Striver's Row, 6, 86
suburban, 116, 110, 172
subway , 1; "Brother from Another Planet," 1; convenience for residents, 147; great subway proposition, 5
Sugar Hill, xv, 6, 80, 133, 165, 171

Theroux, Paul, 107. *See also Mosquito Coast*
Thomas, Clarence, xxi
Trump, Donald, 112
Truth, Sojourner, xv
Turner, Victor, 130

UNIA (United Negro Improvement Association), 7. *See also*: Garvey, Marcus
upward mobility, xi, 130, 148
urban pioneers, 117
urban renewal, xvii, 33, 34, 35, 177

Van Vechten, Carl, 8, 9

Wall Street Journal, 124
Waters, Ethel, 16
White, Walter, 80
Willie, Charles, 62
Wilson, William Julius, 46–47, 66, 131
Wright, Richard, 153, 171

yuppie, x, xi, xii, 60–61, 88, 112

Zweigenhaft, Richard L., 62

Monique M. Taylor is associate professor of sociology at Occidental College. She has written three previous publications on race, history, and identity in Harlem.